D0564075

The Endless Crisis

The Endless Crisis

How Monopoly-Finance Capital Produces Stagnation and Upheaval from the U.S.A. to China

by JOHN BELLAMY FOSTER
and ROBERT W. McCHESNEY

MONTHLY REVIEW PRESS
New York

Library of Congress Cataloging-in-Publication Data
Foster, John Bellamy
The endless crisis : how monopoly-finance capital produces stagnation and upheaval from the U.S.A. to China / by John Bellamy Foster and Robert W. McChesney.
p. cm.
Includes bibliographical references and index.
ISBN 978-1-58367-313-3 (cloth : alk. paper)
1. Capitalism. 2. Stagnation (Economics). 3. Economic development. I. McChesney, Robert Waterman
HB501.F659 2012
332'.041—dc23
2012021925

Monthly Review Press
146 West 29th Street, Suite 6W
New York, New York 10001

www.monthlyreview.org

Table of Contents

Charts and Tables

Charts

Tables

Preface

THE WORLD ECONOMY AS a whole is undergoing a period of slowdown. The growth rates for the United States, Europe, and Japan at the center of the system have been sliding for decades. In the first decade of this century these countries experienced the slowest growth rates since the 1930s; and the opening years of the second decade look no better. Stagnation is the word that economists use for this phenomenon. In human terms it means declining real wages, massive unemployment, a public sector facing extreme budget crises, growing inequality and a general and sometimes sharp decline in the quality of life. It produces all sorts of social and political crises, and these crises and their consequences will likely be the defining events of the coming generation. For the vast majority of the population—excluding the big winners at the top—it feels like an endless crisis. "The trouble with normal," singer and songwriter Bruce Cockburn tells us, "is it always gets worse."

The Great Financial Crisis of 2007–09 was itself linked to this slowdown in the "real economy," referred to by some as the Great Stagnation. China and a handful of emerging economies have continued to expand in recent years, but they too are not immune to the general crisis, and are showing signs of a downward shift and increasing instability. In an increasingly globalized economy the fates of the various nations within it are more and more intertwined.

But while there is a growing acceptance among business leaders and policymakers, not to mention everyday people, of economic stagnation as the state of contemporary capitalism, there is little explanation for the state of affairs. Conventional economics, which cheered on deregulation of financial markets and then slept through the financial meltdown, provides some insights but it has not proven well-suited to the task. Like first-time parachutists grasping their ripcords, most economists cling tightly to the conviction that capitalism's natural state is full employment and rapid growth, so eventually the market will work its magic.

In contrast, we argue that this is an endless crisis, because it flows inexorably from the functioning of what we term monopoly-finance capital. There is no reason to expect growth to improve markedly and for a sustained length of time based on the internal logic of the system, and the existing range of legitimate business-approved options before policymakers. Hence, the *normal* state of a mature capitalist economy dominated by a handful of giant monopolistic corporations is one of stagnation. This has been true for nearly a century (if not longer) and the Great Depression of the 1930s provides, no pun intended, a depressing example. For decades thereafter a variety of mechanisms—generally through government action—allowed the system to stave off stagnation and provide growth, but these mechanisms tended to have deleterious side effects; their usefulness dissipated or was eventually undermined. The most important, and most recent, was the massive increase in debt from 1980–2008 which propped up the economy but was unsustainable and eventually led to the Great Financial Crisis. The factors that induce stagnation are greater today, and globalized, so the future for the economy is grim.

Our objective is not to produce a polemic, or a manifesto; the aim is rather more ambitious and more modest. It is to provide a coherent evidence-based explanation for stagnation, and why it is an endless crisis. Although we believe the evidence points strongly in one political direction—if people want to get off the downward spiral of stagnation and growing human misery, it will require radical change in the economic system—there is no litmus test for who may read this book. We intend that it be of value to anyone, whatever their background or political values, who wishes to understand what may be the central political-economic issue of our lifetimes. We want to do what we can to encourage a broad public debate on the matter, and then participate in that debate. For a crisis of this magnitude, we need all hands on deck.

The book was written between 2009 and 2012, although the research has been done throughout our careers and is the product of discussions that we have had for more than thirty years. The chapters originally appeared in *Monthly Review*, the magazine John Bellamy Foster edits and to which Robert W. McChesney frequently contributes (and was for a time co-editor).

We have many people to thank, whose assistance has been foundational to the book's existence. First and foremost, we must acknowledge the important contribution of R. Jamil Jonna. As we were researching and writing the three articles that now comprise chapters three, four, and five of the book, we quickly realized we needed assistance with gathering data, and using the data to prepare charts and tables for the articles. Jamil, who is the webmaster for *Monthly Review* and a doctoral candidate at the University of Oregon specializing in political-economic research, did such an extraordinary job that he joined us as coauthor of the three articles. His role is acknowledged in each of these chapters below. However, responsibility for the overall conception and analysis in these three chapters, as in the book as a whole, remains ours.

A number of other people have been crucial in the development of this book. Fred Magdoff has helped with every chapter, and particularly with the charts in the Introduction and chapter six. John Mage originally suggested developing this short book based on ongoing work we were doing (part of a bigger project) and we are indebted to him for inspiration and advice. We have benefited throughout from his keen sense of financialized accumulation. William E. Foster helped with the research in chapters five and six, finding key materials. Hannah Holleman, as an *MR* research assistant, helped with the research, fact-checking and proofing in relation to nearly every chapter. Ryan Wishart also helped in proofing some of these chapters and providing us with materials.

Spencer Sunshine and Susie Day, as *MR*'s assistant editors while this book was in production, did the initial copyediting and frequently had specific points that improved the writing. Much of the clarity of this book, despite the difficult topic area, has to do with their immense editorial skills.

Martin Paddio, Michael D. Yates, John J. Simon, Brett Clark, Scott Borchert, and Yoshie Furuhashi at *MR* helped in too many ways to be mentioned. Martha Sweezy has provided unfailing encouragement.

We are also grateful to the large number of heterodox political economists and critical scholars with whom we have had interchanges and/or drawn inspiration in this period. We would especially like to mention Gar Alperovitz, Elmar Altvater, Samir Amin, Beatrice Appay, Amiya Kumar Bagchi, Riccardo Bellofiore, Walden Bello, Michael A. Bernstein, Robert A. Blecker, Daniel Buck, Paul Buhle, Paul Burkett,

Val Burris, William K. Carroll, John Cassidy, Sundiata Cha-Jua, Anita Chan, Ha-Joon Chang, Vivek Chibber, Lim Chin, Noam Chomsky, Keith Cowling, Herman Daly, Mike Davis, Michael Dawson, Doug Dowd, Michael Dreiling, Richard B. Du Boff, Larry Elliott, Gérard Duménil, John W. Farley, Thomas Ferguson, Nancy Folbre, Duncan Foley, James K. Galbraith, Susan George, Jayati Ghosh, Sam Gindin, Cy Gonick, Joseph Halevi, E. K. Hunt, Martin Hart-Landsberg, David Harvey, Doug Henwood, Edward S. Herman, Andrew Higginbottom, Makoto Itoh, Fredric Jameson, Steve Keen, Naomi Klein, Gabriel Kolko, Joyce Kolko, David M. Kotz, Greta R. Krippner, Paul Krugman, Mark Lautzenheiser, Michael A. Lebowitz, Kari Polanyi Levitt, Dominique Lévy, Minqi Li, Michael Lim Mah-Hui, Bill Lucarelli, Joel Magnuson, Jerry Mander, István Mészáros, Branko Milanovic, Bill Moyers, Alan Nasser, John Nichols, Leo Panitch, Robert Pollin, Nomi Prins, Prabhat Patnaik, Thomas I. Palley, Michael Perelman, James Petras, Christos N. Pitelis, William I. Robinson, Allen Ruff, Juliet B. Schor, Nina Shapiro, Howard J. Sherman, John Smith, Eric A. Schutz, Roger Sugden, William K. Tabb, Jan Toporowski, Yanis Varoufakis, Ramaa Vasudevan, Henry Veltmeyer, Richard Walker, Immanuel Wallerstein, Mel Watkins, Edward N. Wolff, Richard York, Robert F. Young, and Michael Zweig. Most of these are friends, a number we have never met, a few we have strong differences with. All, however, have been critical to our thinking.

We are both fortunate to have as our life partners critical intellectuals who are as committed to social change as we are and with whom we have continually discussed the ideas in this book. Our perpetual thanks therefore go out to Carrie Ann Naumoff and Inger L. Stole.

We would like to dedicate this book to the memory of our friends Harry Magdoff and Paul Sweezy.

John Bellamy Foster and
Robert W. McChesney

April 2012

Introduction

> We have had [in England], ever since 1876, a chronic state of stagnation in all dominant branches of industry. Neither will the full crash come; nor will the period of longed-for prosperity to which we used to be entitled before and after it. A dull depression, a chronic glut of all markets for all trades, that is what we have been living in for nearly ten years. How is this?
>
> —Frederick Engels[1]

THE GREAT FINANCIAL CRISIS and the Great Recession arose in the United States in 2007 and quickly spread around the globe, marking what appears to be a turning point in world history. Although this was followed within two years by a recovery phase, the world economy five years after the onset of the crisis is still in the doldrums. The United States, Europe, and Japan remain caught in a condition of slow growth, high unemployment, and financial instability, with new economic tremors appearing all the time and the effects spreading globally. The one bright spot in the world economy, from a growth standpoint, has been the seemingly unstoppable expansion of a handful of emerging economies, particularly China. Yet the continuing stability of China is now also in question. Hence, the general consensus among informed economic observers is that the world capitalist economy is facing the threat of long-term economic stagnation (complicated by the prospect of further financial deleveraging), sometimes referred to as the problem of "lost decades."[2] It is this issue, of the stagnation of the capitalist economy, even more than that of financial crisis or recession, that has now emerged as the big question worldwide.

Within the United States dramatic examples of the shift in focus from financial crisis to economic stagnation are not difficult to find. Ben Bernanke, chairman of the Federal Reserve Board, began a 2011 speech in Jackson Hole, Wyoming, entitled "The Near- and Longer-Term Prospects for the U.S. Economy," with the words: "The financial crisis and the subsequent slow recovery have caused some to question whether the United States... might not now be facing a prolonged period of stagnation, regardless of its public policy choices. Might not the very slow pace of economic expansion of the past few years, not only in the United States but also in a number of other advanced economies, morph into something far more long-lasting?" Bernanke responded that he thought such an outcome unlikely if the right actions were taken: "Notwithstanding the severe difficulties we currently face, I do not expect the long-run growth potential of the U.S. economy to be materially affected by the crisis and the recession if—and I stress *if*—our country takes the necessary steps to secure that outcome." One would of course have expected such a declaration to be followed by a clear statement as to what those "necessary steps" were. Yet this was missing from his analysis; his biggest point simply being that the nation needs to get its fiscal house in order.[3]

Robert E. Hall, then president of the American Economic Association (AEA), provided a different approach in an address to the AEA in January 2011, entitled "The Long Slump." A "slump," as Hall defined it, is the period of above-normal unemployment that begins with a sharp contraction of the economy and lasts until normal employment has been restored. The "worst slump in US history," Hall stated, was "the Great Depression in which the economy contracted from 1929 to 1933 and failed to return to normal until the buildup for World War II." Hall labeled the period of prolonged slow growth in which the U.S. economy is now trapped "The Great Slump." With government seemingly unable to provide the economy with the needed stimulus, he observed, there was no visible way out: "The slump may last many years."[4]

In June 2010, Paul Krugman wrote that the advanced economies were currently caught in what he termed the "Third Depression" (the first two being the Long Depression following the Panic of 1873 and the Great Depression of the 1930s). The defining characteristic of such depressions was not negative economic growth, as in the trough of the business cycle, but rather protracted slow growth once economic recovery had commenced. In such a long, drawn-out recovery "episodes of improvement were never enough to undo the damage of the initial slump, and were followed by relapses." In November 2011,

Krugman referred to "The Return of Secular Stagnation," resurrecting the secular stagnation hypothesis of the late 1930s to early '50s (although in this case, according to Krugman, the excess savings inducing stagnation are global rather than national).[5]

Books too have been appearing on the stagnation theme. In 2011, Tyler Cowen published *The Great Stagnation*, which quickly became a bestseller. For Cowen the U.S. economy has been characterized by a "a multi-decade stagnation.... Even before the financial crisis came along, there was no new net job creation in the last decade.... Around the globe, the populous countries that have been wealthy for some time share one common feature: Their rates of economic growth have slowed down since about 1970."[6] If creeping stagnation has thus been a problem for the U.S. and other advanced economies for some time, Thomas Palley, in his 2012 book, *From Financial Crisis to Stagnation*, sees today's Great Stagnation itself as being set off by the Great Financial Crisis that preceded it, and as representing the failure of neoliberal economic policy.[7]

Such worries are not confined to the United States, given the sluggish economic growth in Japan and Europe as well. Christine Lagarde, managing director of the IMF, gave a speech in Washington in September 2011 in which she stated that the world economy has "entered a dangerous new phase of the crisis.... Overall, global growth is continuing, but slowing down," taking the form of an "anemic and bumpy recovery." Fundamental to this dangerous new phase of crisis was "core instability," or weaknesses in the Triad—North America, Europe, and Japan—along with continuing financial imbalances "sapping growth." The big concern was the possibility of another "lost decade" for the world economy as a whole. In November 2011 Lagarde singled out China as a potential weak link in the world economic system, rather than a permanent counter to world economic stagnation.[8]

The fact that these rising concerns with respect to the slowing down of the wealthy Triad economies have a real basis, not just in the last two decades but also in long-term trends since the 1960s, can be seen in Chart I.1 This shows the declining real growth rates of the Triad economies in the decades from the 1960s to the present. The slowdowns were sharpest in Japan and Europe. But the United States too experienced a huge drop in economic growth after the 1960s, and was unable to regain its earlier trend-rate of growth despite the massive stimuli offered

Chart I.1. Average Annual Real Economic Growth Rates, the United States, European Union, and Japan

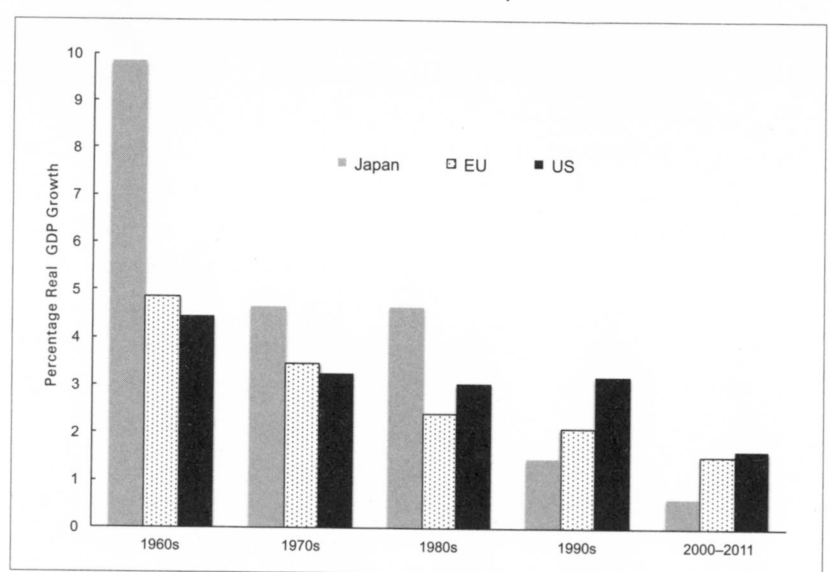

Sources: Data for U.S. from Bureau of Economic Analysis, National Income and Product Accounts, Table 1.1.1. Percent Change from Preceding Period in Real Gross Domestic Product, http://bea.gov/national/nipaweb; Data for Japan and the European Union from World Bank, WDI database, http://databank.worldbank.org.

by military-spending increases, financial bubbles, a growing sales effort, and continuing exploitation of the privileged position of the dollar as the hegemonic currency. The bursting of the New Economy stock market bubble in 2000 seriously weakened the U.S. economy, which was only saved from a much larger disaster by the rapid rise of the housing bubble in its place. The bursting of the latter in Great Financial Crisis of 2007–09 brought the underlying conditions of stagnation to the surface.

Hence, long-term economic slowdown, as Chart I.1 indicates, preceded the financial crisis. In the U.S case, the rate of growth for the 1970s (which was slightly higher than that of the two subsequent decades) was 27 percent less than in the 1960s. In 2000–2011 the rate of growth was 63 percent below that of the 1960s.[9] It was this underlying stagnation tendency, as we shall argue in this book, which was the reason the economy became so dependent on financialization—or a decades-long series of ever-larger speculative financial bubbles.[10] In fact, a dangerous feedback loop between stagnation and financial bubbles has now emerged, reflecting the fact that stagnation and financialization are increasingly interdependent phenomena: a problem that we refer to in this book as the stagnation-financialization trap.

The Denial of History

Although the tendency to stagnation or a long period of anemic growth is increasingly recognized even within the economic mainstream as a major issue, broad historical and theoretical understandings of this and its relation to capitalist development are lacking within establishment circles. The reason for this, we believe, can be traced to the fact that neoclassical economists and mainstream social science generally have long abandoned any meaningful historical analysis. Their abstract models, geared more to legitimizing the system than to understanding its laws of motion, have become increasingly otherworldly—constructed around such unreal assumptions as perfect and pure competition, perfect information, perfect rationality (or rational expectations), and the market efficiency hypothesis. The elegant mathematical models developed on the basis of these rarefied constructions often have more to do with beauty, in the sense of ideal perfection, than with the messy world of material reality. The results therefore are about as relevant to today's reality as the medieval debates on the number of angels that could fit on the end of a pin were to theirs. This is an economics that has gone the way of stark idealism—removed altogether from material conditions. As Krugman put it, "the economics profession went astray because economists, as a group, mistook beauty, clad in impressive-looking mathematics, for truth."[11]

John Kenneth Galbraith, in *The Economics of Innocent Fraud*, provided a still stronger condemnation of prevailing economic and social science, arguing that in recent decades the system itself had been fraudulently "renamed" from capitalism to "the market system." The advantage of the latter term from an establishment perspective was: "There was no adverse history here, in fact no history at all. It would have been hard, indeed, to find a more meaningless designation—this is a reason for the choice.... So it is of the market system we teach the young.... No individual or firm is thus dominant. No economic power is evoked. There is nothing here from Marx or Engels. There is only the impersonal market, a not wholly innocent fraud." Along with this, "the phrase 'monopoly capitalism,' once in common use," Galbraith charged, "has been dropped from the academic and political lexicon." Perhaps worst of all, the growing likelihood of a severe crisis and a long-term slowdown in the economy was systematically hidden from view by this fraudulent displacement of the very idea of capitalism (and even of the corporate system).[12]

The continuing influence of Galbraith's "economics of innocent fraud" and the absurd results it generates can be seen in a 2010 speech by Bernanke at Princeton entitled "Implications of the Financial Crisis for Economics." The primary reason the "standard [macroeconomic] models" had failed to see the Great Financial Crisis coming, Bernanke admitted, was that these models "were designed for... non-crisis periods" only. In other words, the conventional models employed by orthodox economists were constructed (intentionally or unintentionally) so as to *exclude the very possibility* of a major crisis or a long-term period of deepening economic stagnation. As long as economic growth appeared robust, Bernanke told his listeners, the models proved "quite useful." The problem, then, he insisted, was not so much that the models on which economic analysis and policy were based were "irrelevant or at least significantly flawed." Rather the bursting of the financial bubble and the subsequent crisis represented events that were not supposed to happen, and that the models were never meant to explain.[13] This is similar to a meteorologist who has constructed a model that predicts perpetual sunny days interrupted by the occasional minor shower and when the big storm comes claims in the model's defense that it was never intended to account for the possibility of such unlikely and unforeseen events.[14]

All of this points to the lack within mainstream economics and social science of a reasoned historical interpretation. "Most of the fundamental errors committed in economic analysis," Joseph Schumpeter wrote in his *History of Economic Analysis*, "are due to lack of historical experience" or historical understanding. For Schumpeter, this contrasts sharply with the approach of Marx, who "was the first economist of top rank to see and to teach systematically how economic theory may be turned into historical analysis and how the historical narrative may be turned into *histoire raisonnée*."[15] Today conventional social scientists have all too often become narrow specialists or technicians concerned with one little corner of reality—or worse still, developers of models that in their extreme abstraction fall prey to Whitehead's fallacy of misplaced concreteness.[16] They seldom recognize the importance of the old Hegelian adage that "the truth is the whole"—and hence can only be understood genetically in its process of becoming.[17]

These self-imposed blinders of mainstream social science were dramatically evident in the failure of economics and social science generally to recognize *even the possibility* of economic and social catastrophe in today's capitalism. In his presidential address to the American Economic Association in 2003, Robert Lucas flatly declared that the "central problem of depression prevention has been solved." The idea that the economy was now free of major crisis tendencies, due to the advent of new, improved monetary policies, became the conventional macroeconomic wisdom—referred to by none other than Bernanke in 2004 as the coming of the Great Moderation.[18] Yet it took only a few years for the bursting of the housing bubble to prove how illusory these notions of the "end of history" were.

Naturally, not everyone was completely caught off guard by the Great Financial Crisis. As early as 2002, two years before Bernanke coined the term the "Great Moderation," a substantial number of independent, informed political-economic commentators—ourselves amongst them—had drawn attention to the growth of an enormous real estate or housing bubble. Writing as editors of *Monthly Review*, we first mentioned the bursting of the real estate/housing bubble as a potential devastating force in the U.S. economy in November 2002. This was followed up with an article the following spring entitled "What Recovery?" in which we contended, "The housing bubble may well be stretched about as thin as it can get without bursting." As the problem became worse, one of us wrote a piece for the May 2006 issue of *Monthly Review* on "The Household Debt Bubble" pointing to the unsustainable borrowing on home mortgages, with the greatest burden falling on workers and subprime borrowers. The housing bubble, the article argued, had allowed the U.S. economy to recover from the bursting of the stock market bubble, but this pointed to the likelihood of a further and possibly greater "financial meltdown" a little ways down the road, which could be triggered by increases in interest rates then already beginning. So, while some aspects of the crisis that arose in the summer of 2007 came as a surprise to us, the general course of events did not.[19]

Monthly Review had long focused on the problem of financialization and its relation to underlying stagnation tendencies in the economy. But the realization that a devastating crisis was in the making as a result of the buildup of the housing bubble was not unique to us; rather it was quite widespread among heterodox observers, even penetrating into the business literature. This included, most notably, Dean Baker, Stephen Roach, John Cassidy, Robert Shiller, and Kevin Phillips—while also extending to pragmatic business publications like *BusinessWeek* and *The Economist.* In August 2002 Baker wrote a report for the Center for Economic Policy Research entitled "The Run-up in Home Prices: Is It Real or Is It Another Bubble?" The same month *BusinessWeek* warned: "The investors who buy many of the [mortgage] loans they securitize—may soon decide that enough is enough.... If [interest] rates go higher, the burden of debt service will increase.... Approximately 30 percent of outstanding mortgage debt has adjustable rates.... A credit crunch could set in if a rate rise triggers a wave of defaults by holders of adjustable mortgages." On September 22, 2002, Stephen Roach wrote an op-ed piece for the *New York Times* on "The Costs of Bursting Bubbles" in which he stated, "There is good reason to believe that both the property [real estate] and consumer bubbles will burst in the not-so-distant future." In November 2002, *New Yorker* economic columnist John Cassidy published an article entitled "The Next Crash: Is the Housing Market a Bubble that's About to Burst?" The following year, Yale economist Robert Shiller coauthored a prescient Brookings Institution paper entitled "Is There a Bubble in the Housing Market?" *The Economist* in June 2005 stated: "The world-wide rise in house prices is the biggest bubble in history. Prepare for the economic pain when it pops." Political commentator Kevin Phillips continually warned of the dangers of financialization, commenting in 2006 that homes had become "tools of speculative finance" and that "the United States had exchanged a stock-market bubble for the larger credit bubble," presaging financial collapse.[20]

In fact, warnings of a housing bubble and the threat of a severe financial collapse in the four years leading up to the crisis were so numerous as to make it difficult, if not impossible, to catalogue them all. The problem, then, was not that no one saw the Great Financial Crisis coming. Rather the difficulty was that the financial world, driven by their endless desire for more, and orthodox economists, prey to the worship of their increasingly irrelevant models, were simply oblivious to the warnings of heterodox economic observers all around them. Mainstream economists had increasingly retreated back into a Say's Law view (the notion that supply creates its own demand), which argued that severe economic crises were virtually impossible.[21]

The failure of orthodox economics to perceive the financial bubble prior to the Great Financial Crisis is now well established in the literature.[22] What we are suggesting here, however, is something different: that the same economics of innocent fraud has hindered orthodox economists from perceiving until now an even bigger fault line of the mature capitalist economy, the tendency to long-term economic stagnation. Indeed, it is the slow growth or stagnation that has been festering for decades which explains not only financialization, manifested in a string of financial bubbles, but also the deep economic malaise that has set in during the period of financial deleveraging. A realistic analysis today thus requires close examination of the dangerous feedback loops between stagnation and financialization.

In *How Markets Fail* Cassidy argues that the two most prescient economic analyses of our current economic malaise, and its relation to the dual phenomena of financialization and stagnation, were provided by: (1) Hyman Minsky, a heterodox, post-Keynesian economist, who developed a theory of financial instability in relation to contemporary capitalism, and (2) Paul Sweezy, a Marxist economist, who saw what he termed the "financialization of the capital accumulation process" as a response to the stagnation tendency of mature monopoly-capitalist economies.[23]

As Cassidy observes about the tradition that grew up around Sweezy:

> During the 1980s and '90s, a diminishing band of Marxist economists, centered around *The Monthly Review*, a small New York journal that had been eking out an existence since the 1940s, focused on what they termed the "financialization" of U.S. capitalism, pointing out that employment in the financial sector, trading volumes in the speculative markets, and the earnings of Wall Street firms were all rising sharply. Between 1980 and 2000, financial industry profits rose from $32.4 billion to $195.8 billion, according to figures from the Commerce Department, and the financial sector's share of all domestically produced profits went from 19 percent to 29 percent.
>
> Paul Sweezy, a Harvard-trained octogenarian who had emerged from the same Cambridge cohort as Galbraith and Samuelson, and who wrote what is still the best introduction to Marxist economics, was the leader of the left-wing dissidents. To a free market economist, the rise of Wall Street was a natural outgrowth of the U.S. economy's competitive advantage in the sector. Sweezy said it reflected an increasingly desperate

> effort to head off economic stagnation. With wages growing slowly, if at all, and with investment opportunities insufficient to soak up all the [actual and potential] profits that corporations were generating, the issuance of debt and the incessant creation of new objects of financial speculation were necessary to keep spending growing. "Is the casino society a significant drag on economic growth?" Sweezy asked in a 1987 article he cowrote with Harry Magdoff. "Again, absolutely not. What growth the economy has experienced in recent years, apart from that attributable to an unprecedented peacetime military build-up, has been almost entirely due to the financial explosion."[24]

For Cassidy, it was the reasoned historical analysis of capitalism developed by Minsky and Sweezy that allowed each of them to perceive the dramatic transformations leading up to the early twenty-first-century crisis. "Minsky and Sweezy didn't agree on everything, but their highly developed critical faculties allowed them to see, well before many mainstream economists, that a new model of financially driven capitalism had emerged." Indeed, the "worldwide slump" that had its origins in the United States in 2007 "demonstrated that Minsky and Sweezy had been right when they said the fortunes of the economy at large couldn't be divorced from what happened on Wall Street." For Sweezy, in particular, stagnation and financialization represented coevolutionary phenomena caught in a "symbiotic embrace."[25]

Minsky's analysis pointed to what has become known as the Minsky moment, or the advent of financial crisis. In contrast, Sweezy's work on financialization, which he saw as a broad trend encompassing a stream of bubble-bursting events, stressed the causal role of what could be called the "Sweezy normal state" of stagnation in mature monopoly-capitalist economies. It is the Sweezy normal state and its relation to financialization with the rise of monopoly-finance capital—together with the globalized impact of these phenomena on the global South, particularly China—which forms the content of this book.

"Why Stagnation?"

On March 27, 1947, a now legendary debate on the future of capitalism took place at Harvard University between Sweezy and Schumpeter, two of its most popular and influential economists. As Paul Samuelson was to declare decades later, in the early 1970s: "Recent events on college campuses have recalled to my inward eye one of the great happenings in my own lifetime. It took place at Harvard back in the days when giants walked the earth and Harvard Yard. Joseph Schumpeter, Harvard's brilliant economist and social prophet, was to debate Paul Sweezy on 'The Future of Capitalism,' Wassily Leontief was in the chair as the moderator and the Littauer Auditorium could not accommodate the packed house."[26]

The debate between Sweezy and Schumpeter was part of the larger debate on stagnation in the 1930s through the early '50s, brought on by the Great Depression. Sweezy argued on the basis of Marx and Keynes that "accumulation is the primary factor" in capitalist development, yet noted that its influence was waning. "There is no mechanism in the system," he explained, "for adjusting investment opportunities to the way capitalists want to accumulate and no reason to suppose that if investment opportunities are inadequate capitalists will turn to consumption—quite the contrary." Hence, the motor was removed from the capitalist economy, which tended—without some external force, such as "the outside shot in the arm of a war"—toward long-run stagnation. Schumpeter, taking a more conservative and "Austrian" approach, apparently argued that a long cycle (Kondratieff) expansion might commence in the late 1950s, peaking in the late '80s; and yet the wind was likely to go out of the sails of the U.S. economy due to the waning of the entrepreneurial function and the rise of corporations and the state. Schumpeter did not deny the stagnationist tendency of the economy but thought growth was weighed down rather than stimulated by New Deal-type intrusions in the economy.[27]

Nearly twenty years later, Sweezy, writing with Paul Baran, published their now classic study, *Monopoly Capital*, which was to have a strong influence on New Left economics in the 1970s. "The normal state of the monopoly capitalist economy," they declared, "is stagnation."[28] According to this argument, the rise of the giant monopolistic (or oligopolistic) corporations had led to a tendency for the actual and potential investment-seeking surplus in society to rise. The very conditions of exploitation (or high price markups on unit labor costs) meant both that inequality in society increased and that more and more surplus capital tended to accumulate actually and potentially within the giant firms and in the hands of wealthy investors, who were unable to find profitable investment outlets sufficient to absorb all of the investment-seeking surplus. Hence, the economy became increasingly dependent on external stimuli such as higher government spending (particularly on the military), a rising sales effort, and financial expansion to maintain growth.[29] Such external stimuli, as Sweezy was later to explain, were "not part of the internal logic of the economy itself," falling "outside the scope of mainstream economics from which historical, political, and sociological considerations are carefully excluded."[30]

All of these external stimuli were self-limiting, and/or generated further long-run contradictions, leading to the resumption of stagnation tendencies. Sending capital investment abroad did little to abate the problem since the return flow of profits and other business returns, under conditions of unequal exchange between global North and South and U.S. hegemony in general, tended to overwhelm the outward flow. A truly epoch-making innovation, playing the role of the steam engine, the railroad, or the automobile in the nineteenth and early- to mid-twentieth centuries, might alter the situation. But such history-changing innovations of the kind that would alter the entire geography and scale of accumulation were not to be counted on and were probably less likely under mature monopoly-capitalist conditions. The result was that the economy, despite its ordinary ups and downs, tended to sink into a normal state of long-run slow growth, rather than the robust growth assumed by orthodox economics. In essence, an economy in which decisions on savings and investment are made privately tends to fall into a stagnation trap: existing demand is insufficient to absorb all of the actual and potential savings (or surplus) available, output falls, and there is no automatic mechanism that generates full recovery.[31]

Stagnation theory, in this sense, did not mean that strong economic growth for a time was impossible in mature capitalist economies—simply that stagnation was the normal case and that robust growth had to be explained as the result of special historical factors. This reversed the logic characteristic of neoclassical economics, which assumed that rapid growth was natural under capitalism, except when outside forces, such as the state or trade unions, interfered with the smooth operation of the market. Stagnation also did not necessarily mean deep downturns with negative growth, but rather a slowing down of the trend-rate of growth due to overaccumulation. Net investment (i.e., investment beyond that covered by depreciation funds) atrophied, since with rising productivity what little investment was called for could be met through depreciation funds alone. Stagnation thus assumed steady technological progress and rising productivity as its basis. It was not that the economy was not productive enough; rather it was too productive to absorb the entire investment-seeking surplus generated within production.

Baran and Sweezy's *Monopoly Capital* was published at the very height of the post–Second War boom and during the Vietnam War period. In the mid–1970s the U.S. economy slowed down drastically, ending a period of rapid expansion that had been fueled by: (1) the buildup of consumer liquidity during the war; (2) the second great wave of automobilization in the United States (including the construction of the interstate highway system); (3) a period of cheap energy based on the massive exploitation of oil; (4) the rebuilding of the war-torn European and Japanese economies; (5) two regional wars in Asia, and Cold War military spending in general; and (6) a period of unrivaled U.S. hegemony. As the external conditions lifting the economy during these years gradually waned, conditions of stagnation reemerged.

However, in the 1970s growing debt and the related casino economy emerged as a means of propping up U.S. capitalism, and by the 1980s the surplus capital from the entire world was drawn into the speculative whirlwind of a new, financialized economy centered in Wall Street. Paul Sweezy and Harry Magdoff were among the earliest and most persistent analysts of this new process of financialization, seeing it not simply in Minsky-like terms of periodic financial crises, but as a drug or stimulant, akin to those sometimes used by athletes, that had emerged within the system to keep the economy going despite what they called "creeping stagnation."[32] "Finance," they wrote in 1977, "acts as an accelerator of the business cycle, pushing it farther and faster along on the way up and steepening the decline on the way down." Agreeing with Minsky on financial instability, they nonetheless argued that "by focusing almost entirely on the financial aspects he overlooks other long-term factors which give a more solid base to the long wave of prosperity, and he likewise ignores the petering out of the boom-sustaining conditions as well as the resurgence of stagnation tendencies." The underlying problem remained the Sweezy normal state of stagnation, now complicated by an addiction to debt-based stimuli.[33]

On March 22, 1982, almost thirty-five years to the day from his legendary debate with Schumpeter at Harvard, Sweezy delivered a talk at the Harvard Economics Club entitled, "Why Stagnation?"[34] Here he recounted the origins of the great stagnation debate that had arisen at Harvard in the late 1930s, when a deep recession appeared in 1937, before full recovery from the Great Depression had occurred. This raised the question, as Alvin Hansen, Keynes's leading follower in the United States, posed it in his 1938 book, of *Full Recovery or Stagnation?* Schumpeter in his 1942 treatise, *Capitalism, Socialism, and Democracy*, labeled Hansen's stagnationist analysis "the theory of vanishing investment opportunity" and countered it with his own argument that the real problem preventing full recovery was the New Deal itself. It was this that led to the Sweezy-Schumpeter debate in 1947.[35]

In 1982, speaking three and a half decades after his famous debate with Schumpeter, Sweezy told his listeners at the Harvard Economics Club that the stagnation question arising out of the Great Depression had been "dropped without any satisfactory answer.... Reality is now posing it again," demonstrating that "the burial of stagnation was, to say the least, premature." However, what had fundamentally changed things since (beyond the growth in government spending) was the increased reliance on the promotion of credit/debt as a long-term stimulus to counter stagnation:

> Let me digress for a moment to point out that the fact that the overall performance of the economy in recent years has not been much worse than it actually has been, or as bad as it was in the 1930s, is largely owing to three causes: (1) the much greater role of government spending and government deficits; (2) the enormous growth of consumer debt, including residential mortgage debt, especially during the 1970s; and (3) the ballooning of the financial sector of the economy which, apart from the growth of debt as such, includes an explosion of all kinds of speculation, old and new, which in turn generates more than a mere trickledown of purchasing power into the "real" economy, mostly in the form of increased demand for luxury goods. These are important forces counteracting stagnation as long as they last, but there is always the danger that if carried too far they will erupt in an old-fashioned panic of a kind we haven't seen since the 1929–33 period....[36]

There could hardly have been a more far-sighted description of the contradictions of U.S. capitalism, pointing ahead to the Great Financial

Crisis of 2007–09, and to the conditions of severe economic stagnation that arose in its wake. These warnings, however, went unheeded, and no resurrection of the stagnation debate occurred in the 1980s.

Addressing the failure of younger generations of left economists to take up the question, Magdoff and Sweezy observed in *Stagnation and the Financial Explosion* in 1987:

> We both reached adulthood during the 1930s, and it was then that we received our initiation into the realities of capitalist economics and politics. For us economic stagnation in its most agonizing and pervasive form, including its far-reaching ramifications in every aspect of social life, was an overwhelming personal experience. We know what it is and what it can mean; we do not need elaborate definitions or explanations. But we have gradually learned, not altogether to our surprise of course, that younger people who grew up in the 1940s or later not only do not share but also do not understand these perceptions. The economic environment of the war and postwar periods that played such an important part in shaping their experiences was very different. For them stagnation tends to be a rather vague term, equivalent perhaps to a longer-than-usual recession but with no implications of possible grave political and international repercussions. Under these circumstances, they find it hard to relate to what they are likely to regard as our obsession with the problem of stagnation. They are not quite sure what we are talking about or what all the fuss is over. There is a temptation to say: just wait and see, you'll find out soon enough.[37]

Yet, rather than ending with such a pronouncement, Magdoff and Sweezy went on to explain in the remainder of their book why a stagnation tendency was so deeply embedded in mature monopoly-capitalist societies, prone to market saturation, and why financialization had emerged as a desperate and ultimately dangerous savior. In their chapter on "Production and Finance," they introduced a systematic analysis of the relation of the productive base of the economy to the financial superstructure (or as they also called it the relation of the "real economy" to finance), accounting for the increasingly shaky financial structure on top of a "stagnant productive sector."[38]

In his final article, "More (or Less) on Globalization," written in 1997, fifty years after the Sweezy-Schumpeter debate, Sweezy depicted the overaccumulation problem of developed capitalism in terms of three conditions: (1) growing monopolization at the global level with the expansion of multinational corporations, (2) the slowing down (or deepening stagnation) of the Triad economies, and (3) the "financialization of the accumulation process." For Sweezy, these three trends were "intricately related" and anyone wanting to understand the future of the capitalist economy needed to focus on their interrelation, and their presence within a capitalist system that was more and more globalized.[39]

Monopoly-Finance Capital and the Great Stagnation

Our own analysis in this book begins in many ways where Sweezy (and Harry Magdoff) left off, and carries forward as well the analysis of John Bellamy Foster and Fred Magdoff in *The Great Financial Crisis: Causes and Consequences* (2009).[40] What Sweezy called the "intricately related" aspects of monopolization, stagnation, financialization, and globalization have produced a new historical phase, which we refer to as "monopoly-finance capital." In this period the Triad economies are locked in a stagnation-financialization trap, while linked to the growth in the emerging economies via the global labor arbitrage—whereby multinational corporations exploit the differences in wage levels in the world in order to extract surplus profits. The result is the worsening of the overall problem of surplus capital absorption and financial instability in the center of the world economy. In this book we are particularly concerned with how this is working out at the global level, with considerable focus (in the later chapters) on how this is related to the Chinese economy.

Yet the central problem remains overaccumulation within the Triad, where the United States, despite its declining hegemony, still constitutes the trend-setting force in the world system of accumulation. The deepening effects of stagnation in the U.S. economy can be seen in Chart I.2, showing the long-run downward trend in the growth rate of industrial production in the United States.

Nor is the United States alone in this respect. Since the 1960s West Germany, France, the United Kingdom, Italy, and Japan have all seen even larger declines, when compared to the United States, in their trend-rates of growth of industrial production. In the case of Japan industrial production rose by 16.7 percent in 1960–70 and by a mere 0.04 percent in 1990–2010.[41]

Chart I.2. Industrial Production Index

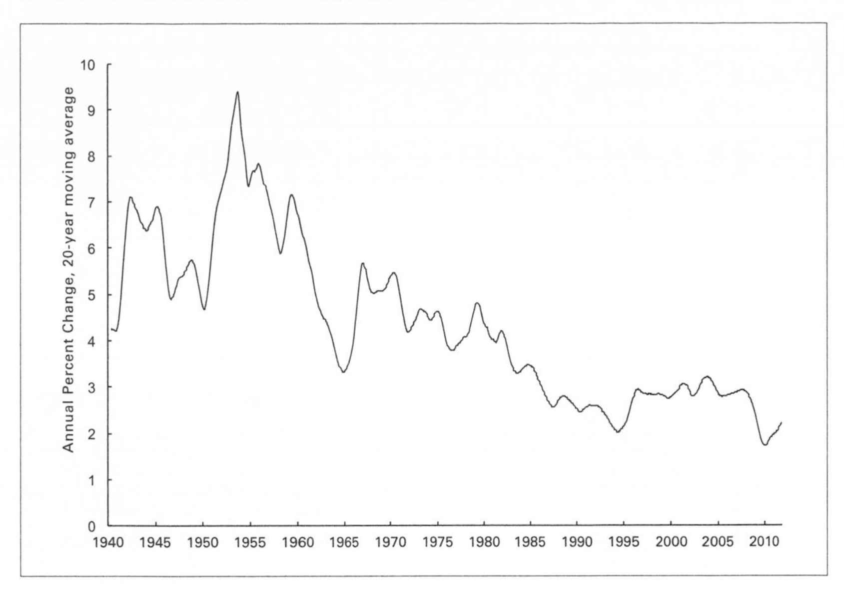

Source: FRED Graph Observations, Economic Research Division, Federal Reserve Board of St. Louis, Industrial Production Index (INDPRO), Index 2007=100, Monthly, Seasonally Adjusted, http://research.stlouisfed.org.

Note: Chart I.2 uses a twenty-year moving average. Moving averages are meant to smooth out fluctuations in order to highlight longer trends.

The story shown in Chart I.2 is one of deepening stagnation of production—already emphasized by Sweezy and Magdoff in the 1970s and '80s. Chart I.3, in contrast, reveals that this led—especially from the 1980s on—to a shift in the economy from production to speculative finance as the main stimulus to growth. Thus the FIRE (finance, insurance, and real estate) portion of national income expanded from 35 percent of the goods-production share in the early 1980s to over 90 percent in recent years. The so-called economic booms of the 1980s and '90s were powered by the rapid growth of financial speculation leveraged by increasing debt, primarily in the private sector.

The dramatic rise in the share of income associated with finance relative to goods production industries has not, however, been accompanied by an equally dramatic rise of the share of jobs in financial services as opposed to industrial production. Thus employment in FIRE as a percentage of employment in goods production over the last two decades has remained flat at about 22 percent. This suggests that the big increase in income associated with finance when compared to production has resulted in outsized gains for a relatively few income recipients rather than a corresponding increase in jobs.[42]

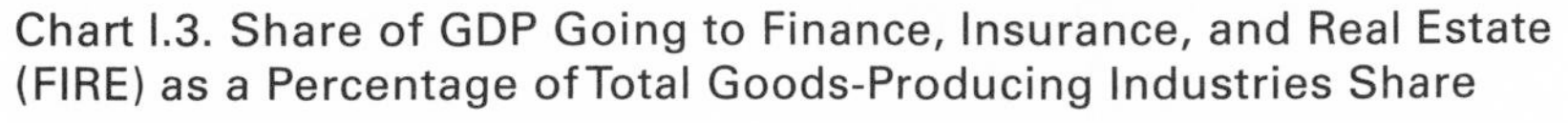
Chart I.3. Share of GDP Going to Finance, Insurance, and Real Estate (FIRE) as a Percentage of Total Goods-Producing Industries Share

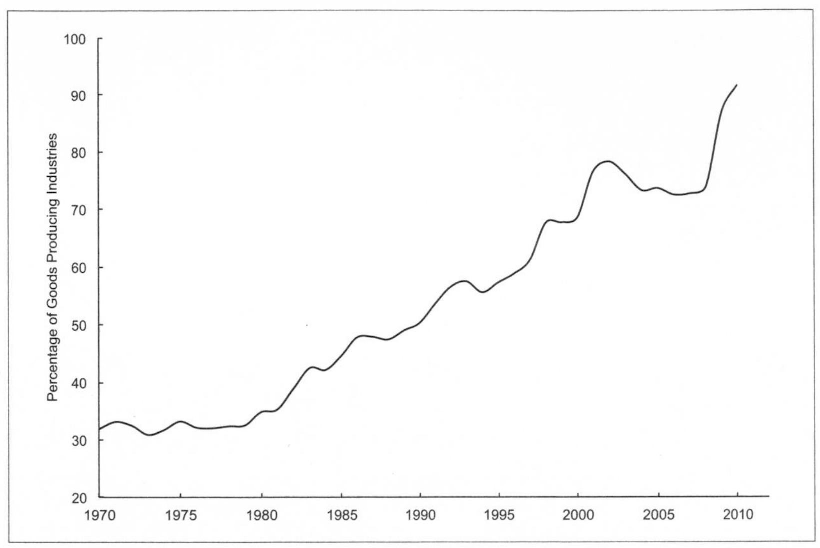

Source: Calculated from Bureau of Economic Analysis, National Income and Product Accounts Table 6.1B-D. National Income without Capital Consumption Adjustment, http://www.bea.gov/national/nipaweb.

Note: "Goods-Producing Industries" include: "Agriculture, Forestry, Fishing, and Hunting; Mining; Utilities; Construction; Manufacturing; Transportation and Warehousing." After 1998 (Table 6.1D), when the NAICS (North American Industrial Classification) replaced the SIC (Standard Industrial Classification) system, "Transportation and Public Utilities" was broken out into "Utilities" and "Transportation and Warehousing."

The rapid expansion of FIRE in relation to goods production in the U.S. economy is a manifestation of the long-run financialization of the economy, i.e., the shift of the center of gravity of economic activity increasingly from production (and production-related services) to speculative finance. In the face of market saturation and vanishing profitable investment opportunities in the "real economy," capital formation or real investment gave way before the increased speculative use of the economic surplus of society in pursuit of capital gains through asset inflation. As Magdoff and Sweezy explained as early as the 1970s, this could have an indirect effect in stimulating the economy, primarily by spurring luxury consumption. This has become known as the "wealth effect," whereby a portion of the capital gains associated with asset appreciation in the stock market, real estate market, etc., is spent on goods and services for the well-to-do, adding to the effective demand in the economy.[43]

Yet the stimulus provided by financialization has not prevented a multi-decade decline in the role of investment in the U.S. economy. Thus net private nonresidential fixed investment dropped from 4 percent of

Chart I.4. Growth Rate of Real Investment in Manufacturing Structures

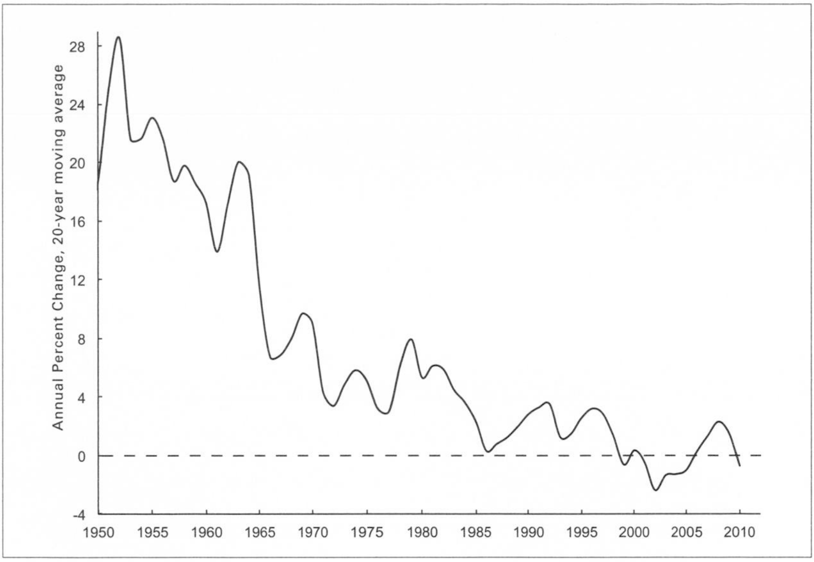

Source: Bureau of Economic Analysis, National Income and Product Accounts, Table 5.4.1. Percent Change from Preceding Period in Real Private Fixed Investment in Structures by Type, http://bea.gov/national/nipaweb.

GDP in the 1970s to 3.8 percent in the '80s, 3 percent in the '90s, and 2.4 percent in 2000–2010.[44] At the heart of the matter is the declining long-term growth rate of investment in manufacturing, and more particularly in manufacturing structures (construction of new or refurbished manufacturing plants and facilities), as shown in Chart I.4.[45]

Even with declining rates of investment growth, productivity increases in industry have continued, leading to the expansion of excess productive capacity (an indication of the overaccumulation of capital). This can be seen in Chart I.5 showing the long-term slide in capacity utilization in manufacturing. High and rising levels of unused (or excess) capacity have a negative effect on investment since corporations are naturally reluctant to invest in industries where a large portion of the existing capacity is standing idle. The U.S. automobile industry leading up to and during the Great Recession (like the worldwide industry) was faced with huge amounts of unused capacity—equal to approximately one-third of its total capacity. A 2008 *BusinessWeek* article underscored the global auto glut: "With sales tanking from Beijing to Boston, automakers find themselves in an embarrassing position. Having indulged in a global orgy of factory-building in recent years, the industry has the capacity to make an astounding 94 million vehicles each year. That's about 34 million too

Chart I.5. Manufacturing Capacity Utilization

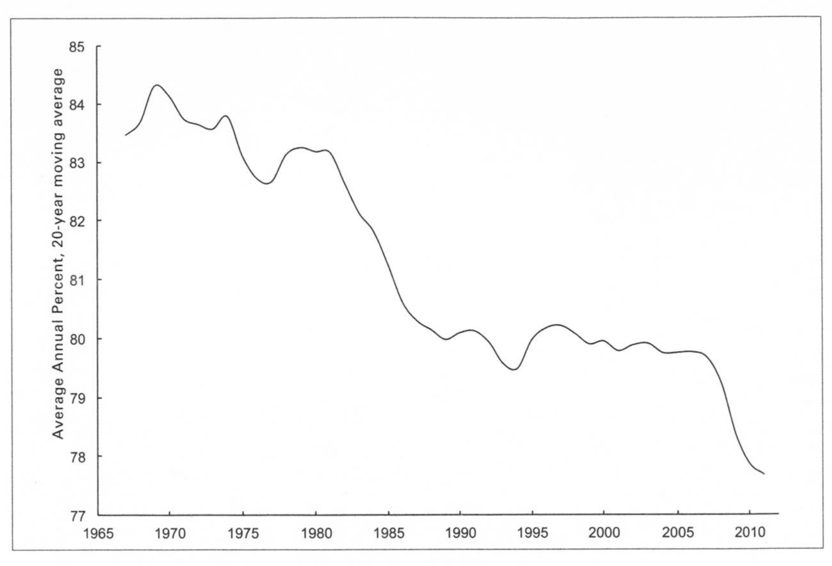

Source: *Economic Report of the President*, 1998, 2005, and 2012, Table B-52.

many based on current sales, according to researcher CSM Worldwide, or the output of about 100 plants."[46]

The decreasing utilization of productive capacity is paralleled by what we referred to in 2004 as "The Stagnation of Employment," or the growing unemployment and underemployment that characterizes both the U.S. economy and the economies of the Triad in general. According to the alternative labor underutilization measure, U6, of the Bureau of Labor Statistics, a full 14.9 percent of the civilian workforce (plus marginally attached workers) were unemployed or underemployed on a seasonally adjusted basis in the United States in February 2012.[47]

In these circumstances, the U.S. economy, as we have seen, has become chronically dependent on the ballooning of the financial superstructure to keep things going. Industrial corporations themselves have become financialized entities, operating more like banks in financing sales of their products, and often engaging in speculation on commodities and currencies. Today they are more inclined to pursue the immediate, surefire gains available through merger, acquisition, and enhanced monopoly power than to commit their capital to the uncertain exigencies associated with the expansion of productive activity. Political-economic power has followed the financial growth curve of the economy, with the economic base of political hegemony shifting from the real economy of production to the financial world, and increasingly serving the interests of the latter, in what became known as the neoliberal age.[48]

The main key to understanding these developments, however, remains the Sweezy normal state. The long-term trends associated with economic growth, industrial production, investment, financialization, and capacity utilization (as shown in Charts I–V above) all point to the same phenomenon of a long-term economic slowdown in the U.S. and the other advanced industrial economies.

A central cause of this stagnation tendency is the high, and today rapidly increasing, price markups of monopolistic corporations, giving rise to growing problems of surplus capital absorption. Taking the nonfarm business sector as a whole, the price markup on unit labor costs (the ratio of prices to unit labor costs) for the U.S. economy over the entire post–Second World War period averaged 1.57, with a low of around 1.50 in the late 1940s. However, from the late 1990s to the present the markup on unit labor costs—what the great Polish economist Michal Kalecki referred to as the "degree of monopoly"—has climbed sharply, to 1.75 in the final quarter of 2011. As stated in *The Economic Report of the President, 2012*: "The markup has now risen to its highest level in post–World War II history, with much of that increase taking place over the past four years. Because the markup of prices over unit labor costs is the inverse of the labor share of output, saying that an increase in the price markup is the highest in postwar history is equivalent to saying that the labor share of output has fallen to its lowest level."[49]

The Ambiguity of Global Competition

In line with the foregoing, the last few decades have seen the intensification of a growing trend today toward monopolization in the U.S. and global economies, reflected in: (1) concentration and centralization of capital on a world scale, (2) growth of monopoly power and profits, (3) the developing global supply chains of multinational corporations, and (4) the rise of monopolistic finance. The total annual revenue of the five hundred largest corporations in the world (known as the Global 500) was equal in 2004–08 to around 40 percent of world income, with sharp increases since the 1990s.[50] This strong monopolization tendency, however, is scarcely perceived today in the face of what is characterized in the conventional wisdom as ever-greater competition between firms, workers, and states.

We call this problem of mistaken identity, in which growing monopolization is misconstrued as growing competition, the "ambiguity of competition." From the days of Adam Smith to the present the development of monopoly power has always been seen as a constraint on free competition, particularly in the domain of price competition. As Smith put it in *The Wealth of Nations*, "The price of monopoly is upon every occasion the highest which can be got. The natural price, or the price of free competition, on the contrary, is the lowest which can be taken."[51] For classical political economists in the nineteenth century competition was only intense if there were numerous small firms. However, Karl Marx had already pointed in *Capital* to the concentration and centralization of capital, whereby bigger firms beat smaller ones and frequently absorb the latter through mergers and acquisitions.[52] This led to a vast transformation of industry in the last quarter of the nineteenth century and the beginning of the twentieth century, as production came to be dominated by a relatively small number of giant corporations. As John Munkirs wrote in 1985 in *The Transformation of American Capitalism*, "The genesis of monopoly capitalism (1860s to 1920s) created a stark dichotomy between society's professed belief in Smith's competitive market structure capitalism and economic reality."[53]

In the 1920s and '30s important innovations in economic theory were introduced designed to account for this new reality, under the rubric of "the theory of imperfect competition." The three most important pioneering attempts to alter mainstream economic theory to take account of monopoly power were developed by Edward H. Chamberlin in *The Theory of Monopolistic Competition* (1933), Joan Robinson in *The Economics of Imperfect Competition* (1933), and Paul Sweezy in "Demand under Conditions of Oligopoly" (1939).[54] As Robinson wrote, "We see on every side a drift toward monopolisation under the names of restriction schemes, quota systems, rationalisation, and the growth of giant companies."[55] In Chamberlin's terms, "The idea of a purely competitive *system* is inadmissible; for not only does it ignore the fact that the monopoly influence is felt in varying degrees throughout the system, but it sweeps it aside altogether.... In fact, as will be shown later, if either element [competition or monopoly] is to be omitted from the picture, the assumption of ubiquitous monopoly has much more in its favor."[56]

These analyses considered a wide variety of monopolistic and semi-monopolistic situations, describing how price competition was diminished with monopoly, how firms were able to set their own prices partly through "product differentiation" (a term coined by Chamberlin), and how industries were increasingly dominated by oligopolies (a few giant firms) with considerable monopoly power.

Chamberlin, who also introduced the concept of oligopoly into economic theory, emphasized its role in the very first chapter of his *Theory of Monopolistic Competition.* Sweezy's "Demand under Conditions of Oligopoly" introduced a theory of oligopolistic pricing, which argued that any price-cutting by giant oligopolistic firms was enormously destructive, leading to actual price warfare, in which firms would each lower their prices in order to retain market share and all would see their profits decline. Hence, large firms in mature, concentrated industries soon learned to collude indirectly in raising rather than lowering prices, with the result that prices (and more importantly profit margins) tended to go only one way—up.[57] The most frequent result of monopolistic (including oligopolistic) competition and the constraints on price competition it imposed, according to Chamberlin, was "excess productive capacity, for which there is no automatic corrective.... The surplus capacity is never cast off, and the result is high prices and waste."[58]

Since these theories of monopolistic competition challenged the notion of a freely competitive system, threatening the whole structure of orthodox economics, they were shunted aside—in an early version of the economics of innocent fraud—into a marginal realm within economics. A set of exceptions to perfect competition was recognized, but this was treated as outside the general model of the economy, which remained a world of perfect and pure competition. At the same time, economists introduced intermediary notions such as "workable competition" (a vague notion that in practice effective competition somehow continued) together with the idea of a new competition geared less to price competition than to innovation, i.e., the perennial gale of Schumpeterian "creative destruction."

Imperfect competition theory itself was reshaped to conform to the needs of economic orthodoxy. Hence, the notion of "monopolistic competition" was redefined simply to relate to conditions where numerous small firms were able to exploit favorable locations or product differentiation, while excluding oligopoly (the typical case) from the concept. Chamberlin himself was driven to object that oligopoly had been the starting point for monopolistic competition theory and its exclusion from the theory of monopolistic competition was absurd. "Monopolistic competition," he complained, was "converted from an almost universal phenomenon, which it surely is.... to the relatively unimportant one of differentiated products in the restricted case of 'large numbers.'"[59]

Competition was therefore redefined in public discourse to mean "workable competition" as a vague analogue to perfect competition, while economists in their basic models continued to hold on to the abstract notion of perfect and/or pure competition. Instances of oligopolistic rivalry—i.e., the intense battles between quasi-monopolistic firms over markets, product differentiation, and low-cost position (but seldom encompassing price cutting in final consumption markets)—were often erroneously treated as if they exemplified Smithian competition. Orthodox figures such as Milton Friedman meanwhile continued to argue that oligopolistic rivalry was the very antithesis of competition.

It is this confused situation that gives rise to the ambiguity of competition.[60] As Munkirs stated in *The Transformation of American Capitalism*: "Within the business community and the economics profession, [John Maurice] Clark's concept of 'workable competition' and Schumpeter's 'gales of creative destruction' were christened 'the new competition.' Simply by assigning a new meaning to the term competition, the ill effects of monopolistically competitive market structures were defined out of existence. Yet the real world does exist."[61]

In contrast, radical and Marxian thinkers were dedicated to a realistic historical outlook, and, as they had no reason to hold on to the notion of free competition where it contradicted such reality, continued to analyze the growing role of monopoly in the modern economic system. For early twentieth-century economist Rudolf Hilferding in Austria and Germany, such monopolization was characterized as the growth of "finance capital."[62] Lenin, following Hilferding, wrote of what he called "the monopoly stage of capitalism"—seeing this as the basis of modern imperialism.[63] The iconoclastic U.S. economist Thorstein Veblen developed an early theory of monopoly capitalism as part of his critique of "absentee ownership."[64]

Within the terrain of critical economics from the 1930s to '70s, Kalecki and Josef Steindl developed theories of the widening degree of monopoly and its relation to maturity and stagnation.[65] The purpose of Baran and Sweezy's *Monopoly Capital*, which drew much of its inspiration from Kalecki and Steindl, was "to begin the process of systematically analyzing monopoly capitalism on the basis of the experience of the most developed monopoly capitalist society"—the United States.[66] Likewise such works as Harry Magdoff's *The Age of Imperialism* (1969), James O'Connor's *The Fiscal Crisis of the State* (1973), and Harry Braverman's *Labor and Monopoly Capital* (1974) relied on the concept of monopoly capital.[67]

Our own line of inquiry in this book builds on such analyses, attempting to understand the current phase of monopoly-finance capital, in which stagnation and financialization have emerged as interrelated trends on a global scale. Here the paradox of an economy where financialization rather than capital accumulation has now become the motor of the system is explored.

The Globalization of Monopoly Capital, U.S. Hegemonic Decline, and the Rise of China

Still, even on the left the role of monopolization is far from universally accepted today, largely because of the changes in perception brought on by increased international competition (or transnational oligopolistic rivalry). In the 1970s core U.S. industries, such as steel and automobiles, began to be affected by international competition, seemingly undermining the power of U.S. monopoly capital.[68] The rise of multinational corporations, primarily in the Triad, was the vehicle for this enhanced world competition. This caused Joan Robinson to quip, "Modern industry is a system not so much of monopolistic competition as of competitive monopolies."[69]

Some observers saw this process of the creation of global oligopolies, which necessarily involved the amalgamation or destruction of the weaker of the national oligopolistic firms, as a return of the nineteenth-century-style competitive system. They were mistaken.

The theory of the multinational corporation, as developed by Stephen Hymer (who is still the definitional economic theorist in this area), saw the rise of these globetrotting firms as the product of the growth of the concentration and centralization of capital and monopoly power worldwide. Rather than a competitive market structure, as envisioned in orthodox economics, what was emerging was a system of global oligopolistic rivalry for the domination of world production by a smaller and smaller number of global corporations. Hymer went on to connect this to Marx's theory of the industrial reserve army of the unemployed, explaining that the monopolistic multinational corporations were in the process of creating a new international division of labor based on the formation of a global reserve army, and the exploitation of wage differentials worldwide (or the global labor arbitrage).[70] This global restructuring of production adopted a divide-and-rule approach to labor worldwide.

These changes were accompanied by a shift of the United States, beginning around 1980, from a massive surplus to a massive deficit country in its current account (the combined balances on trade in goods and services, income, and net unilateral transfers), turning it into the consumption engine of the world economy or "buyer of last resort."[71] All of this was made possible by U.S. dollar hegemony, coupled with financialization, whereby, as Yanis Varoufakis has argued, the United States became the *Global Minotaur*, borrowing and consuming out of proportion to its own production while providing markets for the exports of other countries.[72] This can be seen in Chart I.6, showing the growth of the U.S. current account deficit (a good part of which results from the deficit in the trade in goods and services) as a percent of GDP. During the last thirty years the United States has turned into the world's largest borrower, exploiting its position of financial hegemony and drawing in surplus capital from the rest of the world—while ultimately compounding its underlying problem of overaccumulation.

At the same time, the global labor arbitrage promoted by multinational corporations was restructuring the world economy, transferring much of world production to the global South. The giant corporations developed ever more complex supply chains extending to low-wage countries, with the final goods aimed primarily at markets in the global North, and the surplus capital seized in considerable part by the omnipresent multinational firms themselves. In the 1960s 6 percent of total U.S. corporate profits came from abroad. By the 1990s this had risen to 15 percent, and in 2000–2010 to 21 percent. [73]

Chart I.6. U.S. Current Account Balance

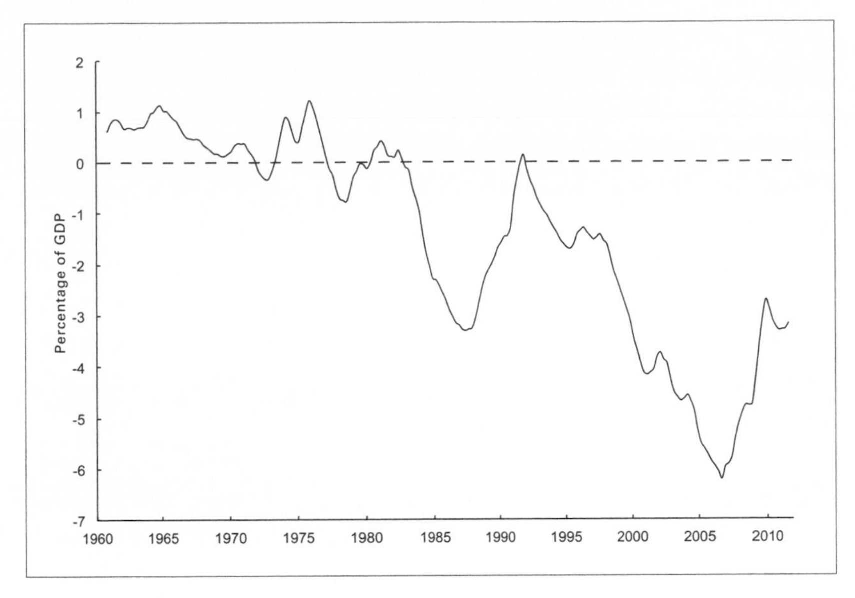

Source: St. Louis Federal Reserve FRED database, http://research.stlouisfed.org.

The biggest question mark generated by this new phase of accumulation today is the rapid growth of a few large emerging economies, particularly China and India. The vagaries of an accumulation system in these countries based on the exploitation of massive reserve armies of workers (in China a "floating population" of peasants) in the hundreds of millions, which cannot be absorbed internally through the standard industrialization process, makes the future of the new Asia uncertain. The imperial rent exacted by multinationals, who also control the global supply chains, means that emerging economies face what may appear to be an open door to the world market, but must proceed along paths controlled from outside.[74] The vast inequality built into a model of export-oriented development based on low-wage labor creates internal fault lines for emerging economies. China is now the site of continual mass protests, occurring on a scale of hundreds of thousands annually. In an article entitled "Is China Ripe for Revolution?" in the February 12, 2012, *New York Times*, Stephen R. Platt wrote that the Taiping Rebellion of the nineteenth century might stand as a historical reminder of the possibility of another major "revolution from within" in that country (in which case, he notes, Washington would most likely find itself "hoping for that revolution to fail").[75]

In many ways the world situation, with minor modifications, conforms to the diagnosis provided by Che Guevara at the Afro-Asian Conference in Algeria in 1965: "Ever since monopoly capital took over the world, it has kept the greater part of humanity in poverty, dividing all the profits among the group of the most powerful countries.... There should be no more talk about developing mutually beneficial trade based on prices forced on the backward countries by the law of value and the international relations of unequal exchange that result from the law of value."[76] If some emerging economies are now developing rapidly, the dominant reality is the global labor arbitrage that is increasing the level of exploitation worldwide, the greatest burden of which is falling on the global South.

An underlying premise throughout our analysis is that imperialist divisions within the world remain and are deep and in many cases deepening, enforcing wide disparities in living conditions. Still, in the age of global monopoly-finance capital working people everywhere are increasingly suffering—a phenomenon that Michael Yates has referred to as "The Great Inequality."[77] Entrenched and expanding monopolies of wealth, income, and power are aimed at serving the interests of a minuscule portion of the world population, now known as the 1%—or the global ruling classes of contemporary monopoly-finance capital. The world is being subjected to a process of monopolistic capital accumulation so extreme and distorted that not only has it produced the "Great Inequality" and conditions of stagnation and financial instability, but also the entire planet as a place of human habitation is being put in peril in order to sustain this very system.[78] Hence, the future of humanity—if there is to be one at all—now lies with the 99%. "If the system itself is at fault," Gar Alperovitz observes in his *America Beyond Capitalism*, "then self-evidently—indeed, by definition—a solution would ultimately require the development of a new system."[79]

CHAPTER 1

Monopoly-Finance Capital and the Crisis

Ironically, the eightieth anniversary of the 1929 Stock Market Crash that precipitated the Great Depression came at the very moment that the capitalist system was celebrating having narrowly escaped falling into a similar abyss. The financial crash and the decline in output, following the collapse of Lehman Brothers in September 2008, was as steep as at the beginning of the Great Depression. "For a while," Paul Krugman wrote in the *New York Times* in August 2009, "key economic indicators—world trade, world industrial production, even stock prices—were falling as fast or faster than they did in 1929–30. But in the 1930s the trend lines kept heading down. This time, the plunge appears to be ending after just one terrible year."[1] Big government, through the federal bailout and stimulus, as well as the shock-absorber effects of the continued payouts of unemployment and Social Security benefits, Medicare, etc., slowed the descent and helped the economy to level off, albeit at a point well below previous output.

Yet if the Great Recession leveled off before plunging into the depths of a second Great Depression, it nonetheless left the U.S. and world economies in shambles. Official U.S. unemployment rose to over 9 percent in 2009, while real unemployment, taking into account all of those wanting jobs plus part-timers desiring full-time work, was close to twice that. Capacity utilization in industry in the United States was at its lowest level since the 1930s. Investment in new plant and equipment faltered. The financial system was a shadow of what it was the year before. The recovery stage of the business cycle was destined to be sluggish.

Indeed, what economists most feared at that point and still continue to fear today was protracted economic stagnation or a long period of slow growth. "Though the economy may stabilize," Thomas Palley wrote for the New America Foundation, "it will likely be unable to escape the pull of stagnation. That is because stagnation is the logical next stage of the existing [economic] paradigm."[2] Judging by the actions of the economic authorities themselves, there seems to be no way out of the present economic malaise that is acceptable to the vested interests, but to restart the financialization process, i.e., the shift in the center of gravity of the economy from production to finance—meaning further financial bubbles. Yet, rather than overcoming the stagnation problem, this renewed financialization will only serve at best to put off the problem, while piling on further contradictions, setting the stage for even bigger shocks in the future.

This paradox of accumulation under today's monopoly-finance capital was captured in a column by Larry Elliott, economics editor of the London-based *Guardian*. He contrasted the Keynesian approach to the crisis, emphasizing fiscal stimulation and financial regulation, to the more conservative approach favored by British Chancellor of the Exchequer Alistair Darling, which sees the revival of a finance-driven economy as crucial. In Elliott's view, the support for the restoration of unfettered finance on the part of leading governmental authorities, such as Darling, may reflect the assessment (shared, ironically, with Marxian economics) that financialization is capital's primary recourse today in countering a basically stagnant economy. As Elliott himself puts it:

> Darling's more cautious approach [in contrast to Keynesian regulatory proposals] is, strangely perhaps, more in tune with the Marxist analysis of the crisis. This argues that it is not the financialisation of Western economies that explains the sluggish growth of recent decades; rather, it is the sluggish growth and the lack of investment opportunities for capital that explains financialisation. From this perspective, the only way capitalists could increase their wealth was through the expansion of a finance sector which, divorced from the real economy, became ever more prone to asset bubbles. Calling time on the casino economy does not mean balanced growth, it just means lower growth.
>
> Those interested in the Marxist perspective should get hold of *The Great Financial Crisis*, written by John Bellamy Foster and Fred Magdoff, published by Monthly Review Press in New York. It is a fascinating read. Whether Darling has read it, I don't know. I suspect,

however, that Treasury caution when it comes to reining in big finance has less to do with Marx and rather more to do with institutional capture.[3]

There are two key points here: (1) the determination of the economic authorities to reinstall the old regime of essentially unregulated financial markets may be due to a perception that the root problem is one of a stagnant real economy, leaving the casino economy as the only practical means of stimulating growth; (2) this attempt to restart financialization may also reflect "institutional capture," i.e., the growing power of financial interests within the capitalist state. These are not contradictory, as (1) invariably leads to (2), as in the case of military spending.

The extreme irrationality of such a solution is not lost on the *Guardian*'s economics editor, who presents the following dismal, but realistic, scenario: "After a short period in which bankers are chastened by their egregious folly there is a return to business as usual. This is the most worrying of all the [various] scenarios [arising from the crash], since it will mean that few—if any—of the underlying problems that caused the crisis have been solved. As a result, we can now start counting down the days to an even bigger financial crisis down the road."[4]

All of this underscores the stagnation-financialization trap of contemporary accumulation, from which it is now increasingly clear there is no easy or complete escape within the system. Such an irrational economic condition and its long-term significance cannot be explained by standard economic models, but only in terms of its historic evolution.

Stages of Accumulation

There has long been a fairly widespread agreement among Marxian political economists and economic historians that the history of capitalism up through the twentieth century can be divided into three stages.[5] The first of these stages is *mercantilism*, beginning in the sixteenth century and running into the eighteenth. In terms of the labor process and the development of productive forces, Marx defined this as the period of "manufacture" (meaning the age of handicraft production prior to the rise of what he called "machinofacture"). Nascent factories were typified by the increasingly detailed division of labor described by Adam Smith in his *Wealth of Nations*. Accumulation took place primarily in commerce, agriculture, and mining. What Marx called Department I (producing means of production) remained small in both absolute and relative terms in this stage, while Department II (producing commodities for consumption) was limited by its handicraft character.

The second stage is an outgrowth of the industrial revolution in Britain, centered at first in the textile trade and then spreading to industry generally. Viewed from the standpoint of the present, this is often conceived of as *competitive capitalism* and as the original age of liberalism. Here the focus of accumulation shifted sharply toward modern industry, and particularly the building up of Department I. This included not only factories themselves, but also a huge infrastructure of transportation and communications (railroads, telegraphs, ports, canals, steamships). This is a period of intense competition among capitals and a boom-and-bust cycle, with price competition playing a central role in governing economic activity.

The third stage, which is usually called *monopoly capitalism* or corporate capitalism, began in the last quarter of the nineteenth century and was consolidated in the twentieth century. It is marked by the spiraling concentration and centralization of capital, and the rise to dominance of the corporate form of business organization, along with the creation of a market for industrial securities. Industries increasingly come under the rule of a few (oligopolistic) firms that, in Joseph Schumpeter's terms, operate "corespectively" rather than competitively with respect to price, output, and investment decisions at both the national and increasingly global levels.[6] In this stage, Department I continues to expand, including not just factories but a much wider infrastructure in transportation and communications (automobiles, aircraft, telecommunications, computers, etc.). But its continued expansion becomes more dependent on the expansion of Department II, which becomes increasingly developed in this stage—in an attempt to utilize the enormous productive capacity unleashed by the growth of Department I. The economic structure can thus be described as "mature" in the sense that both departments of production are now fully developed and capable of rapid expansion in response to demand. The entire system, however, increasingly operates on a short string, with growing problems of effective demand. Technological innovation has been systematized and made routine, as has scientific management of the labor process and even of consumption through modern marketing. The role of price competition in regulating the system is far reduced.

A further crucial aspect of capitalist development, occurring during all three stages, is the geographical expansion of the system, which, over the course of its first three centuries, developed from a small corner in Western Europe into a world system. However, it was only in the nineteenth century that this globalization tendency went beyond one predominantly confined to coastal regions and islands and penetrated into the interior of continents. And it was only in the twentieth century that we see the emergence of monopoly capital at a high level of globalization—reflecting the growing dominance of multinational (or transnational) corporations.

From the age of colonialism, lasting well into the twentieth century, to the present phase of multinational-corporate domination, this globalizing process has operated imperialistically, in the sense of dividing the world into a complex hierarchy of countries, variously described as: developed and underdeveloped, center and periphery, rich and poor, North and South (with further divisions within both core and periphery). As in any complex hierarchy, there is some shifting over time in those that occupy the top and bottom (and in-between) tiers. Nevertheless, the overall level of social and economic inequality between countries at the world level has risen dramatically over the centuries. There is no real "flattening" of the world economy, as presumed by some ideologues of globalization such as Thomas Friedman.[7] Although industrialization has expanded in the periphery, it has generally been along lines determined by global corporations centered in the advanced capitalist countries, and therefore has tended to be directed to the demands of the center (as well as to the wants of the small, internal oligarchies in peripheral countries). Both departments of production in the periphery are thus heavily subject to imperialist influences.

With this thumbnail sketch of capitalism's historical development before us, it is possible to turn to some of the changes in the nature of accumulation and crisis, focusing in particular on transformations occurring at the core of the system. Capitalism, throughout its history, is characterized by an incessant drive to accumulate, leading to what Mark Blaug referred to as the "paradox of accumulation," identified with Marx's critique of capitalist economics. Since profits grow primarily by increasing the rate of exploitation of labor power, i.e., rise by restraining the growth of wages in relation to productivity, this ultimately places limits on the expansion of capital itself. This paradox of accumulation is reflected in what Paul Sweezy called the "*tendency* to overaccumulation" of capital.[8] Those on the receiving end of the economic surplus (surplus value) generated in production are constantly seeking to enlarge their profits and wealth through new investment and further augmentation of their capital (society's productive capacity). But this inevitably runs up against the relative deprivation of the underlying population, which is the inverse of this growing surplus. Hence, the system is confronted with insufficient effective demand—with barriers to consumption leading eventually to barriers to investment. Growing excess capacity serves to shut off new capital formation, since corporations are not eager to invest in new plant and equipment when substantial portions of their existing capacity are idle. This tendency to overaccumulation becomes increasingly dominant in mature, monopolistic capitalism, slowing the trend-rate of growth around which business cycle fluctuations occur, and thus raising the specter of long-term economic stagnation.

Competitive capitalism in the nineteenth century was dynamic at its core, since the tendency to overaccumulation was held at bay by favorable historical factors. In this period, capital was still being built up virtually from scratch. Department I, in particular, emerged to become a major part of the economy (Department II grew also, of course, but less dramatically). In the maturing capitalism of these years, the demand for new capital formation was essentially unlimited. The investment boom that typically occurred in the business cycle upswing did not generate lasting overaccumulation and overproduction. In these conditions it almost seemed possible, as U.S. economist J. B. Clark declared, to "build more mills that should make more mills for ever."[9] At the same time, the freely competitive nature of the system meant that prices, output, and investment levels were largely determined by market forces independent of individual firms. Many of the rigidities later introduced by giant corporations were therefore absent in the nineteenth-century era of free competition.

Although favorable to system-wide accumulation, the repeated boom-and-bust crises of competitive capitalism bankrupted firms, from small to large, throughout the economy. Bankruptcies hit firms even at the center of global financial power (Overend, Gurney in 1866; Jay Cooke in 1873; Baring's in 1890). In contrast, under the mature economy of monopoly capitalism, the dominant U.S. financial firms of 1909 are all still at the center of things a century later: J.P. Morgan, Goldman Sachs, National

City Bank—or in one notable case 99 years later—Lehman Brothers. But offsetting this increased stability at the center of wealth and power was the disappearance of many of the circumstances favorable for system-wide accumulation.

Once industry had been built up and existing productive capacity was capable of expanding output rapidly at a moment's notice (with whatever investment taking place capable of being financed through depreciation funds set aside to replace worn-out plant and equipment), the demand for new net investment for the rapid expansion of Department I was called into question. Hence, in the monopoly stage, capital saturation—the problem of too much capacity, too much production—becomes an ever-present threat. The system tends at all times to generate more surplus than can be easily absorbed by investment (and capitalist consumption). Under these circumstances, as Sweezy put it,

> The sustainable growth rate of Department I comes to depend essentially on its being geared to the growth of Department II.... If capitalists persist in trying to increase their capital (society's productive power) more rapidly than is warranted by society's consuming power...the result will be a build-up of excess capacity. As excess capacity grows, profit rates decline and the accumulation process slows down until a sustainable proportionality between the two Departments is again established. This will occur with the economy operating at substantially less than its full potential. In the absence of new stimuli (war, opening of new territories, significant technological or product innovations), this stagnant condition will persist: there is nothing in the logic of the reproduction process [of capital] to push the economy off dead center and initiate a new period of expansion.[10]

Such a tendency toward maturity and stagnation does not, of course, mean that the normal ups and downs of the business cycle cease—nor does it point to economic collapse. Rather, it simply suggests that the economy tends toward underemployment equilibrium with recoveries typically aborting short of full employment. The classic case is the Great Depression itself during which a full business cycle occurred in the midst of a long-term stagnation, with unemployment fluctuating over the entire period between 14 and 25 percent. The 1929 Stock Market Crash was followed by a recession until 1933, a recovery from 1933 to 1937, and a further recession in 1937–1938 (with full recovery only beginning in 1939 under the massive stimulus of the Second World War).

If, as Paul Baran and Paul Sweezy declared in *Monopoly Capital*, "the *normal* state of the monopoly capitalist economy is stagnation," this is due, however, not merely to the conditions of mature industrialization depicted above, but also to the changed pattern of accumulation associated with the drive to dominance of the giant firm.[11] In orthodox economic theory (both classical and neoclassical), the lynchpin of the so-called "self-regulation" of the economy is price competition, out of which the proverbial "invisible hand" of the system arises. It is this that translates productivity gains into benefits for society as a whole through the cheapening of products. Under monopoly (or oligopoly) capital, however, price competition is effectively banned, with the general price level for industry as a whole (except in the most severe deflationary crises) going only one way—up. Thus, although deflation was normal in nineteenth-century competitive capitalism (the trend of wholesale prices in the United States was downward during most of the century, with the notable exception of the Civil War), inflation was to become the norm in twentieth-century monopoly capitalism (the trend of wholesale prices was upward during most of the century, with the notable exception of the Great Depression).[12]

In the very early years of monopoly capitalism, it was quickly learned, through some spectacular business failures, that the giant firms faced the threat of mutual self-destruction if they engaged in fierce price competition, while an agreement to maintain or to raise prices, basically in tandem, removed this threat altogether. The resulting change in the nature of competition reflected what Schumpeter, as noted above, called the "corespective" nature of big corporations—only a few of which dominate most mature markets, and price their products through a process of indirect collusion (the most common form of which is the price leadership of the biggest firm). The rationality of such collusion can easily be explained in terms of the game-theory orientation often advanced by received economics. Refusal to collude, i.e., continuation of price competition, threatens destruction for all parties; collusion, in contrast, tends to benefit all parties. In such a clear case of coincident interests, collusion can often be indirect.[13]

To be sure, price competition is not entirely excluded in advanced capitalism, and may occur in those instances where firms have reason to think that they can get ahead by such means, such as in new industries not yet dominated by a few firms, i.e., before the shakedown process has occurred leading to oligopolistic conditions. This can clearly be seen in recent decades in computers and digital technology. Prices may also fall and a modicum of price competition may be introduced—albeit aimed at driving smaller firms out of business—due to the increased "global sourcing" of commodities produced in low-wage countries. This is evident, in retail, in the case of Wal-Mart, which relies heavily on goods imported from China. As a general rule, however, genuine price competition comes under a strong taboo in the monopoly stage of capitalism.

The implications of the effective banning of price competition at the center of the modern economy are enormous. Competition over productivity or for low-cost position remains intense, but the drastically diminished role of price competition means that the benefits of economic progress tend to be concentrated in the growing surplus of the big firms rather than disseminated more broadly by falling prices throughout the entire society. This aggravates problems of overaccumulation. Faced with a tendency to market saturation, and hence the threat of overproduction, monopolistic corporations attempt to defend their prices and profit margins by further reducing capacity utilization. This, however, prevents the economy from clearing out its excess capital, reinforcing stagnation tendencies. Idle plant and equipment are also held in reserve in the event that rapid expansion is possible. The monopoly capitalist economy thus tends to be characterized by high levels of unplanned *and planned* excess capacity.[14] Major corporations have considerable latitude to govern their output and investment levels, as well as their price levels, which are not externally determined by the market, but rather with an eye to their nearest oligopolistic rivals.

Competition thus does not altogether vanish under monopoly capitalism, but changes in form. Although today's giant corporations generally avoid genuine price competition (which, when referred to at all in business circles, is now given the negative appellation of price warfare), they nonetheless engage in intense competition for market share through the sales effort—advertising, branding, and a whole panoply of marketing techniques. As Martin Mayer wrote in *Madison Avenue* in the 1950s: "Advertising has been so successful financially because it is an effective, low-risk competitive weapon. It is the modern manner of accomplishing results which were formerly—at least in theory—secured by price-cutting."[15] Despite being a minor factor in nineteenth-century competitive capitalism, advertising thus becomes central to monopoly capitalism. This also reflects problems of market saturation and the need of corporations to expand their final consumption markets, if they are to continue to grow.[16]

The stagnation tendency endemic to the mature, monopolistic economy, it is crucial to understand, is not due to technological stagnation, i.e., any failure at technological innovation and productivity expansion. Productivity continues to advance and technological innovations are introduced (if in a more rationalized way) as firms continue to compete for low-cost position. Yet this, in itself, turns into a major problem of the capital-rich societies at the center of the system, since the main constraint on accumulation is not that the economy is not productive enough, but rather that it is *too productive*. Indeed, in numerous important cases, such as the modern automobile industry, corporations compensate by colluding to promote production platforms and marketing arrangements that maximize inefficiency and waste, while generating big profits. As Henry Ford II once said, "minicars [despite their greater fuel efficiency] make miniprofits."[17]

The appearance of a truly epoch-making innovation with geographical as well as economic scale effects—equivalent to the steam engine and the railroad in the nineteenth century, and the automobile in the twentieth—could, of course, alter the general conditions of the economy, constituting the catalyst for a new, long boom, in which capital accumulation feeds on itself for a considerable time. But epoch-making innovations on the economic scale of the railroad and the automobile have not been seen now for about a century and are obviously not to be counted on. Even the computer-digital revolution since the 1980s has been unable to come close to these earlier epoch-making innovations in stimulating economy-wide capital investment. Economists addressing the information economy see it as characterized by "an enhanced surplus extraction effect" derived from extensive monopoly power. Its capacity to mitigate the surplus absorption problem is thus extremely limited, pointing indeed to the opposite tendency. "Most Web activities," Tyler Cowen writes in *The Great Stagnation*, "do not generate jobs and revenue at the rate of past technological breakthroughs." Google, for example, had only about 20,000 employees overall in 2011.[18]

Monopoly-Finance Capital and the Crisis

The upshot of the preceding analysis is that accumulation under capitalism has always been dependent on the existence of external stimuli, not simply attributable to the internal logic of accumulation. "Long-run development," Michal Kalecki declared in his *Theory of Economic Dynamics*, "is not inherent in the capitalist economy. Thus specific 'development factors' are required to sustain a long-run upward movement."[19] Moreover, this problem of the historical factors behind growth becomes more severe under the regime of monopoly capital, which experiences a strong stagnationist pull. The whole question of accumulation and growth is thus turned upside down. Rather than treating the appearance of slow growth or stagnation as an anomaly that needs explaining by reference to external factors outside the normal workings of the system (as in orthodox economics), the challenge is to explain the anomaly of fast or full-employment growth, focusing on those specific historical factors that serve to prop up the system.

This can be illustrated by looking briefly at the history of accumulation and crisis from the 1930s to the present. Economists discovered the Great Depression as a problem quite late—at the tail end of the 1930s. The early years of the Depression, marked by the 1929 Stock Market Crash and the recession that lasted until 1933, were seen as representing a severe downturn, but not an extraordinary change in the working of capitalism. Schumpeter typified the main response by declaring that recovery would simply come "of itself."[20] It was, rather, the slow recovery that commenced in 1933 that was eventually to alter perceptions, particularly after the recession that began in 1937, and which resulted in unemployment leaping from 14 to 19 percent.

John Maynard Keynes's magnum opus, *The General Theory of Employment, Interest and Money* (1936), had pointed to the possibility of the capitalist economy entering a long-term underemployment equilibrium. As he wrote: "It is an outstanding characteristic of the economic system in which we live that...it seems capable of remaining in a chronic condition of sub-normal activity for a considerable period without any marked tendency either towards recovery or towards complete collapse."[21] This analysis, plus the 1937–38 downturn, induced some economists, such as Alvin Hansen, Keynes's leading early follower in the United States, to raise the question *Full Recovery or Stagnation?*—the title of Hansen's 1938 book.[22]

What followed was an intense but short-lived debate in the United States on the causes of economic stagnation. Hansen raised the issue of maturity, using it to explain the long-term tendency for the capital-rich economy, left to itself, to move "sidewise or even slip down gradually." In contrast, Schumpeter, Hansen's main opponent in the debate, attributed stagnation, not so much to the workings of the economy, but rather to the decline of the sociological foundations of entrepreneurial capitalism with the rise of the modern corporation and state. He ended his *Business Cycles* with the words: "The sociological drift cannot be expected to change."[23] The entire debate, however, came to an abrupt and premature end (it was resurrected briefly after the war but without the same fervor) due to the major stimulus to the economy that ensued with the outbreak of the Second World War in Europe.

As in the case of the Second World War itself, the changed economic conditions in the aftermath of the war were extremely favorable for accumulation. The United States emerged from the war with what Robert Heilbroner described as "the largest reserve of liquid purchasing power [debt-free consumer liquidity] ever accumulated" in its history—if not in the history of capitalism in general. This helped provide the basis, along with heavy government spending on highways, for the second great wave of automobilization in the United States (which included not only the direct effects on industry but also the whole phenomenon of suburbanization). Meanwhile, military spending continued at a much higher level than before the Second World War, with annual U.S. spending on the Korean War rising to about half of peak U.S. spending in the Second World War in both theaters combined.[24] These were also years of the rebuilding of the war-devastated economies in Western Europe and Japan. Finally, the rise of the United States to undisputed hegemony in the world economy was accompanied by the creation of the Bretton Woods institutions (GATT, the World Bank, and the IMF), and the expansion of world trade and finance.

The so-called "golden age" of the 1950s and '60s, however, gradually ran out of steam as the historical forces propelling it waned in influence, turning eventually into what Joan Robinson termed a "leaden age."[25] The consumer liquidity that fed the postwar buying spree dried up. The second-wave automobilization of the country was completed and the automobile industry sank into long-run simple reproduction. Military spending continued to boost the economy with a second regional war in Asia, but with the end of the Vietnam War, this stimulus ebbed. The European and Japanese economies were soon rebuilt, and the new productive capacity that they generated, plus industrial capacity emerging in the periphery, contributed to the growth of international surplus capacity, already becoming evident by the early 1980s.[26] The weakening of U.S. hegemony created growing economic rivalries at the global level.

In 1974–75 the U.S. economy and the world economy as a whole entered a full-fledged structural crisis, ending the long boom, and marking the beginning of decades of deepening stagnation. The worsening conditions of accumulation were to be seen in a downward shift in the real growth rate of the U.S. economy, which was lower in the 1970s than in the 1960s; lower in the 1980s and 1990s than in the 1970s; and lower in 2000–2007 than in the 1980s and 1990s. Since the onset of the Great Financial Crisis in 2007 the economy has descended into a period of protracted stagnation, in the deepest crisis since the Great Depression. As a result, 2000–09 was by far the worst decade in economic performance since the 1930s, while the present decade so far looks no better.[27]

Some analysts, most notably Harry Magdoff and Paul Sweezy in a number of works, described from the very onset of the mid-1970s crisis the resurfacing of overaccumulation and stagnation tendencies.[28] But it was at this time that a new, partial fix for the economy emerged—one that was clearly unanticipated, and yet a logical outcome of the whole history of capitalist development up to that point. This came in the form of the creation of a vast and relatively autonomous financial superstructure on top of the productive base of the capitalist economy.

Financial markets and institutions had, of course, evolved historically along with capitalism. But financial booms were typically short-term episodes coinciding with business cycle peaks, and lacked the independent character that they were to assume in the 1980s and 1990s. Thus, as Sweezy insightfully wrote in 1994 in "The Triumph of Financial Capital":

> Traditionally, financial expansion has gone hand-in-hand with prosperity in the real economy. Is it really possible that this is no longer true, that now in the late twentieth century the opposite is more nearly

> the case: in other words, that now financial expansion feeds not on a healthy economy but a stagnant one? The answer to this question, I think, is yes it is possible, and it is happening. And I will add that I am quite convinced that this inverted relation between the financial and the real is the key to understanding the new trends in the world [economy].[29]

To understand the historical change that took place in this period, it is crucial to recognize that there are, in essence, two price structures in the modern capitalist economy: one related to the pricing of output and associated with GDP and what economists call "the real economy"; the other related to the pricing of assets, composed primarily in the modern period of "financial assets" or paper claims to wealth.[30] Essentially, what occurred was this: unable to find an outlet for its growing surplus in the real economy, capital (via corporations and individual investors) poured its excess surplus/savings into finance, speculating in the increase in asset prices. Financial institutions, meanwhile, on their part, found new, innovative ways to accommodate this vast inflow of money capital and to leverage the financial superstructure of the economy up to ever greater heights with added borrowing—facilitated by all sorts of exotic financial instruments, such as derivatives, options, securitization, etc. Some growth of finance was, of course, required as capital became more mobile globally. This, too, acted as a catalyst, promoting the runaway growth of finance on a world scale.

The result was the creation of mountains of debt coupled with extraordinary growth in financial profits. Total private debt (household and business) rose from 110 percent of U.S. GDP in 1970 to 293 percent of GDP in 2007; while financial profits skyrocketed, expanding by more than 300 percent between 1995 and mid-2007.[31]

This decades-long process of financialization from the 1970s and 1980s up to the present crisis had the indirect effect of boosting GDP growth through various "wealth effects"—the now well-recognized fact that a certain portion of *perceived* increases in assets reenters the productive economy in the form of economic demand, particularly consumption. For example, increased consumer spending on housing occurred as well-to-do individuals benefiting from the upward valuation of assets (real estate and stocks) purchased second homes, contributing to a boom in upper-end home construction.[32] Yet the consequence was the increasing dependence of the entire economy on one financial bubble after another to keep the game afloat. And, with each extension of the quantity of credit-debt, its quality diminished. This whole process meant growing reliance on the Federal Reserve Board (and the central banks of the other leading capitalist powers) as "lenders of last resort" once a major financial bubble burst.

As financialization took hold, first in the 1970s, and then accelerated in the decades that followed, the U.S. and world economies were subject to growing financial crises (euphemistically referred to as credit crunches). At least fifteen major episodes of financial disruption have occurred since 1970, the most recent of which are: the 1998 Malfunctioning of Long-Term Capital Management; the 2000 New Economy crash; and the 2007–2009 Great Financial Crisis. Not only have financial crises become endemic, they have also been growing in scale and global impact.[33]

The symbiotic relation between stagnation and financialization meant that, at each financial outbreak, the Federal Reserve and other central banks were forced to intervene to bail out the fragile financial system, lest the financial superstructure as a whole collapse and the stagnation-prone economy weaken still further. This led to the long-term, piece-by-piece deregulation of the financial system and the active encouragement by state authorities of financial innovation. This included the growth of "securitization"—the transformation of non-marketable debts into marketable securities, under the illusion that credit risk could be reduced and profits expanded by these means. The entire system became internationalized under the leadership of what Peter Gowan called the "Dollar Wall Street Regime." Growth of international finance was facilitated by the rapid development and application of communications technologies, promoting increased competition between financial centers—with Wall Street remaining the world financial hub.[34]

Key to the new financial system in the United States was the emergence of a "financial-industrial complex," as major industrial corporations were drawn into the new system, shifting from equity to debt financing, and developing their own financial subsidiaries. Concentration in finance grew hand over fist—a process that has only accelerated in the present crisis. As recently as 1990, the ten largest U.S. financial institutions held only 10 percent of total financial assets; today they own 50 percent. The top twenty institutions now hold 70 percent of financial assets—up from 12 percent in 1990. At the end of

1985, there were 18,000 FDIC-member banks in the United States. By the end of 2007, this had fallen to 8,534, and since then has dropped still further. Of the fifteen largest U.S. banks in 1991 (together holding at that time $1.5 trillion in assets), only five remained by the end of 2008 (holding $8.9 trillion dollars in assets). As leading financial analyst Henry Kaufman has stated: "In a single generation, our financial system has been transformed. After operating for centuries as a constellation of specialized services, it has melded together rapidly into a highly concentrated oligopoly of enormous, diversified, integrated firms." He continued: "When the current crisis abates, the pricing power of these huge financial conglomerates will grow significantly, at the expense of borrowers and investors."[35]

The foregoing developments can be seen as marking the transformation of the stage of monopoly capital into the new phase of monopoly-finance capital. Characteristic of this phase of accumulation is the stagnation-financialization trap, whereby financial expansion has become the main "fix" for the system, yet is incapable of overcoming the underlying structural weakness of the economy. Much like drug addiction, new, larger fixes are required at each point merely to keep the system going. Every crisis leads to a brief period of restraint, followed by further excesses. Other external stimuli, such as military spending, continue to play a significant role in lifting the economy, but are now secondary in impact to the ballooning of finance.[36]

Today's neoliberal regime itself is best viewed as the political-policy counterpart of monopoly-finance capital. It is aimed at promoting more extreme forms of exploitation—both directly and through the restructuring of insurance and pension systems, which have now become major centers of financial power. Neoliberal accumulation strategies, which function with the aid of a "predator state," are thus directed first and foremost at enhancing corporate profits in the face of stagnation, while providing further needed cash infusions into the financial sector. Everywhere, the advent of neoliberalism has meant an intensification of the class struggle, emanating from both corporations and the state.[37] Far from being a restoration of traditional economic liberalism, neoliberalism is thus a product of big capital, big government, and big finance on an increasingly global scale.[38]

Neoliberalism has also increased international inequalities, taking advantage of the very debt burden that peripheral economies were encouraged to take on, in order to force stringent restructuring on poorer economies: including removal of restrictions on the movement of capital, privatization, deregulation, elimination of state supports to the poor, deunionization, etc.

In the face of financial sector losses, the Federal Reserve Board and U.S. Treasury have explicitly adopted a "too big to fail" policy, giving the lie to the neoliberal notion of a "self-regulating" market economy. The goal has been to prop up the leading financial institutions and to socialize their losses, while retaining an explicit policy of non-intervention during periods when the financial bubble is expanding—thereby allowing corporations to benefit fully from a bubble while it lasts.

Under monopoly-finance capital, we thus see an intensification of the paradox of accumulation. Superimposed on top of the deepening tendency to overaccumulation in the real or productive economy is the further contradiction of a system that increasingly seeks to promote growth in production as a secondary effect of the promotion of speculative financial assets. It is as if, in Marx's famous short-hand, one could indefinitely expand wealth and value by means of M[oney]-M′, instead of M-C[ommodity]-M′—skipping altogether the production of commodities in the generation of surplus value, i.e., profit. This is a potent sign, if there ever was one, of the system's increasing irrationality.

The fact that the root difficulty remains a rising rate of exploitation of workers is indicated by the fact that, in 2006, the real hourly wage rate of private, non-agricultural workers in the United States was the same as in 1967, despite the enormous growth in productivity and wealth in the succeeding decades. In 2000–07, productivity growth in the U.S. economy was 2.2 percent, while median hourly wage growth was -0.1 percent. Wage and salary disbursements as a percentage of GDP declined sharply from approximately 53 percent in 1970 to about 46 percent in 2005. Yet, as if in stark defiance of these trends, consumption at the same time rose as a percent of GDP from around 60 percent in the early 1960s to about 70 percent in 2007.[39] Such contradictory developments were made possible by a massive expansion of household debt and the creation in the end of a household bubble, rooted in the securitization of home mortgages. The bursting of the "housing bubble" was the inevitable result of the destruction of the household finances of the great majority of the working population.[40]

THE SYSTEM'S NO-EXIT STRATEGY

In the Great Financial Crisis and the Great Recession that followed hard upon it, the Federal Reserve and U.S. Treasury, along with the other central banks and treasury departments, have committed tens of trillions of dollars to bailing out financial institutions (by early 2009, over $12 trillion in capital infusions, debt support, and other financial commitments to corporations were provided in the bailout by the U.S. government alone).[41] In order to effect this, in the case of the United States, huge quantities of dollars have been printed, the Federal Reserve's balance sheet has ballooned, and the federal deficit has soared. Although world capital has sought out dollars in the crisis, inflating the dollar's value and seemingly strengthening its position as the hegemonic currency, particularly with the crisis of the euro, there are fears now that the process may go into reverse as world economic recovery takes hold, further destabilizing global finance.[42]

For some economic analysts and investors, the saving grace of the world economy is the rapid economic growth in China and India. This is often seen as eventually pointing toward a new hegemony, based in China, and a new, long upswing in capitalist growth.[43] At present, however, the weight of such emerging capitalist economies is not sufficient to counterbalance the stagnation in the core. And even the most optimistic long-run projections—in which China and India (along with other emerging economies) are able to leap to the next stage of accumulation without further class polarization and destabilization—nonetheless point to insurmountable problems of maturity, stagnation, and financialization (not to mention the overwhelming of planetary resources).

At the core of the system, meanwhile, the forces restraining growth remain considerable. "The current crisis," Kaufman has written, "has brought an end to a decades-long period of private sector debt growth. The institutions that facilitated rapid debt growth in recent decades are now virtually disabled, their borrowers overloaded."[44]

Does this mean that the financialization process, which has been propelling the economy in recent decades, has now come to a standstill, and that a deep, prolonged stagnation is therefore to be expected in the months and years ahead? We believe, as indicated above, that this is the most likely result of the current crisis.

Nevertheless, there are, as we have seen, strong forces pushing for the reinstitution of financialization via the state, with the idea of getting the whole speculative momentum going again. In some cases, this is under the deceptive guise of very modest moves to financial regulation in order to promote confidence and to "legitimize" the system. Indeed, all the indications at present are that financial capital is being put back in the saddle. And with some of the earlier forms of securitization now no longer able to attract investors, the large financial conglomerates are peddling what *BusinessWeek* calls "a new generation of dicey products." For example:

> In recent months such big banks as Bank of America, Citigroup, and JPMorgan Chase have rolled out new-fangled corporate credit lines tied to complicated and volatile derivatives....Some of Wall Street's latest innovations give reason to pause....Lenders typically tie corporate credit lines to short-term interest rates. But now Citi, JPMorgan Chase, and BofA, among others, are linking credit lines both to short-term rates and credit default swaps (CDSs), the volatile and complicated derivatives that are supposed to operate as "insurance" by paying off the owners if a company defaults on its debt....In these new arrangements, when the price of the CDS rises—generally a sign the market thinks the company's health is deteriorating—the cost of the loan increases, too. The result: the weaker the company, the higher the interest rates it must pay, which hurts the company further.... Managers now must deal with two layers of volatility—both short-term rates and credit default swaps, whose prices can spike for reasons outside their control.

BusinessWeek goes on to inform its affluent readers of other new speculative instruments that are being introduced, such as "structured notes" or a form of derivative aimed at small investors, offering "teaser rates"—virtually guaranteeing high returns for small investors for a few years, followed by "huge potential losses" after that.[45]

Whether a major new financial bubble will be generated by such means under current circumstances is at this point impossible to determine. There is no denying, however, that restoring the conditions for finance-led expansion has now become the immediate object of economic policy in the face of a persistently stagnation-prone real economy. The social irrationality of such a response only highlights the paradox of accumulation—from which there is today no exit for capital. The main barrier to the accumulation of capital remains the accumulation of capital itself!

CHAPTER 2

The Financialization of Accumulation

> In the way that even an accumulation of debts can appear as an accumulation of capital, we see the distortion involved in the credit system reach its culmination.
>
> —KARL MARX[1]

IN 1997, IN HIS last published article, Paul Sweezy referred to "the financialization of the capital accumulation process" as one of the three main economic tendencies at the turn of the twenty-first century.[2] Those familiar with economic theory will realize that the phrase was meant to be paradoxical. All traditions of economics, to varying degrees, have sought to separate out analytically the role of finance from the "real economy." Accumulation is conceived as real capital formation, which increases overall economic output, as opposed to the appreciation of financial assets, which increases wealth claims but not output. In highlighting the financialization of accumulation, Sweezy was therefore pointing to what can be regarded as "the enigma of capital" in our time.[3]

To be sure, finance has always played a central, even indispensable, role in capital accumulation. Joseph Schumpeter referred to the credit "created *ad hoc*" as one of the defining traits of capitalism. "The money market," he added, "is always... the headquarters of the capitalist system."[4] Yet something fundamental has changed in the nature of capitalism in the closing decades of the twentieth century. Accumulation—real capital formation in the realm of goods and services—has become increasingly subordinate to finance. Keynes's well-known fear that speculation would come to dominate over production seems to have finally materialized.

When Sweezy made his observation with respect to the financialization of capital accumulation more than a decade ago, it drew very little

Chart 2.1. Net Private Borrowing and Net Private Fixed Investment

Sources: Federal Reserve Board, Flow of Funds Accounts of the United States, Table D.2; Bureau of Economic Analysis, National Income and Product Accounts, Table 5.2.5, Line 9.

attention. But today, following the greatest financial and economic crisis since the Great Depression, we can no longer ignore the question it raises. Now more than ever, as Marx said, "an accumulation of debts" appears as "an accumulation of capital," with the former increasingly effacing the latter. As shown in Chart 2.1, net private borrowing has far overshot total net private fixed investment over the last third of a century—in a process culminating in 2007–2009 with the bursting of the massive housing-financial bubble and the plummeting of both borrowing and investment.[5]

Indeed, since the 1970s we have witnessed what Kari Polanyi Levitt appropriately called "The Great Financialization."[6] Financialization can be defined as the long-run shift in the center of gravity of the capitalist economy from production to finance. This change has been reflected in every aspect of the economy, including: (1) increasing financial profits as a share of total profits; (2) rising debt relative to GDP; (3) the growth of FIRE (finance, insurance, and real estate) as a share of national income; (4) the proliferation of exotic and opaque financial instruments; and (5) the expanding role of financial bubbles.[7] In 1957 manufacturing accounted for 27 percent of U.S. GDP, while FIRE accounted for only 13 percent. By 2008 the relationship had reversed, with the share of manufacturing dropping to 12 percent and FIRE rising to 20 percent.[8] Even with the setback of the Great Financial Crisis, there is every indication that this general trend to financialization of the economy is continuing, with neoliberal economic policy aiding and abetting it at every turn. The question therefore becomes: How is such an inversion of the roles of production and finance to be explained?

Keynes and Marx

In any attempt to address the role of finance in the modern economy, the work of John Maynard Keynes is indispensable. This is especially true of Keynes's achievements in the early 1930s when he was working on *The General Theory of Employment, Interest and Money* (1936). It is here, in fact, that Marx figures centrally in Keynes's analysis.

In 1933 Keynes published a short piece called "A Monetary Theory of Production," which was also the title he gave to his lectures at the time. He stressed that the orthodox economic theory of exchange was modeled on the notion of a barter economy. Although it was understood that money was employed in all market transactions under capitalism, money was nonetheless "treated" in orthodox or neoclassical theory "as being in some sense *neutral*." It was not supposed to affect "the essential nature of the transaction" as "one between real things." In stark opposition, Keynes proposed a monetary theory of production in which money was one of the operative aspects of the economy.

The principal advantage of such an approach was that it established how economic crises were possible. In this, Keynes was launching a direct attack on the orthodox economic notion of Say's Law that supply created its own demand—hence, on the view that economic crisis was, in principle, impossible. Challenging this, he wrote, "booms and depressions are phenomena peculiar to an economy in which... money is not neutral."[9]

In order to develop this crucial insight, Keynes distinguished between what he called a "co-operative economy" (essentially a barter system) and an "entrepreneur economy," where monetary transactions entered into the determination of "real-exchange" relations. This distinction, Keynes went on to explain in his lectures, "bears some relation to a pregnant observation made by Karl Marx....He pointed out that the nature of production in the actual world is not, as economists seem often to suppose, a case of *C-M-C′*, i.e., of exchanging commodity (or effort) for money in order to obtain another commodity (or effort). That may be the standpoint of the private consumer. But it is not the attitude of *business*, which is a case of *M-C-M′*, i.e., of parting with money for commodity (or effort) in order to obtain more money."[10]

"An entrepreneur," Keynes insisted, in line with Marx, "is interested, not in the amount of product, but in the amount of *money* which will fall to his share. He will increase his output if by so doing he expects to increase his money profit." Conversely, the entrepreneur (or capitalist) will decrease the level of output if the expectation is that the money profit will not increase. The monetary aspect of exchange, as depicted by Marx's M-C-M′, thus suggested, not only that monetary gain was the sole object of capitalist production, but that it was also possible for economic crises to arise due to interruptions in the process. Following his discussion of Marx's M-C-M′, Keynes went on to declare in terms similar to Marx: "The firm is dealing throughout in terms of sums of money. It has no object in the world except to end up with more money than it started with. That is the essential characteristic of the entrepreneur economy."[11]

Keynes, as is well known, was no Marx scholar.[12] The immediate inspiration for his references to Marx in his lectures was the work of the American economist Harlan McCracken, who had sent Keynes his book, *Value Theory and Business Cycles*, upon its publication in 1933. McCracken's analysis focused on the problem of effective demand and the role of money, in the tradition of Malthus. But he dealt quite broadly with the history of economic thought. In his chapter on Marx, which Keynes cited in his lecture notes, and which is well worth quoting at length in this context, McCracken wrote:

> In dealing with exchange or the metamorphosis of commodities, he [Marx] first treated C-M-C (Commodity for Money for Commodity). Such an exchange he considered no different in principle from barter since the object of exchange was to transfer a commodity of little or no utility to its possessor for a different commodity of high utility, and money entered in as a convenient medium to effect the transaction. The double transaction indicated no exploitation, for the assumption was that in each transaction there was an exchange of equivalent values, or quantities of embodied labor, so the final commodity had neither more nor less value than the original commodity, but had a

> higher utility for the recipient. Thus the metamorphosis C-M-C represented an exchange of equivalent values and no exploitation....
>
> But the metamorphosis M-C-M′ was fundamentally different. And it was in explaining this formula that Marx treated thoroughly the nature and source of *surplus* value. In this case, the individual starts with money and ends with money. The only possible motive, then, for making the two exchanges was to end with more money than at the beginning. And the extent to which the second M or M′ exceeds the first, is the measure of surplus value. However, surplus value was not created or gained in the circulation of commodities but in production.[13]

In a letter to McCracken, dated August 31, 1933, Keynes thanked him for his book, adding: "For I have found it of much interest, particularly perhaps the passages relating to Karl Marx, with which I have never been so familiar as I ought to have been."[14]

Basing himself on McCracken's exposition of Marx, Keynes proceeded to explain that a crisis could occur if M exceeded M′, i.e., if capitalists were not able, in Marx's terms, to "realize" the potential profits generated in production, and ended up losing money. "Marx," Keynes explained,

> was approaching the intermediate truth when he added that the continuous excess of *M′* would be inevitably interrupted by a series of crises, gradually increasing in intensity, or entrepreneur bankruptcy and underemployment, during which, presumably, *M* [as opposed to *M′*] must be in excess. My own argument, if it is accepted, should at least serve to effect a reconciliation between the followers of Marx and those of Major Douglas [a leading British underconsumptionist], leaving the classical economists still high and dry in the belief that *M* and *M′* are always equal!

Marx's general formula for capital, or M-C-M′, Keynes suggested, not only offered credence to the views of Major Douglas, but also to the underconsumptionist perspectives of "[John] Hobson, or [William T.] Foster and [Waddill] Catchings...who believe in its [the capitalist system's] inherent tendency toward deflation and under-employment."[15] Shortly after reading McCracken's *Value Theory and Business Cycles* and encountering its treatment of Marx's M-C-M′ formula, Keynes made direct reference in his lectures to "the realisation problem of Marx" as related to the problem of effective demand.[16]

Without a great deal of direct knowledge of Marx's analysis, Keynes thus grasped the implications of Marx's general formula for capital, its relation to the critique of Say's Law, and the necessity that it pointed to of integrating within a single system the real and the monetary, production and finance. All of this converged with Keynes's own attempts to construct a monetary theory of production (i.e., *The General Theory*). As Sweezy was to observe more than a half-century later when Keynes's lectures on the monetary theory of production first came to light, these remarks on Marx's general formula for capital indicated that: (1) Keynes "was in important respects closer to Marx's way of thinking about money and capital accumulation than he was to the accepted neoclassical orthodoxy," and (2) "he had an eye for what is important in Marx far keener than any of the other bourgeois economists."[17]

Indeed, it is remarkable, in looking back, just how much of Keynes's thinking here converged with that of Marx. In *Theories of Surplus Value*, Marx pointed to what he called "the abstract possibility of crisis," based on the M-C-M′. "If the *crisis* appears...because purchase and sale become separated, it becomes a *money crisis*," associated with money as a "means of payment... [I]n so far as the development of money as means of payment is linked with the development of credit and of *excess credit* the causes of the latter [too] have to be examined." For Marx, then, a realization crisis, or crisis of effective demand, was always tied to the monetary character of the system, and necessarily extended not just to the phenomenon of credit but also to *excess credit*. It thus pointed to potential crises of overindebtedness.[18]

Hidden within the general formula for capital, M-C-M′, Marx argued, was a tendency of capital to try to transform itself into a pure money (or speculative) economy, i.e., M-M′, in which money begat money without the intermediate link of commodity production. In M-M′, he wrote, "the capital relationship reaches its most superficial and fetishized form."[19] If M-M′ originally referred simply to interest-bearing capital, it metamorphosed in the course of capitalist development into the speculative demand for money more generally. "Credit," Marx explained, "displaces money and usurps its position." Capital more and more took on the "duplicate" forms of: (1) "real capital," i.e., the stock of plant, equipment and goods generated in production, and (2) "fictitious capital," i.e., the structure of financial claims produced by the paper title to this real capital. Insofar as economic activity was directed to the appreciation of "fictitious capital" in the realm of finance rather than the accumulation of real capital within production, Marx argued, it had metamorphosed into a purely speculative form.[20]

Production and Finance

Marx and Keynes both rejected, as we have seen, the rigid separation of the real and the monetary that characterized orthodox economic theory. A monetary theory of production of the sort advanced, in somewhat different ways, by both Marx and Keynes led naturally to a theory of finance as a realm not removed from the workings of the economy, but integrated fully with it—hence, to a theory of financial crisis. Decisions on whether (or where) to invest today in this conception—as developed by Keynes, in particular—were affected by both expected profits on such new investment and by the speculative demand for money and near money (credit) in relation to the interest rate.

The growing centrality of finance was a product of the historical development of the system. During the classical phase of political economy, in capitalism's youth, it was natural enough that economic theory would rest on the simple conception of a modified barter economy in which money was a mere means of exchange but did not otherwise materially affect basic economic relations. By the late nineteenth century, however, there were already signs that what Marx called the "concentration and centralization of production," associated with the emergence of the giant corporation, was giving rise to the modern credit system, based on the market for industrial securities.

This rise of the modern credit system vastly changed the nature of capital accumulation, as the ownership of real capital assets became secondary to the ownership of paper shares or assets—leveraged ever higher by debt. "Speculation about the value of productive assets," Minsky wrote in his book on Keynes, "is a characteristic of a capitalist... economy. The relevant paradigm for the analysis of a [developed] capitalist economy is not a barter economy," but "a system with a City [that is, London's financial center] or a Wall Street where asset holdings as well as current transactions are financed by debt."[21]

Rationally, the rigid separation between the real and the monetary in orthodox economics—continuing even up to the present—has no solid basis. Although it is certainly legitimate to distinguish the "real economy" (and "real capital") from the realm of finance (and what Marx called "fictitious capital"), this distinction should obviously not be taken to imply that monetary or financial claims are not themselves "real" in the normal sense of the word. "There is, in fact, no separation," Harry Magdoff and Paul Sweezy observed, "between the real and the monetary: in a developed capitalist economy practically all transactions are expressed in monetary terms and require the mediation of actual amounts of (cash or credit) money." Rather, "the appropriate analytical separation is between the underlying productive base of the economy and the financial superstructure."[22]

We can picture this dialectic of production and finance, following Minsky, in terms of the existence of two different pricing structures in the modern economy: (1) the pricing of current real output, and (2) the pricing of financial (and real estate) assets. More and more, the speculative asset-pricing structure, related to the inflation (or deflation) of paper titles to wealth, has come to hold sway over the "real" pricing structure associated with output (GDP).[23] Hence, money capital that could be used for accumulation (assuming the existence of profitable investment outlets) within the economic base is frequently diverted into M-M′, i.e., speculation in asset prices.[24] Insofar as this has taken the form of a long-term trend, the result has been a major structural change in the capitalist economy.

Viewed from this general standpoint, financial bubbles can be designated as short periods of extraordinarily rapid asset-price inflation within the financial superstructure of the economy—overshooting growth in the underlying productive base. In contrast, financialization represents a much longer tendency toward the expansion of the size and importance of the financial superstructure in relation to the economic base, occurring over decades. "The final decades of the twentieth century," Jan Toporowski (professor of economics at the University of London) observed in *The End of Finance*, "have seen the emergence of an era of finance that is the greatest since the 1890s and 1900s and, in terms of the values turned over in securities markets, the greatest era of finance in history. By 'era of finance' is meant a period of history in which finance... takes over from the industrial entrepreneur the leading role in capitalist development."[25]

Such an era of finance raises the specter of a pure speculative economy highlighted by Keynes: "Speculators may do no harm as bubbles on a steady stream of enterprise. But the position is serious when enterprise becomes the bubble on a whirlpool of speculation."[26] By the 1990s, Sweezy observed, "the occupants of [corporate] boardrooms" were "to an increasing extent constrained and controlled by financial capital as it operates through the global network of financial markets." Hence, "real power" was to be found "not so much in corporate boardrooms, as in the financial markets." This "inverted relation between the financial and the real," he argued, was "the key to understanding the new trends in the world" economy.[27]

Financial Crises and Financialization

In their attempt to deny any real historical significance to the Great Financial Crisis, most mainstream economists and financial analysts have naturally downplayed its systemic character, presenting it as a "black swan" phenomenon, i.e., as a rare and completely unpredictable but massive event of the kind that might appear, seemingly out of nowhere, once every century or so. (The term "black swan" is taken from the title of Nassim Nicholas Taleb's book published on the eve of the Great Financial Crisis, where a "black swan event" is defined as a game-changing occurrence that is both exceedingly rare and impossible to predict.)[28]

However, some of the more critical economists, even within the establishment, such as Nouriel Roubini and Stephen Mihm in their *Crisis Economics*, have rejected this "black swan" theory, characterizing the Great Financial Crisis instead as a "white swan" phenomenon, i.e., as the product of a perfectly ordinary, recurring, and predictable process, subject to systematic analysis.[29] The most impressive attempt to provide a data-based approach to financial crises over the centuries, emphasizing the regularity of such credit disturbances, is to be found in Carmen Reinhart and Kenneth Rogoff's *This Time Is Different: Eight Centuries of Financial Folly*.[30] (The title of their book is meant to refer to the euphoric phase in any financial bubble, where the notion arises that the business-financial cycle has been transcended and a speculative expansion can go on forever.)

The greatest white swan theorist in this sense was, of course, Minsky, who gave us the financial instability hypothesis, building on Keynes's fundamental insight of "the fragility introduced into the capitalist accumulation process by some inescapable properties of capitalist financial structures."[31]

Nevertheless, what thinkers like Minsky, Roubini and Mihm, and Reinhart and Rogoff tend to miss, in their exclusive focus on the financial cycle, is the long-run structural changes in the accumulation process of the capitalist system. Minsky went so far as to chastise Keynes himself for letting "stagnationist and exhaustion-of-investment-opportunity ideas take over from a cyclical perspective." Thus, Minsky explicitly sought to *correct* Keynes's theory, especially his analysis of financial instability, by placing it entirely in short run business cycle terms, ignoring the long-run tendencies in which Keynes had largely couched his financial-crisis analysis.[32]

Keynes's own argument was therefore quite different from the theory that we have become accustomed to via Minsky. He stressed that the stagnation tendency—or the decline in expected profit on new investment in a capital-rich economy—served to increase the power of money and finance. Thus, for Keynes, Minsky noted, "Money rules the roost as the expected yield of real assets declines."[33] As Keynes put it: "Owing to its accumulation of capital already being larger" in a mature, capital-rich economy, "the opportunities for further investment are less attractive unless the rate of interest falls at a sufficiently rapid rate." The uncertainty associated with the tendency of expected profit on new investment to decline gave an enormous boost to "liquidity preference" (or as Keynes also called it "the propensity to hoard" money) and to financial speculation as an alternative to capital formation, compounding the overall difficulties of the economy.

Underlying all of this was a tendency of the economy to sink into a condition of slow growth and underemployment. "The evidence indicates," Keynes wrote, "that full, or even approximately full, employment is of rare and short-lived occurrence." These conditions led Keynes to his longer-run policy proposals for a "euthanasia of the rentier" and a "somewhat comprehensive socialisation of investment."[34]

Keynes did not develop his long-run theory of stagnation and financial speculation. Yet subsequent elaborations of stagnation theory that built on his insights were to arise in the work of his leading early U.S. follower, Alvin Hansen, and in the neo-Marxian tradition associated with Michal Kalecki, Josef Steindl, Paul Baran, and Paul Sweezy. There were essentially two strands to the stagnation theory that developed based on Keynes (and Marx). The first, emphasized by Hansen, and by the later Sweezy—but characterizing all these thinkers in one way or another—examined the question of the *maturation* of capitalism, i.e., the development of capital-rich economies with massive, unused productive capacity that could be expanded relatively quickly.[35] This enormous potential to build up productive capacity came up against the reality of vanishing outlets for investment, since current investment was hindered (under conditions of industrial maturity) by investment that had occurred in the past. "The tragedy of investment," Kalecki remarked, "is that it causes crisis because it is useful."[36]

The second strand, in which Baran and Sweezy's *Monopoly Capital* is undoubtedly the best-known example, centered on the growing *monopolization* in the modern economy, that is, "the tendency of surplus to rise" in an economy dominated by the giant firm, and the negative effects this had on accumulation.

In both cases, the potential savings or surplus generated by the economy normally outweighed the opportunities for profitable investment of that surplus, leading to a tendency to stagnation (slow growth and rising unemployment/underemployment and idle capacity).[37] Rapid growth could thus not simply be assumed, in the manner of mainstream economics, as a natural outgrowth of the system in the mature/monopoly stage, but became dependent, as Kalecki stated, on "specific 'development' factors" to boost output. For example, military spending, the sales effort, the expansion of financial services, and epoch-making innovations such as the automobile all served as props to lift the economy, outside the internal logic of accumulation.[38]

None of these thinkers, it should be noted, focused initially on the macroeconomic relation between production and finance, or on finance as an outlet for surplus.[39] Although *Monopoly Capital* argued that FIRE could help absorb the economic surplus, this was consigned to the last part of a chapter on the sales effort, and not given strong emphasis.[40] However, the 1970s and '80s saw a deceleration of the growth rate of the capitalist economy at the center of the system, resulting in ballooning finance, acting as a compensatory factor. Lacking an outlet in production, capital took refuge in speculation in debt-leveraged finance (a bewildering array of options, futures, derivatives, swaps, etc.). In the

1970s total outstanding debt in the United States
one-half the size of GDP. By 2005 it was almost tl
GDP and not far from the $44 trillion world GDP.

Speculative finance increasingly took on a life of its own. Although in the prior history of the system financial bubbles had come at the end of a cyclical boom, and were short-term events, financialization now seemed, paradoxically, to feed not on prosperity but on stagnation, and to be long-lasting.[42] Crucial in keeping this process going were the central banks of the leading capitalist states, which were assigned the role of "lenders of last resort," with the task of bolstering and ultimately bailing out the major financial institutions whenever necessary (based on the "too big to fail" principle).

A key contradiction was that the financial explosion, while spurring growth in the economy in the short run, generated greater instability and uncertainty in the long run. Thus, Magdoff and Sweezy, who engaged in a running commentary on these developments from the 1970s to the late 1990s, argued that sooner or later—given the globalization of finance and the impossibility of managing it at that level—the ballooning of the financial superstructure atop a stagnant productive base was likely to lead to a major crash on the level of the 1930s. But whether even such a massive financial collapse, if it were to occur, would bring financialization to a halt remained, in their view, an open question.[43]

"In an era of finance," Toporowski writes, "finance mostly finances finance."[44] Hence, production in recent decades has become increasingly "incidental to the much more lucrative business of balance-sheet restructuring." With the big motor of capital accumulation within production no longer firing on all cylinders, the emergency backup engine of financial expansion took over. Growing employment and profit in the FIRE sector helped stimulate the economy, while the speculative growth of financial assets led to a "wealth effect" by means of which a certain portion of the capital gains from asset appreciation accruing to the well-to-do were funneled into increased luxury consumption, thereby stimulating investment. Even for the broad middle strata (professionals, civil servants, lower management, skilled workers), rapid asset price inflation enabled a large portion of employed homeowners to consume through new debt the apparent "capital gains" on their homes.[45] In this manner, the expansion of debt raised asset prices, which in turn led to a further expansion of debt that raised asset prices, and so on: a bubble.

Debt can be seen as a drug that serves, under conditions of endemic stagnation, to lift the economy. Yet the use of it in ever larger doses, which such a process necessitates, does nothing to overcome the underlying disease, and serves to generate its own disastrous long-run side effects. The result is the stagnation-financialization trap. The seriousness of this trap today is evident, as we have seen, in the fact that capital and its state have no answer to the present Great Financial Crisis/Great Recession but to bail out financial institutions and investors (both corporate and individual) to the tune of trillions of dollars with the object of debt-leveraging up the system all over again. This dynamic of financialization in relation to an underlying stagnant economy is the *enigma of monopoly-finance capital.* As Toporowski has observed, "The apparent paradox of capitalism" at the beginning of the twenty-first century is that "financial innovation and growth" are associated with "speculative industrial expansion," while adding "systematically to economic stagnation and decline."[46]

The Logical End-Point of Capitalism

Hence, financialization, while boosting capital accumulation through a process of speculative expansion, ultimately contributes to the corrosion of the entire economic and social order, hastening its decline. What we are witnessing today in society as a whole is what might be called the "financialization of class." "The credit system," David Harvey observes, "has now become... the major modern lever for the extraction of wealth by finance capital from the rest of the population."[47] In recent years, workers' wages have stagnated along with employment, while both income and wealth inequality have increased sharply. In 1976 the top 1 percent of households in the United States accounted for 9 percent of income generated in the country; by 2007 this share had risen to 24 percent. According to Raghuram Rajan (former chief economist for the IMF), for "every dollar of real income growth that was generated [in the United States] between 1976 and 2007, 58 cents went to the top 1 percent of households." In 2007 a single hedge fund manager, John Paulson, "earned" $3.7 billion, around 74,000 times the median household income in the country. Between 1989 and 2007, the share of total wealth held by the top 5 percent of wealth-holders in the United States rose from 59 percent to 62 percent, far outweighing the wealth of the bottom 95 percent of the population. Middle-class homeowners benefitted for a while in the housing boom, but are now losing ground with the housing bust. This increasing inequality in the distribution of income and wealth in an age of financialization has taken the form of "a growing distinction between the 'balance sheet' rich and the 'balance sheet' poor." It is the "enforced savings" of the latter that help augment the exorbitant gains of the former.[48]

The rapid increase in income and wealth polarization in recent decades is mirrored in the growing concentration and centralization of capital. In 1999, at the peak of the merger and acquisition frenzy associated with the New Economy bubble, the value of global mergers and acquisitions rose to over $3.4 trillion—declining sharply after the New Economy bubble burst. This record was only surpassed (in real terms) in 2007, during the peak of the housing bubble, when the value of global mergers and acquisitions rose to over $4 trillion—dropping off when the housing bubble popped. The result of all this merger activity has been a decline in the number of firms controlling major industries. This increasing monopolization (or oligopolization) has been particularly evident in recent years within finance itself. Thus, the share of U.S. financial-industry assets held by the top ten financial conglomerates increased by six times between 1990 and 2008, from 10 percent to 60 percent.[49]

This analysis of how financialization has heightened the disparities in income, wealth, and power helps us to put into perspective the view, now common on the left, that neoliberalism, or the advent of extreme free-market ideology, is the chief source of today's economic problems. Instead, neoliberalism is best seen as the political expression of capital's response to the stagnation-financialization trap. So extreme has the dominant pro-market or neoliberal orientation of monopoly-finance capital now become that, even in the context of the greatest economic crisis since the 1930s, the state is unable to respond effectively. Hence, the total government-spending stimulus in the United States in the last couple of years has been almost nil, with the meager federal stimulus under Obama negated by deep cuts in state and local spending.[50] The state at every level seems to be stopped in its tracks by pro-market ideology, attacks on government deficits, and irrational fears of inflation. None of this makes any sense in the context of "what," to quote Paul Krugman, "looks increasingly like a permanent state of stagnation and high unemployment."[51] The same basic problem is evident in the other advanced capitalist countries.

At the world level, what can be called a "new phase of financial imperialism," in the context of sluggish growth at the center of the system, constitutes the dominant reality of today's globalization. Extremely high rates of exploitation, rooted in low wages in the export-oriented periphery, including "emerging economies," have given rise to global surpluses that can nowhere be profitably absorbed within production. The exports of such economies are dependent on the consumption of wealthy economies, particularly the United States, with its massive current account deficit. At the same time, the vast export surpluses generated in these "emerging" export economies are attracted to the highly leveraged capital markets of the global North, where such global surpluses serve to reinforce the financialization of the accumulation process centered in the rich economies. Hence, "bubble-led growth," associated with financialization, as Prabhat Patnaik has argued in "The Structural Crisis of Capitalism," "camouflages" the root problem of accumulation at the world level: "a rise in income inequalities across the globe" and a global "tendency of surplus to rise."[52]

Despite "flat world" notions propagated by establishment figures like Thomas Friedman, imperialist divisions are becoming, in many ways, more severe, exacerbating inequalities within countries, as well as sharpening the contradictions between the richest and poorest regions/countries. If, in the "golden age" of monopoly capitalism from 1950–1973, the disparity in per capita GDP between the richest and poorest regions of the world decreased from 15:1 to 13:1, in the era of monopoly-finance capital this trend was reversed, with the gap growing again to 19:1 by century's close.[53]

More and more, the financialization of accumulation in the center of the system, backed by neoliberal policy, has generated a global regime of "shock therapy." Rather than Keynes's "euthanasia of the rentier," we are seeing the threatened euthanasia of almost everything else in society and nature. The consequences of this, as Naomi Klein suggested in her book, *The Shock Doctrine*, extend far beyond the underlying financialized accumulation associated with the neoliberal era, to a much broader set of consequences that can be described as "disaster capitalism"—evident in widening social and economic inequality, deepening instability, expanding militarism and war, and seemingly unstoppable planetary environmental destruction. Never before has the conflict between private appropriation and the social needs (even survival) of humanity been so stark.[54]

CHAPTER 3

Monopoly and Competition in Twenty-First-Century Capitalism

A STRIKING PARADOX ANIMATES political economy in our times. On the one hand, mainstream economics and much of left economics discuss our era as one of intense and increased competition among businesses, now on a global scale. It is a matter so self-evident as no longer to require empirical verification or scholarly examination. On the other hand, wherever one looks, it seems that nearly every industry is concentrated into fewer and fewer hands. Formerly competitive sectors like retail are now the province of enormous monopolistic chains, massive economic fortunes are being assembled into the hands of a few mega-billionaires sitting atop vast empires, and the new firms and industries spawned by the digital revolution have quickly gravitated to monopoly status. In short, monopoly power is ascendant as never before.

This is anything but an academic concern. The economic defense of capitalism is premised on the ubiquity of competitive markets, providing for the rational allocation of scarce resources and justifying the existing distribution of incomes. The political defense of capitalism is that economic power is diffuse and cannot be aggregated in such a manner as to have undue influence over the democratic state. Both of these core claims for capitalism are demolished if monopoly, rather than competition, is the rule.

For all economists, mainstream and left, the assumption of competitive markets being the order of the day also has a striking impact on how growth is assessed in capitalist economies. Under competitive conditions, investment will, as a rule, be greater than under conditions of monopoly, where the dominant firms generally seek to slow down and carefully regulate the expansion of output and investment so as to maintain high prices and profit margins—and have considerable power to do so. Hence, monopoly can be a strong force contributing to economic stagnation, everything else being equal. With the United States and most of the world economy (notwithstanding the economic rise of Asia) stuck in an era of secular stagnation and crisis unlike anything seen since the 1930s—while U.S. corporations are sitting on around $2 trillion in cash—the issue of monopoly power naturally returns to the surface.[1]

In this chapter, we assess the state of competition and monopoly in the contemporary capitalist economy—empirically, theoretically, and historically. We explain why understanding competition and monopoly has been such a bedeviling process, by examining the "ambiguity of competition." In particular, we review how the now dominant neoliberal strand of economics reconciled itself to monopoly and became its mightiest champion, despite its worldview—in theory—being based on a religious devotion to the genius of economically competitive markets.

When we use the term "monopoly," we do not use it in the very restrictive sense to refer to a market with a single seller. Monopoly in this sense is practically nonexistent. Instead, we employ it as it has often been used in economics to refer to firms with sufficient market power to influence the price, output, and investment of an industry—thus exercising "monopoly power"—and to limit new competitors entering the industry, even if there are high profits.[2] These firms generally operate in "oligopolistic" markets, where a handful of firms dominate production and can determine the price for the product. Moreover, even that is insufficient to describe the power of the modern firm. As Sweezy put it, "the typical production unit in modern developed capitalism is a giant corporation," which, in addition to dominating particular industries, is "a conglomerate (operating in many industries) and multi-national (operating in many countries)."[3]

In the early 1980s, an unquestioning belief in the ubiquitous influence of competitive markets took hold in economics and in capitalist culture writ large, to an extent that would have been inconceivable only ten years earlier. Concern with monopoly was never dominant in mainstream economics, but it had a distinguished and respected place at the table well into the century. For some authors, including Baran, Sweezy, and Magdoff, the prevalence and importance of monopoly justified calling the system monopoly capitalism. But by the Reagan era, the giant corporation at the apex of the economic system wielding considerable monopoly power over price, output, investment, and employment had simply fallen out of the economic picture, almost as if by fiat. As Galbraith observed in 2004 in *The Economics of Innocent Fraud* (and as we noted in our introduction): "The phrase 'monopoly capitalism,' once in common use, has been dropped from the academic and political lexicon."[4] For the neoliberal ideologues of today, there is only one issue: state versus market. Economic power (along with inequality) is no longer deemed relevant. Monopoly power, not to mention monopoly capital, is nonexistent or unimportant. Some on the left would in large part agree.

In contrast, we shall demonstrate in what follows that nothing could be further removed from a reality-based social science or economics than the denial of the tendency to monopolization in the capitalist economy: *which is demonstrably stronger in the opening decades of the twenty-first century than ever before.* More concretely, we argue that what we have been witnessing in the last quarter century is the evolution of monopoly capital into a more generalized and globalized system of monopoly-finance capital that lies at the core of the current economic system in the advanced capitalist economies—a key source of economic instability, and the basis of the current new imperialism.

The Real World Trend: Growth of Monopoly Power

The desirability of monopoly, from the perspective of a capitalist, is self-evident: it lowers risk and increases profits. No sane owner or business wishes more competition; the rational move is always to seek as much monopoly power as possible and carefully avoid the nightmare world of the powerless competitive firm of economics textbooks. Once a firm achieves economic concentration and monopoly power, it is maintained through barriers to entry that make it prohibitively costly and risky for would-be competitors successfully to invade an oligopolistic or monopolistic industry—though such barriers to entry remain relative rather than absolute. Creating and maintaining barriers to entry is essential work for any corporation. In his authoritative study, *The Economics of Industrial Organization*, William Shepherd provides a list of twenty-two different barriers to entry commonly used by firms to exclude competitors and maintain monopoly power.[5]

Monopoly, in this sense, is the logical result of competition, and should be expected. It is in the DNA of capitalism. For Karl Marx, capital tended

Chart 3.1. U.S. Manufacturing Industries in which Four Firms Accounted for 50 Percent or More of Shipment Value

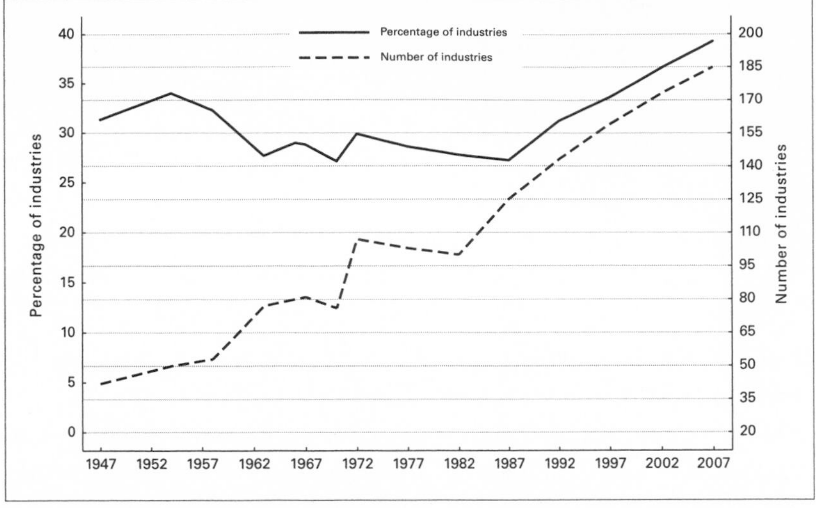

Sources: "Shipments Share of 4, 8, 20, & 50 Largest Companies in each SIC: 1992–1947," Census of Manufactures; and "Economic Census," 1997, 2002, and 2007, American FactFinder (U.S. Census Bureau, 2011), http://census.gov/epcd/www/concentration.html.

Notes: The Census Bureau added new industries (i.e., Standard Industrial Classification [SIC] codes) each year since 1947; in that year there were 134; in 1967, 281; and by 1992, 458. Beginning in 1997, the SIC system was replaced by the North American Industrial Classification System (NAICS) and since this time the number of industries leveled off at approximately 472 (in 1997 and 2002, 473; and 2007, 471).

to grow ever larger in a single hand, partly as a result of a straightforward process of *concentration* of *capital* (accumulation proper), and even more as a result of the *centralization of capital*, or the absorption of one capital by another. In this struggle, he wrote, "the larger capitals," as a rule, "beat the smaller.... Competition rages in direct proportion to the number, and in inverse proportion to the magnitude of the rival capitals. It always ends in the ruin of many small capitalists, whose capitals partly pass into the hands of their competitors, and partly vanish completely. Apart from this, an altogether new force comes into existence with the development of capitalist production: the credit system." Credit or finance, available more readily to large firms, becomes one of the two main levers, along with competition itself, in the centralization process. By means of mergers and acquisitions, the credit system can create huge, centralized agglomerations of capital in the "twinkling of an eye." The results of both concentration and centralization are commonly referred to as economic concentration.[6]

So what do the data tell us about the state of monopoly and competition in the economy today, and the trends since the mid-twentieth century? Chart 3.1 shows that both the number and percentage of

Table 3.1. Percentage of Sales for Four Largest Firms in Selected U.S. Retail Industries

Industry (NAICS code)	1992	1997	2002	2007
Food & beverage stores (445)	15.4	18.3	28.2	27.7
Health & personal care stores (446)	24.7	39.1	45.7	54.4
General merchandise stores (452)	47.3	55.9	65.6	73.2
Supermarkets (44511)	18.0	20.8	32.5	32.0
Bookstores (451211)	41.3	54.1	65.6	71.0
Computer & software stores (443120)	26.2	34.9	52.5	73.1

Source: "Economic Census," 1992, 1997, 2002, and 2007, American FactFinder (U.S. Census Bureau, 2011).
Notes: The transition to the NAICS system means that 1992 cannot be strictly compared to later years (see Chart 1). However, the above industries were matched using "NAICS Concordances" provided by the U.S. Census Bureau.

U.S. manufacturing industries (for example, automobile production) that have a four-firm concentration ratio of 50 percent or more have risen dramatically since the 1980s. More and more industries in the manufacturing sector of the economy are tight oligopolistic or quasi-monopolistic markets characterized by a substantial degree of monopoly. And, if anything, the trend is accelerating.

Concentration is also proceeding apace in most other sectors of the economy, aside from manufacturing, such as retail trade, transportation, information, and finance. In 1995 the six largest bank holding companies (JPMorgan Chase, Bank of America, Citigroup, Wells Fargo, Goldman Sachs, and Morgan Stanley—some of which had somewhat different names at that time) had assets equal to 17 percent of U.S. GDP. By the end of 2006, this had risen to 55 percent, and by 2010 (Q3) to 64 percent.[7]

In retail, the top fifty firms went from 22.4 percent of sales in 1992 to 33.3 percent in 2007. The striking exemplar of retail consolidation has been Wal-Mart, which represents what Joel Magnuson in his *Mindful Economics* (2008) has called "Monopsony Capitalism." Wal-Mart uses its power as a "single buyer" (thereby monopsony, as opposed to monopoly or "single seller") to control production and prices.[8] The trends, with respect to concentration in retail, can be seen in Table 3.1, which shows the rise in four-firm concentration ratios in six key retail sectors and industries, over the fifteen-year period, 1992–2007. Most remarkable was the rise in concentration in general merchandise stores (symbolized by Wal-Mart), which rose from a four-firm concentration ratio of 47.3 percent in 1992 to 73.2 percent in 2007; and in information goods—with bookstores going from a four-firm concentration ratio of 41.3 percent in 1992

Chart 3.2. Revenue of Top 200 U.S. Corporations as a Percentage of Total Business Revenue

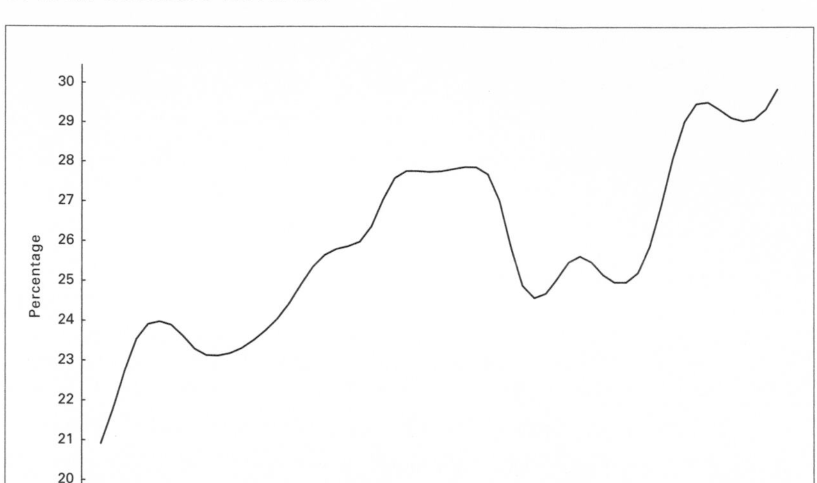

Sources: Data for the top 200 corporations (see notes) were extracted from COMPUSTAT, "Fundamentals Annual: North America" (accessed February 15, 2011). Total revenue was taken from "Corporate Income Tax Returns" (line item "total receipts") Statistics of Income (Washington, DC: Internal Revenue Service, 1950–2008).

Notes: "Total revenues" (COMPUSTAT) and "total receipts" (SOI) are equivalent. Since the COMPUSTAT dataset contains only conglomerate-level data all foreign companies—defined as those not incorporated in the United States—were dropped. In this Chart, as well as for Charts 3.3, 3.4, and 3.5, a robust linear smoother was used so the line approximates a five-year moving average. COMPUSTAT data was extracted from Wharton Research Data Services (WRDS). WRDS was used in preparing this article. This service and the data available thereon constitute valuable intellectual property and trade secrets of WRDS and/or its third-party suppliers.

to 71 percent in 2007, and computer and software stores from a four-firm concentration ratio of 26.2 percent in 1992 to 73.1 percent in 2007.

Concentration ratios for individual industries are important, but are of more limited value today than in the past in getting at the full range of monopoly power of the giant corporation. This is because the typical giant firm operates not in just one industry, but is a conglomerate, operating in numerous industries. The best way to get an overall picture of the trend toward economic concentration that takes into account the multi-industry nature of the typical giant firm is to look at some measure of aggregate concentration, e.g., the economic status of the two hundred largest firms compared to all firms in the economy.[9]

To put the top two hundred firms in perspective, in 2000 there were 5.5 million corporations, 2.0 million partnerships, 17.7 million nonfarm sole proprietorships, and 1.8 million farm sole proprietorships in the U.S. economy.[10] Chart 3.2 shows the revenue of the top two hundred

Chart 3.3. Gross Profits of Top 200 U.S. Corporations as a Percentage of Total Gross Profits in U.S. Economy

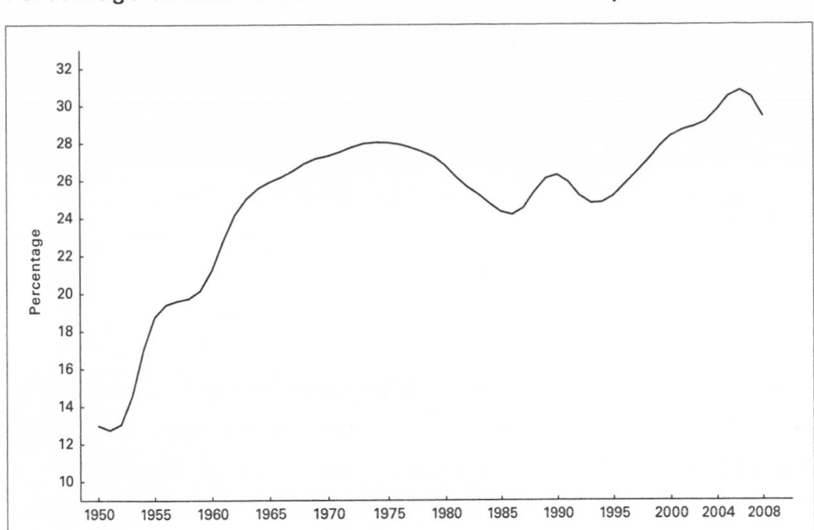

Source: See Chart 3.2. Total gross profits (see notes for calculations) were taken from "Corporate Income Tax Returns," Statistics of Income (Washington, DC: Internal Revenue Service, various years).

Notes: Total gross profits were calculated by subtracting "cost of goods sold" (or "cost of sales and operations" for earlier years) from "business receipts." This follows the definition used in the COMPUSTAT database. Business receipts are defined as gross operating receipts of a firm reduced by the cost of returned goods and services. Generally, they include all corporate receipts except investment and incidental income. Also see notes to Chart 3.2.

U.S. corporations as a percentage of the total business revenue in the economy since 1950. What we find is that the revenue of the top two hundred corporations has risen substantially from around 21 percent of total business revenue in 1950 to about 30 percent in 2008.[11]

The capacity of the giant firms in the economy to obtain higher profits than their smaller competitors is the main indicator of the degree of monopoly exercised by these megacorporations. Chart 3.3, above, shows the total gross profits of the top two hundred U.S. corporations as a percentage of total business profits in the U.S. economy, from 1950 to 2008, during which their share rose from 13 percent in 1950 to over 30 percent in 2007.

The share of profits of the top two hundred corporations turned down briefly in 2008, reflecting the Great Financial Crisis, which hit the largest corporations first and then radiated out to the rest of the economy. Nonetheless, the largest corporations rebounded in 2009 and 2010, gaining back what they had lost and probably a lot more. Referring to the top five hundred firms, *Fortune* magazine (April 15, 2010) indicated that their earnings rose 335 percent in 2009, the second largest increase in the fifty-six years of the Fortune 500 data. Returns on sales more than quadrupled in 2009. As *Fortune* writes: "Hence, the 500's profits virtually returned to normal after years of extremes—bubbles in 2006 and 2007, collapse in 2008—despite a feeble overall recovery that's far from normal." There is little doubt that this recovery of the giant firms was related to their monopoly power, which allowed them to shift the costs of the crisis onto the unemployed, workers, and smaller firms.[12]

A New Wave of Competition?

The evidence we have provided with respect to the U.S. economy suggests that economic concentration is greater today than it has ever been, and it has increased sharply over the past two decades. Why then is this not commonly acknowledged—and even frequently denied? Why indeed have so many across the political spectrum identified the past third of a century as an era of renewed economic competition? There are several possible explanations for this that deserve attention. For starters, the past three decades have seen dramatic changes in the world economy and much upheaval. Four major trends have occurred that, individually and in combination, have appeared to foster new economic competition, while at the same time leading inexorably to greater concentration: (1) economic stagnation; (2) the growth of the global competition of multinational corporations; (3) financialization; and (4) new technological developments.

The slowdown of the real growth rates of the capitalist economies, beginning in the 1970s, undoubtedly had a considerable effect in altering perceptions of monopoly and competition. Although monopolistic tendencies of corporations were not generally seen in the economic mainstream as a cause of the crisis, the post–Second World War accommodation between big capital and big unions, in manufacturing in particular, was often presented as a key part of the diagnosis of the stagflation crisis of the 1970s. Dominant interests associated with capital insisted that the large firms break loose from the industrial relations moorings they had established. The restructuring of firms to emphasize leaner and meaner forms of competition in line with market pressures was viewed by the powers-that-be as crucial to the revitalization of the economy. The result of all of this, it was widely contended, was the launching of a more competitive global capitalism.

The giant corporations that had arisen in the monopoly stage of capitalism operated increasingly as multinational corporations on the plane of the global economy as a whole—to the point that they confronted each other with greater or lesser success in their own domestic markets as well as in the global economy. The result was that the direct competitive pressures experienced by corporate giants went up. Nowhere were the negative effects of this change more evident than in relation to U.S. corporations, which in the early post-Second World War years had benefitted from the unrivaled U.S. hegemony in the world economy. Multinational corporations encouraged worldwide outsourcing and sales as ways of increasing their profit margins, relying less on national markets for their production and profits. Viewed from any given national perspective, this looked like a vast increase in competition—even though, on the international plane as a whole, it encouraged a more generalized concentration and centralization of capital.

The U.S. automobile industry was the most visible manifestation of this process. The Detroit Big Three, the very symbol of concentrated economic power, were visibly weakened in the 1970s with renewed international competition from Japanese and German automakers, which were able to seize a share of the U.S. market itself. As David Harvey has noted: "Even Detroit automakers, who in the 1960s were considered an exemplar of the sort of oligopoly condition characteristic of what Baran and Sweezy defined as 'monopoly capitalism,' found themselves seriously challenged by foreign, particularly Japanese, imports. Capitalists have therefore had to find other ways to construct and preserve their much coveted monopoly powers. The two major moves they have made" involve "massive centralization of capital, which seeks dominance through financial power, economies of scale, and market position, and avid protection of technological advantages... through patent rights, licensing laws, and intellectual property rights."[13]

One of the most important historical changes affecting the competitive conditions of large industrial corporations was the reemergence of finance as a driver of the system, with power increasingly shifting in this period from corporate boardrooms to financial markets.[14] Financial capital, with its movement of money capital at the speed of light, increasingly called the shots, in sharp contrast to the 1950s and '60s during which industrial capital was largely self-financing and independent of financial capital. In the new age of speculative finance, it was often contended that an advanced and purer form of globalized competition had emerged, governed by what journalist Thomas Friedman dubbed "the electronic herd," over which no one had any control.[15] The old regime of stable corporations was passing and, to the untrained eye, that looked like unending competitive turbulence—a veritable *terra incognita.*

Technological changes also affected perceptions of the role of the giant corporations. With new technologies associated in particular with the digital revolution and the Internet giving rise to whole new industries and giant firms, many of the old corporate powers, such as IBM, were shaken, though seldom experienced a knockout punch. John Kenneth Galbraith's world of *The New Industrial State*, where a relatively small group of corporations ruled imperiously over the market based on their own "planning system," was clearly impaired.[16]

All of these developments are commonly seen as engendering greater competition in the economy, and could therefore appear to conflict with a notion of a general trend toward monopolization. However, the reality of the case is more nuanced. Most of these skirmishes were being fought out by increasingly centralized global corporations, each aiming to maintain or advance its relative monopoly power. Such globalized oligopolistic rivalry has more to do, as Harvey says, with constructing and conserving "much-coveted monopoly powers" than promoting competition in the narrow sense in which that term is employed in received economics. Twentieth-century monopoly capitalism was not returning to its earlier nineteenth-century competitive stage, but evolving into a twenty-first century phase of globalized, financialized monopoly capital. The booming financial sector created turmoil and instability, but it also expedited all sorts of mergers and acquisitions. In the end, finance has been—as it invariably is—a force for monopoly. The worldwide merger and acquisition deals in 1999, as noted in the previous chapter, rose to over $3.4 trillion. This was equivalent at the time to 34 percent of the value of all industrial capital (buildings, plants, machinery, and equipment) in the United States.[17] In 2007, just prior to the Great Financial Crisis, worldwide mergers and acquisitions reached a record $4.38 trillion, up 21 percent from 2006.[18] The long-term result of this process is a ratcheting up of the concentration and centralization of capital on a world scale.

Chart 3.4 shows net value of acquisitions of the top five hundred global corporations (with operations in the United States and Canada)

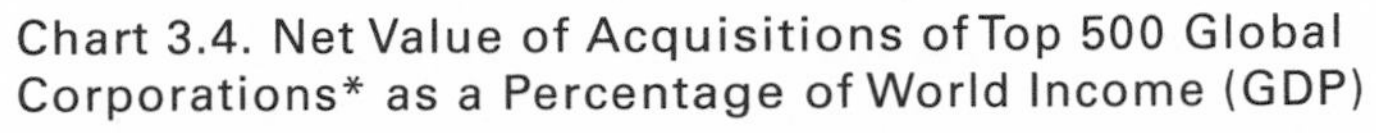

Chart 3.4. Net Value of Acquisitions of Top 500 Global Corporations* as a Percentage of World Income (GDP)

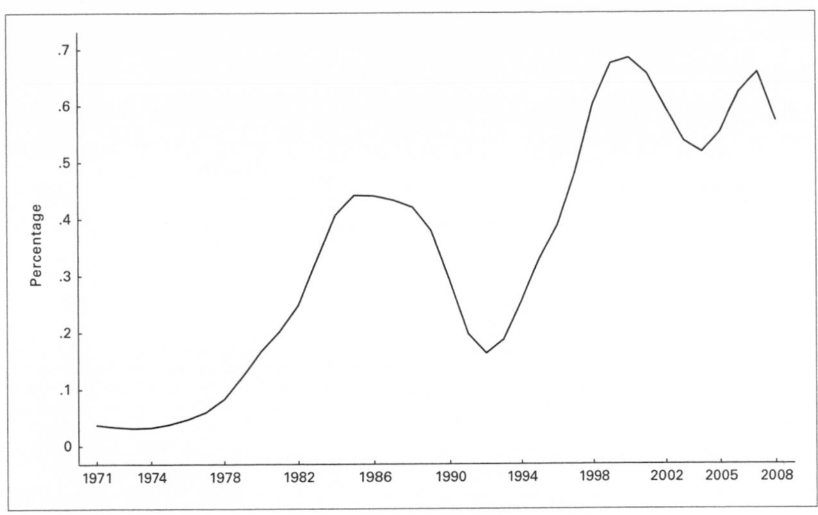

Source: See Chart 3.2. World Bank, "World Development Indicators," http://databank.worldbank.org.

Notes: The COMPUSTAT North America dataset does not technically cover all global corporations, only those required to file in the United States or Canada. Therefore, the value of acquisitions, as well as total revenues (Chart 3.5), are understated to some degree. In 2009, revenues for the top 500 global corporations operating in the United States totaled $18 trillion; in comparison, Fortune's "Global 500," which includes the top corporations operating inside and outside North America, gives a total of $23 trillion (Chart 3.5 compares the two series on revenues). The COMPUSTAT series is incomparable in terms of its length and consistency of measurement, however, which is why we report it here.

* Includes only those corporations with operations in the United States and/or Canada.

as a percentage of world income. The upward trend in the graph, most marked since the 1990s, shows that acquisitions of these giant multinational corporations are centralizing capital at rates in excess of the growth of world income. Indeed, as the chart indicates, there was a tenfold increase in the net value of annual global acquisitions by the top five hundred firms (operating in the United States and Canada) as a percentage of world income from the early 1970s through 2008.

To assess all the new competition that the aforementioned four factors ostensibly encouraged and the result to which this leads, let us return to the automobile industry. As the dust cleared after the upheaval of the 1970s and 1980s, there was no longer a series of national automobile industries but rather a global oligopoly for automobile production, where five multinational firms—all of which were national powerhouses at the beginning of the process—produced nearly half the world's motor vehicles, and the ten largest firms produced 70 percent of the world's motor vehicles. There is a power law distribution thereafter; the twenty-fifth largest motor vehicle producer now accounts for around one-half of 1 percent of the global market, and the fiftieth largest global producer accounts for less than one-tenth of 1 percent of production.[19] The logic of the situation points to another wave of mergers and acquisitions and consolidation among the remaining players. There are no banks lining up to cut $50 billion checks to the fiftieth ranked firm so it can make a play to join the ranks of the big five. There is little to no chance that newcomers will arise out of the blue or from another planet to challenge the dominance of the handful of firms that rule global automobile production.

As Chart 3.5 shows, the share of revenues of the largest five hundred corporations in the world (with operations in the United States and Canada) have been trending upward since the 1950s. In 2006, just prior to the Great Financial Crisis, the world revenues of these firms equaled about 35 percent of world income, and then dipped when the crisis hit. In recent years, *Fortune* has been compiling its own list of the top five hundred corporations in the world known as the "Global 500" (this consists not just of those global corporations operating in the United States and Canada, as in the COMPUSTAT data used in the longer time series, but rather the top five hundred operating in the world at large). This shows Global 500 revenues on the order of 40 percent of world GDP (falling slightly in 2008). The percentages shown by these two series are highly significant. Were the five hundred largest shareholders in a company to own 35–40 percent of the shares of a firm, they would be considered to have the power to control its operations. Although the analogy is not perfect, there can be no doubt that such giant corporate enterprises increasingly represent a controlling interest in the world economy, with enormous consequences for the future of capitalism, the population of the world, and the planet.

In 2009 the top twenty-five global private megacorporations by revenue rank were: Wal-Mart Stores, Royal Dutch Shell, Exxon Mobil, BP, Toyota Motor, AXA, Chevron, ING Group, General Electric, Total, Bank of America, Volkswagen, ConocoPhillips, BNP Paribus, Assicurazioni Generali, Allianz, AT&T, Carrefour, Ford Motor, ENI, JPMorgan Chase, Hewlett-Packard, E.ON, Berkshire Hathaway, and GDF Suez.[20] Such firms straddle the globe. Samir Amin aptly calls this "the late capitalism of generalized, financialized, and globalized oligopolies." There is no doubt that giant global corporations are able to use their disproportionate power to leverage monopoly rents, imposed on populations, states, and smaller corporations.[21] So much for that new wave of competition.

Chart 3.5. Revenues of Top 500 Global Corporations as a Percentage of World Income (GDP)

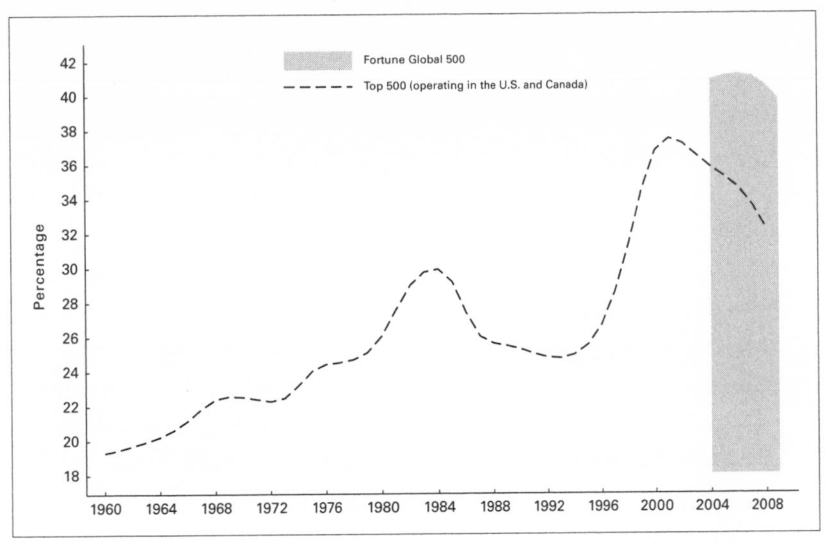

Source: See Chart 3.4 sources and notes. "Fortune Global 500," *Fortune*, 2005–2010 (data are for previous fiscal year).

The Ambiguity of Competition

In our view, the best explanation for the continuing confusion about the degree of monopoly in the economy is due to what we call the "ambiguity of competition." This refers to the opposite ways in which the concept of competition is employed in economics and in more colloquial language, including the language of business itself. It is best explained by Milton Friedman, in his conservative classic *Capitalism and Freedom*, first published in 1962: "Competition," Friedman writes,

> has two very different meanings. In ordinary discourse, competition means personal rivalry, with one individual seeking to outdo his known competitor. In the economic world, competition means almost the opposite. There is no personal rivalry in the competitive market place. There is no personal higgling. The wheat farmer in a free market does not feel himself in personal rivalry with, or threatened by, his neighbor, who is, in fact, his competitor. No one participant can determine the terms on which other participants shall have access to goods or jobs. All take prices as given by the market and no individual can by himself have

> more than a negligible influence on price though all participants together determine the price by the combined effect of their separate actions.[22]

Competition, in other words, exists when, because of the large number and small size of firms, the typical business unit has no significant control over price, output, investment, which are all given by the market—and when each firm stands in a non-rivalrous relation to its competitors. An individual firm is powerless to intervene in ways that change the basic competitive forces it or another firm faces. The fate of each business is thus largely determined by market forces beyond its control. Such assumptions are given a very restrictive and determinate form in neoclassical economic notions of perfect and pure competition, but the general view of competition in this respect is common to all economics. This *is* the principal meaning of competition in economics.

Yet, as Friedman emphasizes, the above economic definition of competition conflicts directly with the way in which the concept of competition is used more generally and in business analyses to refer to *rivalry*, particularly between oligopolistic firms. Competition in the business sense of rivalry, he says, is "the opposite" of the meaning of competition in economics associated with the anonymity of one's competitors.

The same problem arises exactly the other way around with respect to what is taken to be the inverse of competition: monopoly. As Friedman states: "Monopoly exists when a specific individual or enterprise has sufficient control over a particular product or service to determine significantly the terms on which other individuals shall have access to it. *In some ways, monopoly comes closer to the ordinary concept of competition since it does involve personal rivalry*" (italics added).[23] In economic terms, he is telling us, monopoly can be said to exist when firms have "significant" monopoly power, able to affect price, output, investment, and other factors in markets in which they operate, and thus achieve monopolistic returns. Such firms are more likely to be in *rivalrous* oligopolistic relations with other firms. Hence, monopoly, ironically, "comes closer," as Friedman stressed, to the "ordinary concept of competition."

The ambiguity of competition evident in Friedman's definitions of competition and monopoly illuminates the fact that today's giant corporations are closer to the monopoly side of the equation. Most of the examples of competition and competitive strategy that dominate economic news are in fact rivalrous struggles between quasi-monopolies (or oligopolies) for greater monopoly power. Hence, to the extent to which we speak of competition today, it is more likely to be oligopolistic rivalry, i.e., battles between monopoly-capitalist firms. Or to underline the irony, the greater the amount of discussion of cutthroat competition in media and business circles and among politicians and pundits, the greater the level of monopoly power in the economy.

What we are calling "the ambiguity of competition" was first raised as an issue in the 1920s by Schumpeter, who was concerned early on with the effect of the emergence of the giant, monopolistic corporation on his own theory of an economy driven by innovative entrepreneurs. The rise of big business in the developed capitalist economies in the early twentieth century led to a large number of attempts to explain the shift from competitive to what was variously called trustified, concentrated, or monopoly capitalism. Marxist and radical theorists played the most prominent part in this, building on Marx's analysis of the concentration and centralization of capital. The two thinkers who were to go the furthest in attempting to construct a distinct theory of monopoly-based capitalism in the early twentieth century were the radical American economist Thorstein Veblen in *The Theory of Business Enterprise* (1904) and the Austrian Marxist Rudolf Hilferding in his *Finance Capital* (1910). In his *Imperialism, the Highest Stage of Capitalism*, Lenin depicted imperialism in its "briefest possible definition," as "the monopoly stage of capitalism."[24] The Sherman Antitrust Act was passed in the United States in 1890 in an attempt to control the rise of cartels and monopolies. No one at the time doubted that capitalism had entered a new phase of economic concentration, for better or for worse.

In 1928 Schumpeter addressed these issues and the threat they represented to the whole theoretical framework of neoclassical economics in an article entitled "The Instability of Capitalism." "The nineteenth century," he argued, could be called "the time of *competitive*, and what has so far followed, the time of increasingly '*trustified*,' or otherwise 'organized,' 'regulated,' or 'managed,' capitalism." For Schumpeter, conditions of dual monopoly or "multiple monopoly" (the term "oligopoly" had not yet been introduced) were much "more important practically" than either perfect competition or the assumption of a single monopoly, and of more general importance "in a theoretic sense." The notion of pure competition was, in fact, "very much in the nature of a crutch" for orthodox economics, and due to overreliance on it, the undermining of economic orthodoxy was "a rather serious one." Trustified capitalism raised the ambiguity of competition directly: "Such things as bluffing, the use of non-economic force, a will to force the other party to their knees, have much more scope in the case of two-sided monopoly—just as cut-throat methods have in the case of limited competition—than in a state of perfect competition."

Schumpeter's own solution to this in "The Instability of Capitalism" (and much later in his 1942 *Capitalism, Socialism, and Democracy*) was to introduce the concept of "corespective pricing." This meant that the giant firms in a condition of "multiple monopoly" (or oligopoly) acted as corespectors, determining their actions in relation to those of others, deliberately seeking to restrict their rivalry, particularly in relation to price, by various forms of collusion, in order to maximize group advantage.[25] Yet there was no hiding the fact that such a solution constituted a serious "breach" in the wall of economics, introducing a notion of the basic economic unit that was foreign to the entire corpus of received economics in both its classical and neoclassical phases.[26]

This breach in the established doctrine was only to widen in subsequent decades. In mainstream economics the theory of imperfect competition, introduced almost simultaneously by Joan Robinson and Edward Chamberlin in the 1930s, dealt not only (or even mainly) with oligopoly but rather emphasized the influence of monopolistic factors of all kinds in firms at every level, particularly in the form of product differentiation.[27] It was found that monopoly elements were much more pervasive in the economy than the orthodox neoclassical analysis of perfect competition allowed. In 1939, Sweezy, as we have seen, developed the most influential theory of oligopolistic pricing, known as the "kinked-demand curve" analysis. He argued that there was a "kink" in the demand curve at the existing price such that oligopolistic firms would find themselves facing competitive price warfare, and hence would experience no gain in market share if they sought to lower prices, which would then only squeeze profits.[28] These contributions to imperfect competition theory constituted an important qualification to conventional economics. Yet they were largely excluded from the core analytical framework of orthodox economics, which continued to rest on the unrealistic and increasingly preposterous assumptions of perfect competition, with its infinitely large numbers of buyers and sellers. Hence, small firms, able to enter and exit freely from industries, enjoyed perfect information, and produced homogeneous products.[29]

The essential challenge facing conventional economics, in the face of the rise of the giant, monopolistic or oligopolistic firm, was either to hold on to its economic model of perfect competition, on which its overall theory of general equilibrium rested, and therefore forgo any possibility of a realistic assessment of the economy—or to abandon these make-believe models in favor of greater realism. The decision at which neoclassical theorists generally arrived—reinforced over and over throughout the twentieth century and into the twenty-first century—was to retain the perfect competition model, despite its inapplicability to real world conditions. The reasons for this were best stated by John Hicks in his *Value and Capital* (1939):

> If we assume that the typical firm (at least in industries where the economies of large scale are important) has some influence over the price at which it sells... [it] is therefore to some extent a monopolist.... Yet it has to be recognized that a general abandonment of the assumption of perfect competition, a universal adoption of the assumption of monopoly, must have very destructive consequences for economic theory. Under monopoly the stability conditions become indeterminate; and the basis on which economic laws can be constructed is therefore shorn away....
>
> It is, I believe, only possible to save anything from this wreck—and it must be remembered that the threatened wreckage is the greater part of [neoclassical] general equilibrium theory—if we can assume that the markets confronting most of the firms with which we shall be dealing do not differ very greatly from perfectly competitive markets.... Then the laws of an economic system working under perfect competition will not be appreciably varied in a system which contains widespread elements of monopoly. At least, this get-away seems well worth trying. We must be aware, however, that we are taking a dangerous step, and probably limiting to a serious extent the problems with which our subsequent analysis will be fitted to deal. Personally, however, I doubt if most of the problems we shall have to exclude for this reason are capable of much useful analysis by the methods of economic theory.[30]

The choice economists faced was thus a stark one: dealing seriously with the problem of monopoly as a growing factor in the modern economy and thus undermining neoclassical theory, or denying the essential reality of monopoly and thereby preserving the theory—even at the risk of taking the "dangerous step" of "limiting to a serious extent the problems" with which any future economics would be "fitted to deal." Establishment economic theorists have generally chosen the latter course—but with devastating consequences in terms of their ability to understand and explain the real world.[31]

In the United States in the 1930s, the issues of economic concentration and monopoly took on greater significance in the context of the Great Depression, with frequent claims that administrative prices imposed by monopolistic firms and restraints on production and investment had contributed to economic stagnation. The result was a large number of studies and investigations in the period, including Adolf A. Berle and Gardiner C. Means's seminal *The Modern Corporation and Private Property* (1932) on concentration and the managerial revolution, and Arthur Robert Burns's forgotten classic, *The Decline of Competition* (1936), addressing the effective banning of price competition in oligopolistic industries. These studies were followed by hearings on economic concentration conducted by the Roosevelt administration's Temporary National Economic Committee, which, between 1938 and 1941, produced forty-five volumes and some thirty-three thousand pages focusing, in particular, on the monopoly problem.[32] After the Second World War, additional investigations were conducted by the Federal Trade Commission and the Department of Commerce. In the words of President Roosevelt in 1938, the United States was experiencing a "concentration of private power without equal in history," while the "disappearance of price competition" was "one of the primary causes of our present [economic] difficulties."[33]

In his 1942 *Capitalism, Socialism, and Democracy*, Schumpeter famously responded to these New Deal criticisms of monopoly by trying to combine realism with a defense of "monopolistic practices," viewed as logically consistent with competition in its most important form: "the perennial gale of creative destruction," or what Marx had called the "constant revolutionizing of production." Schumpeter argued that what mattered most were the waves of innovation that revolutionized "the economic structure *from within*, incessantly destroying the old one, incessantly creating a new one. This process of Creative Destruction is the essential fact about capitalism." Yet such creative destruction, he recognized, also led to consolidation of capitals.

Pointing to oligopolistic industries, such as U.S. automobile production, he contended that "from a fierce life and death struggle three concerns emerged that by now account for over 80 per cent of total sales." In this "edited competition," firms clearly enjoyed a degree of monopoly power, behaving "among themselves...in a way which should be called corespective rather than competitive." Nevertheless, such oligopolistic firms remained under "competitive pressure" from the outside in the sense that failure to continue to innovate could lead to a weakening of the barriers to entry, protecting them from potential competitors. It was precisely innovation or creative destruction that made the barriers surrounding the giant monopolistic firms vulnerable to new competitors. Indeed, if there were a fault in the giant corporation for Schumpeter, it lay not in "trustified capitalism" per se, but rather in the weakening of the entrepreneurial function that this often brought about.[34]

But it was Galbraith who best voiced the public sentiment with respect to monopoly and competition in the post–Second World War United States, leading the heterodox liberal assault on the conventional view in three influential, iconoclastic works: *American Capitalism* (1952); *The Affluent Society* (1958); and *The New Industrial State* (1967). Significantly, he launched his critique in *American Capitalism* with the concept of the ambiguity of competition. In neoclassical economics, the very rigor of the concept of competition was the Achilles heel of the entire analysis. This was best explained, he argued, by quoting Friedrich Hayek, who had insisted: "The price system will fulfill [its] function only if competition prevails, that is, if the individual producer has to adapt himself to price changes and cannot control them." It was this definition of competition, as used by economists, Galbraith contended, that led to

> an endless amount of misunderstanding between businessmen and economists. After spending the day contemplating the sales force, advertising agency, engineers, and research men of his rivals the businessman is likely to go home feeling considerably harassed by competition. Yet if it happens that he has measurable control over his prices he obviously falls short of being competitive in the foregoing sense. No one should be surprised if he feels some annoyance toward scholars who appropriate words in common English usage and, for their own purposes, give them what seems to be an inordinately restricted meaning.[35]

Galbraith argued that the typical industry in the United States was now highly concentrated economically, dominated by a handful of "very, *very* big corporations." As long as the firms in the economy could be viewed in "bipolar classification" as consisting of either perfect competitors (small and numerous, with no price control) or monopolists (single sellers—a phenomenon practically nonexistent), the ideal competitive model worked well enough. But once oligopoly or "crypto-monopoly" was recognized as the typical case, all of this changed. "To assume that oligopoly was general in the economy was to assume that power akin to that of a monopolist was exercised in many, perhaps even a majority of markets." Prices were no longer an impersonal force, and power and rivalry could no longer be excluded from economic analysis. "Not only does oligopoly lead away from the world of competition...but it leads toward the world of monopoly."[36]

The reality-based view of monopoly had considerable currency in the postwar decades, even in economics departments, as Keynesians and liberals enjoyed prominence. Harvard economist Sumner Slichter, a free market advocate, lamented that "the belief that competition is dying is probably accepted by a majority of economists."[37] How much influence it had over government antitrust policies is another matter, but it is striking that a leading scholar and critic of monopolistic markets, John M. Blair, served as the chief economist for the Senate's Subcommittee on Anti-Trust and Monopoly from 1957 to 1970. Blair was somewhat disappointed with the government's inability to arrest monopoly power during these years, but in retrospect it seems like a period of robust public interest activism, compared with the abject abandonment of antitrust enforcement that began in the 1980s.[38]

Monopoly and 1960s U.S. Radical Political Economy

Marxian theory, as we noted, pioneered the concept of the monopoly stage of capitalism with the contributions of Hilferding and Lenin, but work in the area had languished in the early decades of the twentieth century. The more traditional Marxian theorists were content to rest on the case established by Marx in *Capital* based on nineteenth-century market conditions, with no attempt to extend the critique of capitalism to new developments associated with the monopoly stage.

The crucial step in the development of an essentially Marxist (or neo-Marxist) approach, however, arose with Kalecki's introduction of the concept of "degree of monopoly" (the power of a firm to impose a price markup on prime production costs) into the analysis of the capital accumulation process. Kalecki took the markup on costs as a kind of index of the degree of monopoly, and hence a reflection of the degree of concentration, barriers to entry, etc. His innovation, which was characteristically presented in just a few paragraphs in his *Theory of Economic Dynamics* (1952), was to show that the effect of an increased degree of monopoly/oligopoly would not only be to concentrate economic surplus (surplus value) in monopolistic firms, as opposed to competitive firms, but would also increase the rate of surplus value at the expense of wages (that is, the rate of exploitation).[39]

From here it was clear, as Steindl was to demonstrate in *Maturity and Stagnation in American Capitalism* (1952), that the growth of monopolization created an economy biased toward overaccumulation and stagnation.[40]

The work of Kalecki and Steindl, evolving out of the concept of the "degree of monopoly," became the crucial economic basis for Baran and Sweezy's 1966 *Monopoly Capital: An Essay on the American Economic and Social Order*, which became the theoretical foundation on which radical political economics was to emerge, with the rise of the Union for Radical Political Economics (URPE), in the United States in the 1960s. Thus, the first major economic crisis reader published by URPE in the mid-1970s was entitled *Radical Perspectives on the Economic Crisis of Monopoly Capitalism.*[41]

For Baran and Sweezy, a fundamental change had occurred in the competitive structure of capitalism. "We must recognize," they wrote at the outset of their book,

> that competition, which was the predominant form of market relations in nineteenth-century Britain, has ceased to occupy that position, not only in Britain but everywhere else in the capitalist world. Today the typical economic unit in the capitalist world is not the small firm producing a negligible fraction of a homogeneous output for an anonymous market but a large-scale enterprise producing a significant share of the output of an industry, or even several industries, and able to control its prices, the volume of its production, and the types and amounts of its investments.

> The typical economic unity, in other words, has the attributes which were once thought to be possessed only by monopolies. It is therefore impermissible to ignore monopoly in constructing our model of the economy and to go on treating competition as the general case. In an attempt to understand capitalism in its monopoly stage, we cannot abstract from monopoly or introduce it as a mere modifying factor; we must put it at the very center of the analytical effort.[42]

Building on Kalecki's degree of monopoly concept, Baran and Sweezy argued that Marx's law of the tendency of the profit rate (as determined at the level of production) to fall, specific to competitive capitalism, had been replaced, in monopoly capitalism, by the tendency for the rate of potential surplus generated within production to rise. This led to a gravitational pull toward overaccumulation and stagnation: for which the main compensating factors were military spending, the expansion of the sales effort, and the growth of financial speculation.[43] By exercising a tighter control over the labor process, and thus appropriating more labor power from a given amount of work—as Braverman demonstrated in *Labor and Monopoly Capital* (1974)—and by being so much better able to search the globe for cheaper labor, the system was able to generate greater profits. So it was not just that more profits shifted to the monopolies—more profit was generated in the system itself.[44]

At the core of this analysis was the notion that price competition had been effectively banned by monopoly capital—as earlier depicted by Sweezy in his kinked-demand curve analysis. At the time Baran and Sweezy were writing *Monopoly Capital*, this had received strong confirmation in U.S. government hearings directed at the steel industry. Steel executives testified that they could only increase prices in tacit or indirect collusion with their oligopolistic competitors, adding that "we are certainly not going to go down" in price because that "would be met by our competitors"—resulting in cutthroat competition and a drop in profits. As Sweezy stated in the margins of his copy of the 1958 steel hearings: "They all but draw the kinky curve!"[45] The result in oligopolistic markets, as Baran and Sweezy wrote, was a "powerful taboo" on price cutting.[46] Through tacit collusion corporations tended increasingly toward a price system, which, as famously summed up by *Business Week*, "works only one way—up."[47] Giant oligopolistic firms were price *makers*—not price *takers*, as postulated by orthodox economics.

The value of this perspective is perfectly evident today. As billionaire Warren Buffett, the voice of monopoly-finance capital, declared in February 2011: "The single most important decision in evaluating a business is pricing power. If you've got the power to raise prices without losing business to a competitor, you've got a very good business. And if you have to have a prayer session before raising the price by 10 percent, then you've got a terrible business." For Buffett, it is all about monopoly power, not management. "If you own the only newspaper in town, up until the last five years or so, you had pricing power and you didn't have to go to the office" and worry about management issues.[48]

However, the corespective pricing strategies that turned oligopolistic markets into shared monopolies developed only gradually in the early twentieth century. It took time, Baran and Sweezy observed in *Monopoly Capital*, before corporate executives "began to learn the advantages of corespective behavior." This often only occurred after a period of destructive price warfare. Indirect collusion, such as following the price leader, eventually solved this problem, generating widening gross profit margins for the giant corporations.[49]

In the *Monopoly Capital* perspective, competition was not eliminated, but rather its forms and methods changed, departing significantly from competitive capitalism. The powerful taboo against price competition did not extend to competition over low-cost position in the industry, most importantly through the reduction of unit labor costs—the main weapon of which was constant revolutionization of the means of production.[50] Yet, under monopoly capital, cost reductions did not normally lead to price reductions, but simply to wider profit margins.

In place of the formerly predominant role occupied by price competition, other forms of competition, borne of oligopolistic rivalry, prevailed: product differentiation, sales management, advertising, etc. (what Baran and Sweezy called "the sales effort") became the main means, outside of technological developments, in which firms sought in the short-run to increase their profits and market share. All such forms of competition, however, fell closer to the monopoly side of the spectrum, challenging both classical economic notions of free competition and, even more so, neoclassical notions of perfect competition.

At the same time, the giant corporations often held back on the development and release of new technologies if these did not fit with their long-term profit maximization strategies, an option unavailable under atomistic competition. Here Baran and Sweezy confronted Schumpeter's claim that the "perennial gale of creative destruction"—the new method, the new technology—was the really significant aspect of competition, constantly threatening the giant corporations, "their foundation and their very lives." In contrast, they argued that the modern giant corporations, or "corespectors" as Schumpeter called them, "as he knew well, were not in the habit of threatening each other's foundations or lives—or even profit margins. The kinds of non-price competition which they do engage in are in no sense incompatible with the permanence of monopoly profits and their increase over time.... Schumpeter's perennial gale of creative destruction has subsided into an occasional mild breeze which is no more a threat to the big corporations than is their own corespective behavior toward each other."[51]

Central to the *Monopoly Capital* thesis was the notion that the tendency toward a system-wide average rate of profit, as depicted in classical and neoclassical economics, had lost its former meaning. The reality was one of a "hierarchy of profit rates," highest in those industries where firms were large and concentrated, and lowest in those industries that were most atomistically competitive.[52] The growth in the size of firms, economic concentration, and barriers to entry therefore served to feed ever larger agglomerations of corporate power. But this did not mean that there was no movement within this hierarchy, that large capitals would not come and go, some dropping out of the picture and new firms arising. Individual monopolistic firms were not invulnerable; industry levels of concentration could shift. The rise of new industries could lead to increased competition for a time, until a shakedown process occurred. But overall, the theory pointed to greater and greater concentration and centralization of capital, monopolization, and a hierarchy of profits.

Monopoly Capital was based on a Marxian-derived *accumulation analysis* of the growth of the modern firm in which the increase in firm size and monopoly power went hand in hand with the drive to greater accumulation. From this perspective, it was hardly surprising that the typical giant corporation grew to be not only vertically integrated (embracing subsidiaries along its entire stream of production and distribution), and horizontally integrated (combining with firms in the same industry and at the same stage of production), but also evolved into a conglomerate and a multinational corporation. Conglomerates such as the DuPont Corporation had already begun to appear in the early part of the twentieth century. However, there was a qualitative difference in the post-Second World War U.S. economy in this respect. As Willard Mueller, a longtime analyst of the phenomenon, declared in 1982, "Now in much of the [U.S.] economy, conglomerate enterprise is no longer the exception but the rule."[53]

Much more significant than even conglomeration, however, was the rapid growth of "multinational corporations"—a term coined by David Lilienthal, previously director of the Tennessee Valley Authority, in 1960, and then subsequently taken up by *BusinessWeek* in a special report in April 1963. Multinational corporations, particularly emanating from the United States, were widely seen as increasingly menacing to states and peoples, not only in the periphery of world capitalism but also in some states of the developed core. For Baran and Sweezy, the rise of this phenomenon was not difficult to explain: multinational corporations represented *monopoly capital abroad*, with the giant corporations moving beyond their home countries, in the developed core of the system, to control resources and markets elsewhere. What multinational corporations wanted was "*monopolistic control* over foreign sources of supply and foreign markets, enabling them to buy and sell on specially privileged terms, to shift orders from one subsidiary to another, to favor this country or that depending on which has the most advantageous tax, labor, and other policies—in a word, they want to do business on their terms and wherever they choose."[54]

In the 1960s orthodox economists scrambled desperately to address the new core reality of a world economy increasingly dominated by multinational corporations, within the framework of a competitive model that left little room for monopoly power. They invariably sought to emphasize that such corporations were efficient instruments aimed at optimal allocation and were consistent with competitive markets, leading to a general equilibrium. Initial strategies to explain the growth of multinational corporations in the mainstream focused on such elements as: (1) different factor endowments of labor and capital between countries; (2) risk premiums in international equity markets; and (3) the need to expand firms' markets while relying on internally generated funds. None of this, however, got at the reality of multinational corporations in terms of accumulation and power.

It is in this context that economist Stephen Hymer, who was to become one of the leading radical economists of his generation before his tragic death in 1974, wrote his 1960 dissertation, *The International Operations of National Firms: A Study of Direct Foreign Investment*. He used the economics of industrial organization to uncover the reality of the multinational corporation, and directly inspired much of the critical work on the subject internationally.[55] Breaking out of orthodox international trade and investment theory, Hymer saw the multinational corporation in terms of the search for global monopolistic power, in conflict with the traditional theory of competition. Although far less critical than Hymer, others such as Charles Kindleberger in his *American Business Abroad*, moved toward greater realism, adopting in part Hymer's "monopolistic theory of direct investment."[56] Hymer's work on the monopolistic influences in multinational corporate investment became so important that the United Nations volume on *The Theory of Transnational Corporations*, edited by John Dunning in 1993, begins with Hymer's work as the first major source of a realistic theory.[57]

Magdoff and Sweezy's "Notes on the Multinational Corporation," published in 1969, depicted multinational capital as exhibiting the basic characteristics of monopoly capital, and reflecting the problem of overaccumulation in the advanced capitalist countries. The result was that "the monopolistic firm...is driven by an inner compulsion to go outside of and beyond its historical field of operations.... [Hence,] the great majority of the 200 largest nonfinancial corporations in the United States today—corporations which together account for close to half the country's industrial activity—have arrived at the stage of both conglomerates and multinationality."[58]

Financial corporations were to follow in subsequent decades in adopting multinational fields of operation. Indeed, a key question today in understanding the evolution of the giant corporation is its relation to finance. Here the classical Marxian analysis was ahead of all others. In Marx's concept of the modern corporation or joint-stock company, the most important lever—other than the pressure of competition itself (and abstracting from the role of the state)—in promoting the centralization of capital, was the development of the credit or finance system. The rise of the modern firm, first in the form of the railroads, and then more generally in the form of industrial capital, was made possible by the growth of the market for industrial securities.[59] Finance thus led to centralization. In 1895, just before his death, Engels was working on a two-part supplement to Marx's *Capital*, the second part of which, entitled "The Stock

Exchange," remained only in outline form. It started with observations on the rise of the industrial securities market, tied this rise to the fact that "in no industrial country, least of all in England, could the expansion of production keep up with accumulation, or the accumulation of the individual capitalist be completely utilised in the enlargement of his own business," and saw this tendency toward overaccumulation as the general economic basis of the *founding* of giant capital and the acceleration of an outward movement toward world colonization/imperialism.[60] Both Hilferding's *Finance Capital* and Veblen's *The Theory of Business Enterprise* focused on finance as a lever of monopoly.

Although industrial corporations were later to generate so many internal funds that they became, for a time, largely free of external financing for their investment, their very existence was associated with a vast expansion of the role of finance generally within the accumulation process. With the slowing down of economic growth beginning in the 1970s, corporations, unable to find outlets in productive investment for the enormous surplus they generated, increasingly turned to mergers and acquisitions and the associated speculation in the financial superstructure of the economy. The financial realm responded with a host of financial innovations, encouraging still further speculation leading to an economy that, while increasingly stagnant—i.e., prone to slow growth at its base—was being continually lifted by the growth of credit/debt. This phase in the development of monopoly capital is, as we argue throughout this book, best described as a shift to *monopoly-finance capital*.[61]

Neoliberal Newspeak: Monopoly Is Competition

The left embrace of monopoly at the heart of its critique of capitalism was hardly emulated by mainstream economists. To the contrary, over the course of the 1970s and certainly by the early 1980s, the field went in precisely the opposite direction. The neoliberal shift to a "leaner, meaner" capitalist system brought the "free market" economics of the Chicago School into a position of dominance. The ideas of Hayek, Friedman, George Stigler, and a host of other conservative economists now ruled the profession. Traditional Keynesians and institutionalists—those more sympathetic to reality-based assessments of monopoly—not to mention left economists, found themselves marginalized.

The victory of neoliberal economics was not the result of superior debating techniques or stellar research. It is best viewed as the necessary political-economic policy counterpart to the rise of monopoly-finance capital.[62] More specifically, it can be described as a response to the changes in accumulation and competition associated with a new phase of stagnant accumulation in the capitalist core, and to the associated financialization of the global economy. The general transformation in capital's global imperatives in the 1970s and '80s was powerfully described by Joyce Kolko in 1988 in *Restructuring the World Economy*:

> Capital continues to flow in quest of profit, and this process itself objectively restructures the economy—through accretion, not as a consequence of a strategy or a plan. But profit since the 1970s is found primarily in financial speculation and commercial parasitism, and in other ephemeral services, rather than in production.... The phenomenal growth of financial "product innovations" in the 1980s, the internationalization of equity markets, the stampedes of currency speculations by banks and corporations gambling for a quick return...all follow the laws of capitalism.... The banks themselves have been transformed from being lending units to being financial speculators.... At the same time that capital is being concentrated in huge conglomerates and trading companies.... Growing competition in the capitalist world economy has created overcapacity in all sectors—finance, basic industry, and commodities—inhibiting investment and encouraging nonproductive financial speculation.[63]

These changes initially came about, as Kolko said, through "accretion"—as a result of capital's drive to overcome all limits to operations in the context of a global economic crisis, beginning in the mid-1970s. But they soon led to the development, through the state and international organizations, of a political-economic counterattack against all forms of restraints on capital, including the welfare state, business regulation, recognition of unions, antitrust, controls on foreign investment, etc. This then became the neoliberal project of economic restructuring. Increasingly, corporations contracted out labor in order to weaken unions and reduce costs, and relied on greater global sourcing of inputs, taking advantage of low wages in the periphery.[64] Global competition between corporations increased, but it did so in Marx's sense of constituting a lever, along with finance, for the greater centralization of capital.

Key to this resurrection of neoliberal ideology was the newly articulated claim that perfect competition existed effectively in reality, and not simply on the blackboard. Economic concentration and monopoly were no longer to be considered significant, despite more than a century of growing concentration. This aspect of neoliberal economics, which deftly exploited the ambiguity of competition, was crucial in changing the entire debate about monopoly among scholars, policymakers, activists, and the general public.

The most important theoretical development in sidelining the traditional issue of monopoly power was a new theory of the emergence of the firm rooted in the concept of transaction costs. In 1937 Ronald Coase (who was to join the University of Chicago economics department in 1964) had written his now famous article "The Nature of the Firm," which argued that the reasons for corporate integration (particularly vertical integration) had to do with reducing external transaction costs arising from purchasing inputs within the market, as opposed to producing them internally within a given firm. Vertical integration, when it took place, was then seen as a way in which firms optimized on costs and "efficiency" by reducing transaction costs rather than an attempt to generate monopoly power.

The introduction of transaction costs into economics was an important innovation. But Coase's purpose was clear. As he later recalled, "my basic position was (and is)... that our economic system is in the main competitive. Any explanation therefore for the emergence of the firm had to be one which applied in competitive conditions, although monopoly might be important in particular cases. In the early 1930s I was looking for an explanation of the existence of the firms which did not depend on [the drive to] monopoly. I found it, of course, in transaction costs."[65]

Coase's argument in "The Nature of the Firm" had little influence until the late 1970s and '80s, but was increasingly seized, with the ascendance of free market conservatism, to attack all notions of monopoly power, and to challenge traditional industrial organization theory and antitrust actions.[66] With the new emphasis on transaction costs, all developments in firm integration were interpreted as optimizing "efficiency," while the question of monopoly power was largely set aside as irrelevant.

It should be noted that recourse to arguments on "efficiency" in this sense is suspect since circular in nature, justified in terms of "market exchange" as the benchmark, which is seen as efficient by definition. In this perspective, greater profits and accumulation are presumed to be indicators of efficiency and then justified because they are... efficient. It is not fewer hours of some standard labor that are "efficient" by this criterion, but less costly labor, since this directly enhances profits.[67]

Coase's transaction cost analysis was later carried forward in Oliver Williamson's influential 1975 *Markets and Hierarchies*, which extended its putative claims with respect to "efficiency," and was aimed specifically at moderating antitrust attacks on monopolies, oligopolies, vertically integrated firms, and conglomerates.[68]

In the analysis of the growth of multinational corporations at the global level, transaction cost analysis was heavily emphasized by those sympathetic to corporations. It also provided a basis for rejecting and ultimately ignoring the interpretation based on monopoly, pioneered by Hymer, Baran, Sweezy, Magdoff, and radical critics across the globe. Transaction costs were presented as external to the multinationals. Global corporations were thus said simply to be operating more "efficiently" by incorporating elements of the global economy into their internal processes, and thereby reducing their external transaction costs. Monopoly rents were no longer deemed central. Placing a disproportionate emphasis on transaction costs, mainstream economists increasingly criticized Hymer's theory of monopoly power as the key to understanding the growth of multinational corporations. Power was no longer a central issue in the analysis of the global corporation.[69]

A more concerted attempt to bring back perfect competition to its former glory as part of the new neoclassical-neoliberal program was promoted and advocated by George Stigler. In his *Memoirs of an Unregulated Economist* (1988), Stigler emphasized that a central objective of Chicago school economics was the destruction of the concept of monopoly power in all of its aspects (including its connection to advertising). He also made it clear that his own work had been particularly concerned with countering "the growing socialist critique of capitalism [which] emphasized monopoly; 'monopoly capitalism' is almost one word in that literature."[70] Although Stigler claimed that Marx's theory of concentration and centralization was a deviation from the main line of Marxist theory, he nonetheless thought it a considerable threat to neoclassical economics and the ideology of capitalism.[71]

In an article titled "Competition" for the *New Palgrave Dictionary of Economics* in 1987, Stigler started with a broad definition of competition as "rivalry" between individuals, groups, and nations in order to paper over the ambiguity of competition, and then quickly slipped into competition in economic terms, without clearly distinguishing the two. Perfect competition was then brought in as the real content of competition and as a "first approximation" to the real world of competition. While "workable competition," as it prevailed in the economy, was depicted as essentially in reality what perfect competition was in pure theory: i.e., an economy that operated *as if* numerous small firms constituted the representative case. He concluded: "The popularity of the concept of perfect competition in theoretical economics is as great today as it has ever been."[72]

At the same time, operating from the opposite tack, a Chicago School argument on the positive aspects of monopoly, building on Stigler's 1968 *The Organization of Industry*, was developed. This approach invariably saw monopoly power as (1) reflecting greater "efficiency"; (2) collapsing quickly and reverting to the competitive case; and (3) involving short-term monopoly profits that were eaten up in advance by the costs of obtaining a monopoly. Monopoly was thus naturally fleeting and rapidly turned into competition, so it could be ignored. This was accompanied by a considerable rewriting of history, with Stigler and his colleagues, for example, attempting to deny the predatory pricing policies that had led to the rise to dominance of Rockefeller's Standard Oil.[73]

In general, neoclassical economics in the era of neoliberal triumph, beginning in the late 1970s, promoted versions of economics that eschewed reality for pure market conceptions. Rational expectations theory (in which the ordinary economic actor was credited with absolute rationality, to the point of utilizing higher mathematics in making everyday economic decisions) was designed to deny that government could play an affirmative role in regulating the economy. The efficient market hypothesis was designed to deny categorically at the theoretical level anything but "efficient" outcomes in the realm of finance.[74]

With respect to competition, the conservative vogue became "contestable markets theory." Billed as a "new theory of industrial organization," the goal of this theory, as explained by its foremost proponent, William Baumol, was to demonstrate that competition and efficiency did not require "large numbers of actively producing firms, each of whom bases its decisions on the belief that it is so small as not to affect price," as in perfect competition theory. Rather, contestable markets theory posited "costlessly reversible entry" or absolutely free entry and exit to industries by *potential* competitors.[75] The barriers to entry that constituted the basis of conceptions of monopoly power were abolished by fiat at the level of pure theory. In particular, economies of scale were no longer seen as an advantage for a given firm, constituting a substantial barrier to entry. Instead, what was postulated was ultra-free entry even in such cases. Antitrust actions were therefore no longer necessary. Contestability theory was used in the 1980s to promote airline deregulation; which then proceeded to produce exactly the opposite of what the theory had suggested, leading to shared monopoly or oligopoly. In the end, "the theory of purely contestable markets," as industrial organization theorist Stephen Martin observed, "is presented as a generalization of the theory of perfectly competitive markets." In effect, perfectly competitive markets exist, even where the conditions of perfect competition do not pertain. Markets are inherently free, except in cases of state or labor interference.[76]

Antitrust law enforcement in the new neoliberal period was heavily influenced by the arguments of Robert Bork in his book *The Antitrust Paradox*. Bork was a student of Williamson's work (though focusing on "efficiency" and not transactions costs) and that of the Chicago School. He claimed that monopoly was rational, fleeting, and readily dissipated by new entry. Referring to monopolistic and oligopolistic market structures, Bork wrote: "My conclusion is that the law should never attack such structures, since they embody the proper balance of forces for consumer welfare."[77] Since consumer welfare was the object of public policy in this area, any antitrust actions threatened to go against the consumer interest by generating "inefficiency." The issue of monopoly power was simply irrelevant.

To give some sense of how mainstreamed the new neoliberal mantra became, nearly all of the major conservative economists making the case that the corporate status quo was by definition competitive and the best of all possible worlds—Hicks, Hayek, Friedman, Stigler, Coase, and Williamson—were all awarded the Bank of Sweden's Prize in Economic Sciences in Memory of Alfred Nobel.[78]

Monopoly and the Left

Above all else, it was the growth of global competition that seemed to make the monopoly question less pressing to economists. For Stigler, it was the "potential competition" from multinational corporations in other countries, symbolized by the declining national and international position of the U.S. steel and automobile industries in the 1970s, that led to widespread "skepticism about the pervasiveness of monopoly."[79]

Ironically, many of neoliberalism's foremost critics on the left came to agree with Stigler and the Chicago School on the irrelevance of monopoly, particularly in view of increased global multinational competition. Three prominent radical economists, Thomas Weisskopf, Samuel Bowles, and David Gordon, argued in 1985 that aggregate concentration in the U.S. economy was increasing only slowly, and that international competition had made the issue of monopoly capital, in the sense presented in Baran and Sweezy's analysis, no longer as significant in the United States. U.S. automakers, they pointed out, "surely have far less monopoly power than they did twenty years ago. And this is by no means an exceptional industry."[80] In their 1990 book *Global Capitalism*, Robert Ross and Kent Trachte pronounced "the death of monopoly capitalism," hypothesizing (though devoid of evidence) that capitalism was now characterized by "vigorous price competition" between "global firms," and suggesting that the entry of foreign competitors into the U.S. market meant that the U.S. auto industry no longer had oligopolistic characteristics.[81]

We would like to be able to characterize this as the beginning of a major schism among left economists, one visited by extensive research and debate, but we cannot. The topic received little more debate on the left than it did in the faculty lounge of the University of Chicago Department of Economics. The energy and attention of most radical economists—a heterogeneous group on any number of other issues—went over to the "monopoly is no longer a big deal" camp and, with that, most left economists no longer concerned themselves with the matter.

Some part of this abandonment of the concept of monopoly can be attributed not to the adoption of a definite theoretical position, but to considerable confusion across the left concerning the contours of a globalizing economy. In what was then widely regarded as a pathbreaking treatment of the subject, David Gordon wrote an article for *New Left Review* in 1988 on "The Global Economy: New Edifice or Crumbling Foundations?" which read like a compilation of uncertainties: was globalization about a vast increase in international competition, or was it a process governed by multinational corporations, obtaining a new level of domination? Despite a very careful analysis of conflicting trends, Gordon found it difficult to answer the questions he raised. Nor did anyone else have easy answers. In this situation, a rather general and undifferentiated notion of international competition took over in much of left analysis.[82]

Part of the reason for the decreased interest in the issue of monopoly capital on the left may also have been the growth of a fundamentalist strain within Marxian economics that increasingly rejected any reference to monopoly capital in its analysis—since that approach attempted to go on historical grounds beyond Marx's *Capital.* As John Weeks flatly declared in *Capitalism and Exploitation* in 1981: "The monopolies that stalk the pages of the writings of Baran and Sweezy have no existence beyond the work of these authors."[83]

Yet there is little doubt that, for the left as a whole, the dominant reason for the shift away from the consideration of monopoly power was that it fell prey to the ambiguity of competition, pretty much in the manner neoliberal economics scripted. With large corporations increasingly mobile and expanding in global markets, the tendency was to see these, not in Magdoff and Sweezy's terms, as "monopoly multinationals," but as competitors pure and simple.[84] Important treatises in Marxian political economy by thinkers as various as Giovanni Arrighi, David Harvey, Robert Brenner, and Gérard Duménil and Dominique Lévy were written with no systematic references to problems of economic concentration and monopoly, whether at the national or international level—sharply distinguishing their work in this respect from early generations of Marxian political economists.[85]

Consider the work of two important contributors to recent Marxist political economy: Giovanni Arrighi and Robert Brenner. Arrighi's *The Long Twentieth Century* showed how far left political economy had devolved in this respect. Not only is there no discussion of monopoly power or monopoly capital in his account of the development of twentieth-century capitalism, but the growth of the giant corporation and multinational firm is explained entirely in terms of transaction cost analysis derived directly from Coase, Williamson, and Alfred Chandler.[86] A century of left analysis of the growth of monopoly capital was conspicuous in its absence. Brenner replicated the spirit of the times by simply dismissing concerns about monopoly in 1999.[87]

There were, of course, holdouts in this shift away from the consideration of monopoly power. Several radical political economists continued to develop aspects of the monopoly capital argument during these years.

Magdoff and Sweezy, as we discuss above, addressed the problem of explaining how the stagnation associated with monopoly capital had led to the financialization of the economy. They examined the shift toward monopoly-finance capital in great detail in a series of articles and books in the 1970s, '80s, and early '90s.[88] The central problem, from this perspective, was to understand how transnational production was altering the nature of monopolistic rivalry, and the consequences for the world economy. As Magdoff wrote in *Imperialism: From the Colonial Age to the Present* in 1978: "What needs to be understood is that the very process of concentration and centralization of capital is spurred by competition and results in intensifying the struggle among separate aggregates of capital, albeit on a different scale and with altered strategies."[89] Rather than seeing the crisis of the U.S. steel industry in 1977 as a refutation of the monopoly capital thesis, Magdoff and Sweezy focused on the growth of international surplus capacity in steel, the relation of this to economic stagnation, the resulting competitive struggle, and the role of this struggle in generating further concentration and centralization of capital on a global scale. Instead of the end of monopoly capital, this struggle represented its elevation to another level.[90]

In this regard, industrial organization economist Eric Schutz has cogently observed with respect to international competition: "[O]nce a market expands to include producers from across the entire world, no further countertendency [to concentration from competition entering from abroad] can exist, and any tendency toward concentration must predominate, as it obviously has, for example with mergers in the auto industry worldwide."[91] As we noted earlier, five multinational corporations now account for nearly half of world motor vehicle production, while ten firms account for 70 percent of global auto production. Concentration in this area can be expected to go up—not down. Indeed, commercial aircraft production worldwide is now essentially a duopoly.

Other left economists pursued the monopoly approach as well. British theorist Keith Cowling took the argument further in 1982 in his prescient work, *Monopoly Capitalism*. For Cowling, oligopoly was moving from a primarily national plane to an international one. "Changes on the international scene, such as the creation of a smaller, tighter, international oligopoly group," he wrote, "will serve to sustain the degree of international collusion.... Each member of the international oligopoly will anticipate that any attempt [on the part of a given firm] to secure a bigger market share as a consequence [for example] of... tariff reduction will lead to an immediate response [by the other firms] which will imply that such a move is unprofitable, and thus the degree of monopoly in each country is sustained." It was taken as a given among the global corporate giants, he pointed out, that "free trade would lead to the increasing dominance of transnational corporations, implying a shift to profits" at the expense of global labor and smaller firms.[92] Moreover, "the growth of international firms means that stagnation tendencies generated in any one country... will be immediately translated across many countries.... The growth of the dominance of transnational corporations may have accentuated stagnation tendencies already endemic in monopoly capitalism," giving these a more global range.[93]

In two iconoclastic works, *Capitalism and Its Economics* (2000) and *Inequality and the Global Economic Crisis* (2009), Doug Dowd has usefully explained this historical change as a shift from Monopoly Capitalism I to Monopoly Capitalism II. If Monopoly Capitalism I was preeminently the system of oligopolistic production in the United States up to around 1975, Monopoly Capitalism II, in contrast, is dominated by much larger multinational corporations, linked more intimately to finance (and information technology), and part of an increasingly global, integrated production at the apex of the world economy. What Baran and Sweezy "analyzed in 1966," he suggests, "now applies to *global* capitalism and Monopoly Capitalism *II*. Why *II*? Because the relationships and processes taken up in the 1960s have altered greatly and swiftly: from the 1970s to the 1980s and 1990s and even more since 2000, the power and practices of giant business have picked up both their reach and speed, and in doing so have greatly deepened their dangerous consequences."[94]

Central to our entire argument is the notion that the phase of monopoly capitalism that has emerged since the mid-1970s is best characterized as *global monopoly-finance capital.* The larger political implications of this were recently spelled out by Samir Amin: "The following phenomena are inextricably linked to one another: the capitalism of oligopolies; the political power of oligarchies; barbarous globalization; financialization; U.S. hegemony; the militarization of the way globalization operates in the service of oligopolies; the decline of democracy; the plundering of the planet's resources; and the abandoning of development for the South."[95]

Our hope is that there can be a greater recognition of the monopoly capital issue in general, and far greater study and debate about it, by all principled scholars and economists who believe in reality-based social science. This is particularly important for scholars on the left. Radical economists quickly grasped the sharp growth in economic inequality wrought by neoliberalism, and did the most to examine its causes and effects and publicize its existence. Over the past one or two decades, a number of exceptional left political economists gradually have come to appreciate and assess the growing importance of financialization and debt for the economy.[96] Reconsideration of the question of monopoly is the next link in the chain, and indispensable for a meaningful and comprehensive understanding of both inequality and financialization, not to mention twenty-first-century capitalism. The research to date has barely scratched the surface of what is needed.[97]

In our view, the stakes are high. Understanding monopoly power is not only indispensable to understanding how the capitalist system works and the problems of stagnation and financialization; it is also vital to understanding the real world of politics and governance, and to any meaningful analysis of imperialism. The struggle for democracy requires that we face up to the reality of ever more concentrated political and economic power held by a plutocracy that owns and controls the giant monopolistic corporations. We on the left must learn to speak intelligibly and effectively to people who experience the consequences of this power in their lives each and every day—or reconcile ourselves to irrelevance.

CHAPTER 4

The Internationalization of Monopoly Capital

THE THREE KEY TRENDS of the capitalist economy in modern times, outside of globalization, are the slowing down of economic growth rates, the expansion of monopolistic multinational corporations, and the "financialization of the capital accumulation process."[1] The first and third of these—economic stagnation in the rich economies and the financialization of accumulation—have been the subjects of widespread discussion since the onset of severe financial crisis in 2007–09. Yet the second underlying trend, which might be called the "internationalization of monopoly capital," has received much less attention. Indeed, the dominant, neoliberal discourse—one that has also penetrated the left—assumes that the tendency toward monopoly has been vanquished. In this narrative, as explained in the previous chapter, the oligopolistic structure of early post–Second World War capitalism in the United States and elsewhere was broken down and replaced by a new era of intense global competition.

We do not intend to argue that those perceptions of growing global competition were all wrong. Rather, we suggest that renewed international competition evident since the 1970s was much more limited in range than often supposed. It has since given way to a new phase of global monopoly-finance capital in which world production is increasingly dominated by a relatively few multinational corporations able to exercise considerable monopoly power. In short, we are confronted by a system of international oligopoly. We present the broad contours of our argument with empirical evidence and explanation. Our treatment of these issues will no doubt raise as many questions as it will answer. Nevertheless, our objective is to demonstrate that addressing the internationalization of monopoly capital is a necessary prerequisite to understanding present global economic trends, including the period of slow growth and financialization in the mature economies.

Evidence of the internationalization of monopoly capital has been mounting for decades. As Richard Barnet and Ronald Müller wrote in 1974 in their book, *Global Reach: The Power of the Multinational Corporations*: "The rise of the global corporation represents the globalization of oligopoly capitalism.... The new corporate structure is the culmination of a process of concentration and internationalization that has put the economy under the substantial control of a few hundred business enterprises which do not compete with one another according to the traditional rules of the classic market."[2]

The typical or representative firm today is a monopolistic multinational corporation—a firm that operates in numerous countries, but is headquartered in one. In recent years, there has been a growth of multinational corporations in the periphery of the capitalist economy, but in the main such global firms are predominantly headquartered in the rich nations of the center (the more so the larger the firm). As the United Nations Conference on Trade and Development (UNCTAD) stated in its 2010 *World Investment Report*, "The composition of the world's top 100 TNCs [transnational corporations] confirms that the triad countries [the United States, the European Union, and Japan] remain dominant," although "their share has been slowly decreasing."[3]

Mark Casson, a leading mainstream analyst of the global corporation, observed in 1985: "From a broad long-run perspective, the postwar MNE [multinational enterprise] may be regarded simply as the latest and most sophisticated manifestation of a tendency towards the international concentration of capital. This view emerges most clearly from the work of Lenin [in *Imperialism, the Highest Stage of Capitalism*]."[4]

Today this tendency is manifested most concretely in the growth of international oligopolies. For Louis Galambos, a business historian at Johns Hopkins University, "global oligopolies are as inevitable as the sunrise."[5] Indeed, as the *Wall Street Journal* put it in 1999:

> In industry after industry the march toward consolidation has seemed inexorable.... The world automobile industry is coalescing into six or

Chart 4.1. Foreign Direct Investment as a Percentage of World Income, 1980–2009

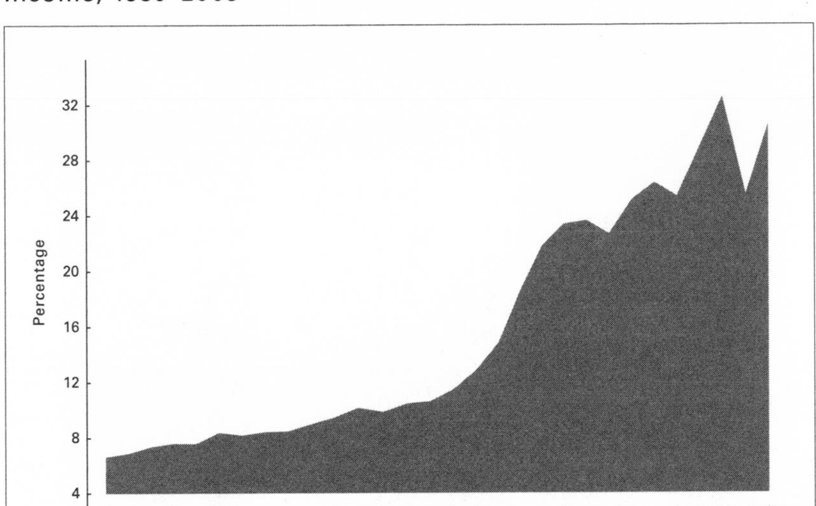

Source: UNCTADStat, United Nations Conference on Trade and Development (UNCTAD), http://unctadstat.unctad.org (Geneva: Switzerland, 2011). GDP and FDI are in current U.S. dollars.

Note: FDI stock (inward) is the value of the share of capital and reserves (including retained profits) of affiliates attributable to their parent enterprises, plus the net indebtedness of affiliates to parent enterprises.

> eight companies. Two U.S. car makers, two Japanese and a few European firms are among the likely survivors.
>
> The world's top semiconductor makers number barely a dozen. Four companies essentially supply all of the world's recorded music. Ten companies dominate the world's pharmaceutical industry, and that number is expected to decline through mergers as even these giants fear they are too small to compete across the globe.
>
> In the global soft drink business, just three companies matter, and the smallest, Cadbury Schweppes PLC, in January sold part of its international business to Coca-Cola Co., the leader. Just two names run the world market for commercial aviation: Boeing Co. and Airbus Industrie.[6]

The same tendency is evident across the board: in areas such as telecommunications, software, tires, etc. This is reflected in vast increases in foreign direct investment (FDI), which is rising much faster than world income. Thus FDI inward stock grew from 7 percent of world GDP in 1980 to around 30 percent in 2009, with the pace accelerating in the late 1990s. (See Chart 4.1.) Even these figures are conservative

Chart 4.2. Share of Foreign Affiliates in the Assets, Sales, and Employment of the World's Top 100 Non-bank Multinational Corporations

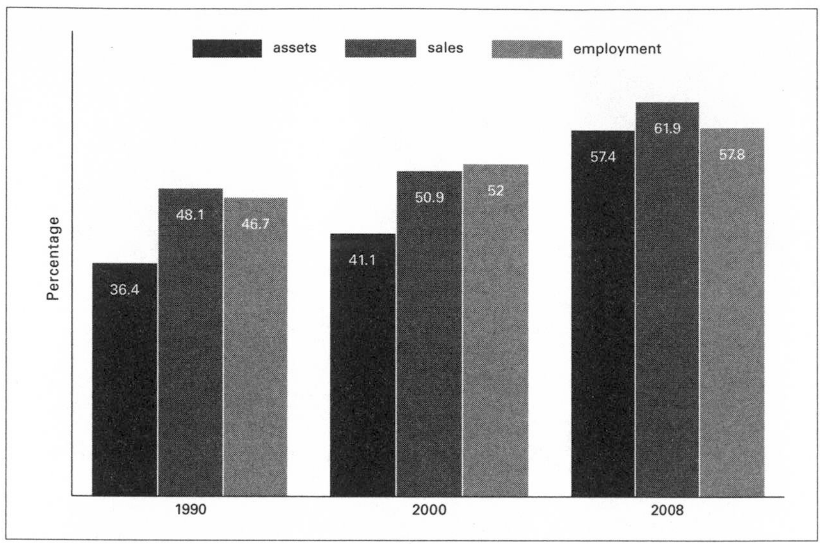

Source: UNCTAD, *World Investment Report* (New York: UNCTAD, 1993, 2002, and 2010).

Notes: The list is made up of nonfinancial multinational corporations (MNC) ranked by foreign assets. "Foreign affiliates" are defined by at least 10 percent ownership by the parent. If no foreign assets, sales or employment were reported, the non-reporting MNC was dropped. This primarily affected assets in 1990, reducing the total to 78 MNCs.

in demonstrating the growing power of multinationals since they do not capture the various forms of collusion, such as strategic alliances and technological agreements that extend the global reach of such firms. Nor is there any accounting of the massive subcontracting done by multinational corporations, extending their tentacles into all areas of the global economy.[7]

As giant corporations operate more and more, not in one but in twenty or even fifty or more countries, production has shifted to a global plane. This is shown in Chart 4.2 by the rapid growth in the proportion of assets, sales, and employment accounted for by the foreign affiliates of the top one hundred nonfinancial (non-bank) multinational corporations—ranked according to the assets of their foreign affiliates. As recently as 1990, the foreign affiliates of the world's top one hundred nonfinancial multinationals accounted for only a little over a third of the total assets and less than half of the sales and employment of these firms, with production still largely based in their parent companies headquartered in their home countries. By 2008, however, these top one hundred global corporations had shifted their production more decisively to their

Table 4.1. Top 18 U.S. Nonfinancial Multinational Corporations Ranked by Foreign Affiliate Assets

	Total Foreign Assets				Total Sales				Total Employment			
	2000		2008		2000		2008		2000		2008	
	Billions USD	Percent Foreign	Billions USD	Percent Foreign	Billions USD	Percent Foreign	Billions USD	Percent Foreign	Total	Percent Foreign	Total	Percent Foreign
General Electric (GE)	437	36	798	50	130	38	183	53	313,000	46	323,000	53
Exxon	149	68	228	71	206	69	460	70	97,900	65	79,900	63
Chevron	78	55	161	66	117	56	273	56	69,265	31	67,000	52
Ford	283	7	223	46	170	30	146	59	350,117	53	213,000	58
Conoco	16	53	143	55	32	33	241	31	17,579	47	33,800	45
Procter & Gamble	34	50	135	47	40	50	79	61	*102,000	*43	135,000	73
Wal-Mart	78	33	163	38	191	17	401	25	1,300,000	23	2,100,000	31
IBM	88	49	101	47	88	58	104	65	316,303	54	398,455	71
Pfizer	34	57	111	44	29	34	48	58	90,000	62	81,800	61
Hewlett-Packard	*33	*52	113	43	49	56	118	69	*86,200	*52	321,000	65
General Motors	303	25	91	45	185	26	149	49	386,000	43	243,000	52
Johnson & Johnson	34	42	85	47	30	41	64	49	101,901	48	118,700	59
Liberty Global			34	100			11	100			22,300	59
Alcoa	*28	*35	38	71	*23	*34	27	47	*72,500	*56	87,000	66
United Technologies	†35	†47	57	47	†31	†46	59	52	†203,000	†70	223,100	65
Kraft Foods			63	41			42	49			98,000	60
Coca-Cola	21	80	41	62	21	62	32	75	37,000	76	92,400	86
Schlumberger Ltd.			32	78			27	75			87,000	78

Source: UNCTAD, *World Investment Report* (New York: UNCTAD, various years).
* Figures are for 2001; † Figures are for 2003.

foreign affiliates, which now account for close to 60 percent of their total assets and employment, and more than 60 percent of their total sales.

U.S. corporate giants have, in recent decades, made the transition to production on a truly global scale. Table 4.1 presents data on the total assets, sales, and employment of the eighteen U.S. multinational corporations in the top one hundred multinationals worldwide. (Because the U.S. domestic market is so large and because the ranking of the top one hundred multinational corporations is based solely on foreign affiliate assets, there are only eighteen U.S. corporations among the top one hundred multinationals worldwide when ranked in this way.) These eighteen corporations represent a substantial share of the assets, sales, and employment of all U.S. nonfinancial multinational corporations: holding close to 16 percent of the total assets, raking in 28 percent of the sales, and accounting for nearly 23 percent of employment.[8] Around half or more of the total assets and production of nearly all of these U.S. firms is attributable to their foreign affiliates.

As Table 4.1 shows, a majority of these U.S. corporations in the top one hundred multinationals experienced, between 2000 and 2008, substantial (and, in some cases, huge) increases in the share of assets, sales, and employment of their foreign affiliates. To take a few examples, the share of foreign assets, sales, and employment represented by General Electric's foreign affiliates rose from 36 percent, 38 percent, and 46 percent, respectively, in 2000, to 50 percent, 53 percent, and 53 percent in 2008—making GE primarily a global, as opposed to U.S., producer. For Ford, the share of foreign affiliate assets/sales/employment rose even more dramatically, with foreign affiliate assets climbing from 7 percent to 46 percent of Ford's total assets between 2000 and 2008, and the sales and employment of its foreign affiliates rising from 30 percent and 53 percent, respectively, to 59 percent and 58 percent. In 2008, the Ford parent company accounted for only a little over 40 percent of both sales and employment. A full 86 percent of Coca-Cola's total workforce in 2008 was employed by its foreign affiliates.

These firms represent an extreme in terms of the internationalization of U.S. multinational corporations. For U.S. multinationals as a whole (which includes smaller firms and financial as well as nonfinancial corporations), U.S. parents in 2008 still accounted for more than two-thirds, and foreign affiliates less than one-third, of their combined valued added, capital expenditures, and employment. Nevertheless, the share of the parental companies in value added in 2008 had fallen by about 10 percentage points over the two preceding decades, suggesting a strong trend toward greater internationalization for U.S. multinationals as a whole.[9]

The concentrated economic power of international monopoly capital is also evident in the various kinds of strategic alliances that global corporations construct. This led Joseph Quinlan, senior economist of Morgan Stanley Dean Witter, to coin the term "Alliance Capitalism" in 2001. "Foreign direct investment and trade," Quinlan wrote, "are the primary, although not the only, means of global engagement." Other means include "subcontracting agreements, management contracts, turnkey deals, franchising, licensing, and product sharing. Of particular importance…has been the rise of strategic alliances and partnerships, which have become nearly as prominent—if not more so in some industries—over the past decade as global mergers and acquisitions." In the 1980s and '90s, Ford, for example, formed dozens of global technology agreements with the suppliers of inputs for its components, its manufacturing technology providers, its equipment suppliers, and other auto manufacturers.

The world's major airlines have "coalesced into a handful of mega-alliances." For example, just one of these, the Star Alliance, includes United Airlines and US Airways (United States); Air Canada (Canada); BMI (United Kingdom); Lufthansa (Germany); Brussels Airlines (Belgium); Swiss (Switzerland); Austrian (Austria); Spanair (Spain); Tap Portugal (Portugal); Lot Polish Airlines (Poland); Croatia Airlines (Croatia); Adria (Slovenia); SAS (Scandinavia); Blue1 (Finland); Aegean (Greece); Turkish Airlines (Turkey); Egyptair (Egypt); Thai (Thailand); Singapore Airlines (Singapore); Tam (Brazil); Air New Zealand (New Zealand); South African Airways (South Africa); ANA (Japan); Asiana Airlines (Korea); and Air China (China). "United and its counterparts" in the Star Alliance, Quinlan explained, "have achieved greater economies of scale by alliance building—pooling assets, whether they are planes, code-sharing capabilities, frequent-flyer programs, catering services, training, maintenance, or even aircraft buying programs." The result is, in effect, a global fleet of aircraft operating under the leadership of a single dominant carrier, in this case United. Mega-alliances of this sort serve to enhance international oligopoly.

"Even Microsoft, arguably one of the most powerful companies in the world," Quinlan continues, "has had to enter into multiple strategic alliances (with Ericsson, British Telecommunications, Telmex, and others).... Like many other companies, Microsoft hopes to position itself in the center of a global constellation, thereby leveraging global resources."[10]

A large part of world trade is now dominated by the outsourcing of multinational corporations. One crude estimate is that at least 40 percent of world trade is linked to outsourcing.[11] Of that, subcontracting has assumed a large role. According to the United Nations, subcontracting agreements of multinational corporations now number in the hundreds of thousands.[12] Global corporations and their affiliates frequently rely on sweatshops run by subcontractors to obtain lower unit labor costs. A well-known example is Nike, which, as a "hollow corporation," outsources all of its production to subcontractors in Asia in such countries as South Korea, China, Indonesia, Thailand, and Vietnam. In 1996 a single Nike shoe contained 52 different components produced by subcontractors in five different countries.

In Indonesia in the 1990s, where Nike manufactured seventy million pairs of shoes in 1996 alone, young girls were being paid as little as fifteen cents an hour for an eleven-hour day. Indonesian workers as a whole made an average of around $2.00 per day, well below a living wage. The *Multinational Monitor* calculated in the late 1990s that the entire labor cost for the production of a pair of $149.50 basketball shoes (if produced entirely in Vietnam), would be $1.50—1 percent of the final retail price in the United States.[13]

By using subcontractors, which removes its direct involvement in production, Nike has been able to take advantage of extreme forms of labor coercion, while defusing much of the criticism associated with such gross exploitation. For example, in 1997, a labor investigator visiting a factory in Ho Chi Minh City operated by a Nike subcontractor firm from Taiwan, saw a manager ordering fifty-six workers to run around the factory grounds until fifteen collapsed from the heat. In early 1998, an ESPN film crew was in Ho Chi Minh City and witnessed a manager at one of Nike's Korean subcontractor firms slapping a worker for not spreading glue properly, and another hurling a shoe at a worker. In response to criticisms directed at similar abuses, Nike billionaire Phil Knight responded by declaring that these were subcontractors, not companies that Nike owned or managed.[14] Although Nike subsequently voluntarily adopted new labor standards in its outsourcing, it continues to rely on subcontracting through sweatshops, where exploitation of labor is at its highest.[15]

Nike's oligopolistic rivals, like Reebok, are compelled to use the same forms of outsourcing—and coercion—through sweatshop subcontractors in order to achieve similar high profit margins derived from low unit labor costs, if they are to stay in business. A recent report by the National Labor Committee indicates that in 2010, women workers employed in El Salvador by the Singapore-based subcontractor Ocean Sky to make National Football League (NFL) T-shirts, commissioned by Reebok, were "paid just eight cents for every $25 NFL T-shirt" they produced—meaning their wage amounted to "three-tenths of one percent of the NFL's retail price."[16]

As "more and more firms externalize non-strategic activities," relying less exclusively on FDI or direct ownership, French political economist Beatrice Appay argues, they continue to maintain a "high level of control through subcontracting." Yet this tendency is not captured in the standard definition of multinational corporations based on FDI, which excludes all indirect forms of control and therefore masks the true extent of MNC power. Firms like Nike and Apple (which subcontracts its production to China) are rightly seen as monopolistic multinational corporations—capturing extremely high profit margins through their international operations and exerting strategic control over their supply lines—regardless of their relative lack of actual FDI.

Further, many of those firms with high levels of FDI, like GE, are themselves major international subcontractors. Thus, GE relies heavily on the Singapore-based subcontractor Flextronics and China's Kelon to provide it with electronic parts. A characteristic of the world of subcontracting is that the same subcontractor may work simultaneously for several different giant corporations, which collude rather than compete in this respect. Thus Flextronics, one of the world's largest subcontractors in electronics manufacturing, supplies parts not only to GE, but also to Honeywell, Compaq, Pratt and Whitney, Nortel, and others.[17]

Blockages to Understanding International Oligopoly

Oddly, so focused have economic and political discussions been on ever increasing international competition, that the actual growth of a more monopolistic world economy has been largely overlooked, even by those on the left. What has made the shift toward a world economy dominated by international oligopolistic rivalry/collusion so difficult to understand has to do primarily with five common blockages in our thinking: (1) the tendency to think of economic categories exclusively in national, rather than international, terms; (2) a fetishism of "the market," excluding the analysis of corporate power; (3) what we have called "the ambiguity of competition"; (4) the notion that financialization and new communication technologies have engendered unstoppable global competition; and (5) a common category mistake at the international level that confuses competition between capitals with competition between workers.

In discussing international competition from the standpoint of any given nation-state—particularly from the standpoint of the United States, which long enjoyed unrivaled economic hegemony in the world economy—it is assumed that international competition is simply going up when it appears to impinge on industrial concentration and the degree of monopoly in that country. The most famous example of this, as we saw in the previous chapter, is the weakening of the tight oligopoly of U.S. automakers in Detroit as a result of the invasion of foreign, particularly Japanese, firms. What is less frequently recognized, however, is that this weakening was part of the shift to concentration and centralization of production on an international plane. "As U.S. companies fell by the wayside in several industries" in the competition of the 1970s and '80s, Galambos observed in 1994 in "The Triumph of Oligopoly," "new global oligopolies began to emerge.... Whatever the outcome of this competition, the form that seems most likely to emerge is that of global oligopoly."[18]

A second blockage to our thinking is the common designation of economic relations in terms of abstract economic forces and flows—the market—while ignoring the role of giant corporations in shaping the economic terrain. The notion of the free market in today's economic theory has little real meaning other than the fact that it explicitly excludes the state, and implicitly excludes all considerations of institutional power within the economy: namely, the role played by giant corporations.[19]

Third, a serious blockage to our thinking is to be found in the confusions surrounding the concept of competition—as this is commonly understood in economics, on the one hand, and in more colloquial (including business) terms, on the other. In economic theory, competition in the fullest sense rests on the existence of large numbers of small firms, none of which has any power to control the market. Other competitors, though they exist, are essentially anonymous. Hence, direct rivalry between firms is minimal. Viewed from this standpoint, as numerous economists, including Milton Friedman, have pointed out, the intense rivalry that often characterizes oligopolistic markets—with which competition is almost exclusively associated today—is closer to monopoly in economic terms than to competition.[20] Hence, *the ambiguity of competition*.

Indeed, the dialectical counterpart of such oligopolistic rivalry (often mistaken for simple competition) is a tendency toward collusion, particularly where threat of destructive price competition between the giants is concerned. The logic of this process was well described by Baran and Sweezy in *Monopoly Capital* over forty years ago:

> The typical giant corporation...is one of several corporations producing commodities which are more or less adequate substitutes for each other. When one of them varies its price, the effect will immediately be felt by the others. If firm A lowers its price, some new demand may be tapped, but the main effect will be to attract customers away from firms B, C, and D. The latter, not willing to give up their business to A, will retaliate by lowering their prices, perhaps even undercutting A. While A's original move was made in the expectation of increasing its profit, the net result may be to leave all the firms in a worse position....
>
> Unstable market situations of this sort were very common in the earlier phases of monopoly capitalism, and still occur from time to time, but they are not typical of present-day monopoly capitalism. And clearly they are anathema to the big corporations with their penchant for looking ahead, planning carefully, and betting only on the sure thing. To avoid such situations therefore becomes the first concern of corporate policy, the *sine qua non* of orderly and profitable business operations.
>
> The objective is achieved by the simple expedient of banning price cutting as a legitimate weapon of economic warfare. Naturally this has not happened all at once or as a conscious decision. Like other powerful taboos, that against price cutting has grown up gradually out of long and often bitter experience, and it derives its strength from the fact that it serves the interests of powerful forces in society. As long as it is accepted and observed, the dangerous uncertainties are removed from the rationalized pursuit of maximum profits.[21]

This process was not confined to the national level. With concentration and centralization on a world scale and the proliferation of multinational corporations, which now increasingly govern world production, the nature of competition changed—not only at the national but now at the international level as well.[22] Thus, for economists Edward Graham and Paul Krugman, writing in 1995 in *Foreign Direct Investment in the United States*, the direction of FDI is, to a substantial extent, a product of "oligopolistic rivalry."[23] Today's now-dominant firms strive for ever greater monopolistic advantages derived from strategic control of the various elements of production and distribution, while resisting genuine price competition, not only at the national but also the international level.

A fourth common blockage in our thinking is the notion that the growth of finance and the new digital communication technologies have greatly increased market competition at the expense of the tendency toward monopoly/oligopoly. But financialization and digitalization are, in fact, integrally related to the development and maturation of the giant corporation. Finance made the modern corporation possible and accelerated the centralization of capital, particularly through mergers and acquisitions. In today's era of global monopoly-finance capital, financial capital, which once promoted national consolidations of economic power, is now extending its role in corporate consolidation to the global level. Moreover, financial corporations themselves have been increasingly subject to concentration and centralization on a world scale, becoming part of the transnational migration of capital. Information technology, which was once thought to be the great leveler, is itself undergoing global monopolization, while augmenting monopolization trends generally.[24]

A final blockage to comprehending the tendency toward global monopolization consists of a simple category mistake, wherein *competition between firms*—what economists primarily have in mind when they discuss competition—is confused with *competition between workers*.[25] Corporations seek, by means of divide-and-rule strategies, to gain advantages over different local, regional, and national labor markets, benefitting from the reality that, while capital is globally mobile, labor—due to a combination of cultural, political, economic, and geographical reasons—for the most part, is not. Consequently, workers increasingly feel the crunch of worldwide job and wage competition, and giant capital enjoys widening profit margins as the world races to the bottom in wages and working conditions. In neither mainstream nor radical economics is such competition between workers considered to be economic competition, which has to do primarily with the firm and price determination.

In Marxian theory, competition between workers, as distinct from competition between capitals (or competition proper), is related to the class struggle. The conflict between workers is engendered by capital through the creation of an industrial reserve army of the unemployed. This divide-and-rule strategy integrates disparate labor surpluses, ensuring a constant and growing supply of recruits to the global reserve army, which is made less recalcitrant by insecure employment and the continual threat of unemployment.[26] For French sociologist Pierre Bourdieu, "the *structural violence* of unemployment," including the "*fear* provoked by the threat of losing employment," is the "condition of the 'harmonious' functioning of the individualist micro-economic model." Or, as legendary U.S. capitalist Samuel Insull put it nearly a century ago, with the candor of a pre-public-relations era, "My experience is that the greatest aid to efficiency of labor is a long line of men waiting at the gate."[27]

Today we often hear—in the ideology of national competition so often used to channel class dissatisfaction—that U.S. workers are facing increased competition for jobs with Mexican workers, Chinese workers, Indian workers, etc. In our view, this is not a reflection of increased competition—certainly not in the sense that this term is used in economics—but of the growth of monopolistic multinational corporations, which, through their much larger number of foreign affiliates, their still larger numbers of subcontractors, and their corrupt domination of national governments and policymaking, are able to employ a strategy of divide-and-rule with respect to the workers of the world. Competition between workers is aggravated as the internationalization of monopoly capital grows more certain: they are two sides of the same coin. The result is a worldwide heightening of the rate of exploitation (and of the degree of monopoly). Tariffs and capital controls were battered down through GATT and WTO under the leadership of capital from the center because imperial corporations believed they were strong enough to outcompete firms in the periphery. The resulting free movement of capital has contributed to real wage stagnation or actual wage decrease for the relatively privileged workers in the countries of capitalism's core, while worsening the conditions of the vast majority of the much poorer workers in the periphery.

The Law of Increasing Firm Size and the Rise of the Multinational Corporation

From its inception, capitalism has been a system driven above all by the accumulation of capital, based on control over and exploitation of the labor force—with competition between capitals representing the mechanism that makes rapid accumulation into a law imposed on each and every individual capital. As Marx wrote: "The development of capitalist production makes it necessary constantly to increase the amount of capital laid out in a given industrial undertaking, and competition subordinates every individual capitalist to the immanent laws of capitalist production, as external and coercive laws. It compels him to keep extending his capital, so as to preserve it, and he can only extend it by means of progressive accumulation."[28] Accumulation naturally goes hand in hand with the concentration and centralization of capital and the monopolization of the main means of production in a relatively few hands.

Looking back over the history of capitalism, we can see evidence of what the most famous analyst of the multinational corporation, radical economist Stephen Hymer, called "The Law of Increasing Firm Size." In his words: "Since the beginning of the Industrial Revolution, there has been a tendency for the representative firm to increase in size from the *workshop* to the *factory* to the *national corporation* to the *multi-divisional corporation* and now to the *multinational corporation.*"[29] In early mercantilist capitalism, one of the principal ways of carrying out production was the putting-out system, whereby a capitalist provided workers with the means of production and the raw materials to produce goods in their homes, and then went around and collected the products of the workers' labor, paying them a minimal sum. This system, however, had the disadvantage of not allowing the capitalist to supervise the labor process of the worker directly.[30] As a result, the organization of production moved to the workshop—or to what Marx called the phase of "cooperation"—whereby the workers were brought together and subjected to a single owner-manager. This set the stage for a more developed division of labor (exemplified by Adam Smith's famous discussion of pin manufacture). This internalization of previous market relations was the beginning of the factory system, which preceded the widespread introduction of machinery.[31]

In Marx's terms, the division of labor under capitalism could be seen as evolving broadly from the period of "manufacture," i.e., the creation of goods simply through human labor applied to raw materials, to the period of "modern industry" (or machinofacture), marked by the subordination of labor to machinery, and corresponding to the Industrial Revolution itself. The essence of this process throughout was the evolution of capital's control of labor power in the factory, which then generated a greater surplus product or profit.

The initial development of the division of labor in the workshop and under factory conditions was associated with the small family-owned and -managed firm.[32] However, the concentration and centralization of capital meant that the small family firm was soon replaced by the large industrial corporation. Thus, the representative individual capital grew in size. This was due not only to the straightforward amassing of wealth (or concentration proper), but also to centralization: the fact that big capitals generally beat (and absorb) smaller ones. Centralization was greatly enhanced by finance, which facilitated gargantuan mergers and acquisitions. In 1901, for example, 165 steel firms were combined in a single year to create U.S. Steel, the first billion-dollar corporation, with J.P. Morgan's financial empire providing the necessary credit.[33]

Large firms enjoyed enormous advantages over small firms: not only economies of scale of all kinds, but also specifically monopolistic advantages resulting from barriers to entry, and the capacity, therefore, to acquire monopoly rents. Moreover, once a corporation became big enough to impact the economy generally, it exercised its power in the political sphere, enabling it to draw more fully on state subsidies and support—as the whole history of monopoly capitalism has demonstrated.[34] Consequently, by the twentieth century, the typical business enterprise was no longer the small-family firm celebrated in Alfred Marshall's *Principles of Economics* but a large monopolistic corporation.[35]

Managerial control of labor in the competitive stage of capitalism was fairly simple or crude.[36] But as firms increased in size along with the expansion of the market, a more complex and systematic division of labor became possible under the new regime of monopoly capitalism. Frederick Winslow Taylor's well-known introduction of scientific management at the beginning of the twentieth century, in which knowledge and control of the labor process was increasingly removed from the laborer and concentrated in management, along with the enormous intensification of actual labor that this brought about, represented the historical emergence of what Marx had called the "real" as opposed to the "formal subsumption" of labor under capital.[37]

It was this, along with the banning of price competition among oligopolies, and a host of other factors, that led to the triumph of monopoly capital. It was in this era that the modern multidivisional corporation (first developed by railroad capital), oligopoly, horizontal integration, vertical integration, conglomeration, the market for industrial securities, and the multinational corporation all arose. The "three cardinal attributes of business enterprise—investment expansion, concentration of corporate power, and the growth of the world market—are," Harry Magdoff observed in 1978, "eventually uniquely fulfilled in the multinational corporation." However, the rise of the multinational, he added, could not "take shape until the concentration of capital" had reached "the stage conveniently called monopoly capitalism (as distinguished from competitive capitalism), in which competition among only a few giant corporations is the typical pattern in each of the leading industries."[38]

Since the multinational corporation in this sense is a product of the inner development of capital—involving the struggle to control labor, the drive to accumulation, the force of competition, the leverage of credit/finance, and the growth of the world market—there can, in the Marxian vision, be no simple theory of the global firm.[39] A number of factors, however, can be singled out. Some of the first multinational firms were primarily organized around the search for raw materials, of which the oil and rubber companies are obvious examples. This continues to be an important factor in global corporate activities. A bigger factor, however, lies in the fact that capital in mature monopolistic (or oligopolistic) markets seeks carefully to regulate the expansion of output and investment in industries it controls in order to maintain higher prices and wider profit margins. Consequently, there is a constant search for new outlets for the potential economic surplus generated within production. Thus, the monopolistic corporation is "driven by an inner compulsion [i.e., by the accumulation process itself] to go outside of and beyond its historical field of operations. And the strength of this compulsion is the greater the more monopolistic the firm and the greater the amount of surplus value it disposes over and wishes to capitalize."[40]

A corporation with surplus to invest and seeking profits in other industries and other countries has the choice of indirect portfolio investment (i.e., a mere monetary investment) or direct ownership and control of subsidiaries.[41] To choose the latter course usually means that the corporation has certain monopolistic advantages vis-à-vis competitors that it believes it can exploit—for example, economies of scale in production, access to capital/finance on more favorable terms, technological (or research and development) advantages, patents, managerial assets, a more developed sales effort, etc.—all of which will allow it to erect barriers to entry, and obtain monopoly profits. A corporation may believe it is able to achieve increased strategic control over its worldwide operations, creating greater stability for the firm.[42] Intrafirm trade between parents and affiliates of multinational corporations (and between various affiliates) often allows a corporation to elude taxes, by apportioning profits/losses between one unit and another in such a way as to take advantage of the differences in national laws.

The oligopolistic nature of multinational corporate expansion means that firms are constantly strategizing ways to outmaneuver their rivals. Thus, Graham and Krugman argue that FDI commonly takes the form of an "'exchange of threat,' in which firms invade each other's home markets as part of an oligopolistic rivalry."[43]

A crucial factor determining the operations of multinational corporations—already referred to above—is the phenomenon that some analysts—beginning with Hymer, and continuing more recently with James Peoples and Roger Sugden—have called "divide and rule."[44] In the neoliberal age, corporations are able to roam the world, with most obstacles to "free trade" (that is, the free mobility of capital) removed, while labor, unable to move easily, is rooted in particular nations and localities due to immigration laws, language, custom, and numerous other factors.

What David Harvey has called "accumulation by dispossession," associated with the mass global removal of peasants from the land by agribusiness and peasant migration to overcrowded cities, has greatly increased the industrial reserve army of labor worldwide. On top of this, the fall of the Soviet bloc and the integration of China into the capitalist world economy increased the number of workers competing with each other worldwide. All of this has led some corporate analysts to speak of the "great doubling" of the global capitalist workforce.[45] This means that the global reserve army of labor has grown by leaps and bounds in the last couple of decades, making it easier to play increasingly desperate workers in different regions and nations off against each other.

A key element in this strategy of divide and rule, as noted, is the reliance by multinationals on subcontracting firms, which often utilize the most brutal forms of exploitation, outside of all forms of regulation, particularly in the global South. For example, the production of almost all of Apple's iPhones and iPads is outsourced to the Taiwanese manufacturing firm Foxconn, which owns and operates factories in (mainland) China. In the first five months of 2010, sixteen workers jumped (with twelve dying) from the high buildings at Foxconn's

Longhua, Shenzhen factory, where over three hundred thousand to four hundred thousand employees eat, work, and sleep under horrendous conditions. Compelled to carry out the same rapid hand movements for long hours and for months on end, workers find themselves twitching all night. As a symbol of their plight, they have twisted Foxconn's Chinese name so that it sounds like "Run to Your Death."[46]

The threat to move production abroad to areas where wages are cheaper and working conditions are worse is directed at workers almost everywhere, even in the low-wage periphery of the world capitalist system, anytime workers try to organize. A classic case can be found in Britain in 1971, when Henry Ford II declared, in response to strikes by British auto workers, that parts of the Ford Escort and Cortina models would, in the future, be manufactured in Asia. Surveys of the management of multinational corporations in the United States have indicated that they are not averse to using such threats of shifting production abroad in disputes with unions (while surveys of unions suggest this even more strongly). The result of this strategy, euphemistically called flexible production, is to fragment and weaken labor organization globally.[47] All of this is part of the control of the labor process that is inseparable from the division of labor and the system of exploitation under capitalism. Flexible production represents a new international division of labor, based on dispersed global production, which is often justified in technological terms, but has as its core the search for cheaper, more exploitable labor.[48]

As Keith Cowling wrote almost three decades ago in *Monopoly Capitalism*:

> Capitalism has become increasingly nomadic, leaving a trail of social disruption in its wake. It will be privately efficient for each transnational corporation to adopt such a nomadic existence, reflecting as it does an appropriate response to rising labour costs and the opportunities offered by a more flexible technology, which in turn implies a reduced demand for broadly based skills in the workforce.... Wherever workers act to raise wages or control the intensity or duration of work they will lose their jobs to other groups of less well organised and less militant workers in other countries. Thus de-industrialisation [in some industries of advanced capitalism] is a consequence of class struggle in such a world.[49]

This means that outsourcing production through foreign affiliates and subcontractors in the lower-wage sectors of the world economy is requisite in international oligopolistic rivalry. A "new nomadism" has emerged within production, with locational decisions determined largely by where labor is cheapest, and with imperial corporations pulling up stakes and moving elsewhere at the first signs of labor resistance.[50]

For today's oligopolistic multinationals, global expansion is understood to be an imperative for accumulation, and hence survival. If one major corporation moves into a new market, its rivals have to follow quickly or risk being shut out. Some economic theorists such as Graham and Krugman call this the "'follow the leader' pattern" of multinational corporate investment.[51]

Trade itself is no longer to be seen realistically as resulting primarily from free market forces—as in neoliberal theory—but as more and more the product of the interactions between the parent companies of multinationals and their affiliates, and therefore increasingly taking the form of intrafirm trade. In the United States, trade is completely dominated by multinationals. As John Dunning and Sarianna Lundan observe in *International Enterprises and the Global Economy* (2008): "Combining the share of US MNE parents and that of foreign affiliates in the US, MNEs accounted for 77 percent of US exports and 65 percent of imports in 2002."[52] Hence, where U.S. international trade is concerned, it is fast approaching the situation where multinational corporations are the only actors.[53] "Transnationalisation," Cowling wrote in 2005, referring to the global growth of multinational or transnational corporations, "introduced an added dimension of control over the market—it brings control by giant firms to the pattern and dimensions of trade and therefore undermines the possible impact of trade in restraining monopoly or oligopoly pricing behaviour within national markets."[54]

The Contradictions of International Monopoly Capital

The main consequences of the internationalization of monopoly capital for accumulation are the intensification of world exploitation and a deepening tendency to stagnation. Since the 1970s, as explained at the very beginning of this book, there has been a worsening slowdown in the rate of growth of the world economy centered in the advanced capitalist economies—while many of the most dire effects of the world crisis are falling on the poorest countries of the world. The growth of international monopoly-finance capital has not only spread stagnation across much of the globe but has also given rise to financialization, as the giant firms, unable to find sufficient investment outlets for their enormous economic surpluses within production, increasingly turn to speculation within the global financial sphere.[55] As a result, financial crises have become both more common and more severe, while state systems everywhere are increasingly subject to the whims of giant capital and are forced to bail out corporations that are deemed "too big to fail." Governments at the national, regional, and local levels seek to clear up the resulting fiscal crises by hammering the general public, cutting back on social services while creating more regressive tax systems, thereby ratcheting up the effective level of exploitation in society. Hence, the internationalization of monopoly capital, rather than contributing to the stabilization of the world system, is generating ever-greater crises, not only for the private economy but also for state systems.

Inequality, in all its ugliness, is, if anything, deeper and more entrenched. Today the richest 2 percent of adult individuals own more than half of global wealth, with the richest 1 percent accounting for 40 percent of total global assets.[56] From 1970 to 1989, the annual per capita GDP of the developing countries (excluding China) averaged a mere 6.1 percent of the per capita GDP of the G7 countries (the United States, Japan, Germany, France, the United Kingdom, Italy, and Canada). From 1990 to 2006 (just prior to the Great Financial Crisis), this dropped to 5.6 percent. Meanwhile, the average GDP per capita of the forty-eight or so Least Developed Countries (a UN-designated subset of developing countries) as a share of average G7 GDP per capita declined from 1.4 percent in 1970–1989, to .96 percent in 1990–2006.[57] The opening decade of the twenty-first century has seen waves of food crises, with hundreds of millions of people chronically food-deprived, in an era of rising food prices and widespread speculation.[58]

The supreme irony of the internationalization of monopoly capital is that this entire thrust toward monopolistic multinational-corporate development has been aided and abetted at every turn by neoliberal ideology, rooted in the "free market" economics of Hayek and Friedman. The rhetoric invariably proclaims human freedom, economic growth, and individual happiness—or "democracy" in popular parlance—as arising on a global scale, with no outposts of "tyranny" remaining. There are, in the Hayekian view, two enemies of this rosy future: labor and the state (insofar as the latter serves the interest of labor and the general population).[59]

This neoliberal campaign for the internationalization of monopoly capital is not merely an attack on the working class. Rather it must be understood, more broadly, as an attack on the potential for political democracy, that is, on the capacity of the people to organize as an independent force to counteract the power of corporations. With no clear notion they are contradicting themselves, much less denying reality, neoliberals paint a picture of a small "libertarian" state that gets out of the way of individuals, business, and free markets worldwide. Yet, to paraphrase the old calypso song, this millionaire's "libertarian" heaven is the poor person's hell.

In fact, state spending across the planet has hardly shrunk. Instead, states increasingly serve the needs of national and international monopoly capital, by aiding and abetting "the take" of their "own" giant corporations—with political elites corrupted by payoffs, which come in innumerable forms. At the same time, these quasi-privatized state systems have become ever more preoccupied with incarcerating and oppressing their domestic populations.[60]

Just as, nationally, any state programs that aid the working-class majority are targeted by neoliberalism, so, internationally, the primary goal is to remove—in the name of "free trade"—any limits on the power of multinational corporations exercised by nation-states. This mainly hurts the weaker states, where such rules are more stringently imposed by international organizations (principally the IMF, the World Bank, and the WTO) controlled by the rich countries—and where there is less capacity to resist the intrusion of global corporations. The very reality of economic stagnation in the neoliberal era has been used as a further justification for the freeing up of the market on behalf of the giant firms.

The domination in our time of global monopoly-finance capital means that every new crisis is a financial crisis, taking the form of a debt bubble that expands, only to burst in the end. Only those states large enough and strong enough to resist the full force of neoliberalism are able to prosper to some degree in these circumstances, though often the "prosperity" does not extend much beyond the plutocracies that rule them. Meanwhile, the so-called failed states that now dot the world are a manifestation of the crushing blows that international monopoly capital (backed up, when needed, by the military force of imperial nations) has inflicted on most of the world's population.

CHAPTER 5

The Global Reserve Army of Labor and the New Imperialism

IN THE LAST FEW decades there has been an enormous shift in the capitalist economy in the direction of the globalization of production. Much of the increase in manufacturing and even services production that would have formerly taken place in the global North—as well as a portion of the North's preexisting production—is now being offshored to the global South, where it is feeding the rapid industrialization of a handful of emerging economies. It is customary to see this shift as arising from the economic crisis of 1974–75 and the rise of neoliberalism—or as erupting in the 1980s and after, with the huge increase in the global capitalist labor force resulting from the integration of Eastern Europe and China into the world economy. Yet the foundations of production on a global scale, we will argue, were laid in the 1950s and 1960s, and were already depicted in the work of Stephen Hymer, the foremost theorist of the multinational corporation, who died in 1974.

For Hymer multinational corporations evolved out of the monopolistic (or oligopolistic) structure of modern industry in which the typical firm was a giant corporation controlling a substantial share of a given market or industry. At a certain point in their development (and in the development of the system) these giant corporations, headquartered in the rich economies, expanded abroad, seeking monopolistic advantages—as well as easier access to raw materials and local markets—through ownership and control of foreign subsidiaries. Such firms internalized within their own structure of corporate planning the international division of labor for their products. "Multinational corporations," Hymer observed, "are a substitute for the market as a method of organizing international exchange." They led inexorably to the internationalization of production and the formation of a system of "international oligopoly" that would increasingly dominate the world economy.[1]

In his last article, "International Politics and International Economics: A Radical Approach," published posthumously in 1975, Hymer focused on the issue of the enormous "latent surplus-population" or reserve army of labor in both the backward areas of the developed economies and in the underdeveloped countries, "which could be broken down to form a constantly flowing surplus population to work at the bottom of the ladder." Following Marx, Hymer insisted that "accumulation of capital is, therefore, increase of the proletariat." The vast "external reserve army" in the third world, supplementing the "internal reserve army" within the developed capitalist countries, constituted the real material basis on which multinational capital was able to internationalize production—creating a continual movement of surplus population into the labor force, and weakening labor globally through a process of "divide and rule."[2]

A close consideration of Hymer's work thus serves to clarify the essential point that "the great global job shift"[3] from North to South, which has become such a central issue in our time, is not to be seen so much in terms of international competition, deindustrialization, economic crisis, new communication technologies—or even such general phenomena as globalization and financialization—though each of these can be said to have played a part. Rather, this shift is to be viewed as the result primarily of the internationalization of monopoly capital, arising from the global spread of multinational corporations and the concentration and centralization of production on a world scale. Moreover, it is tied to a whole system of polarization of wages (as well as wealth and poverty) on a world scale, which has its basis in the global reserve army of labor.

The international oligopolies that increasingly dominate the world economy avoid genuine price competition, colluding instead in the area of price. For example, Ford and Toyota and the other leading auto firms do not try to undersell each other in the prices of their final products—since to do so would unleash a destructive price war that would reduce the profits of all of these firms. With price competition—the primary form of competition in economic theory—for the most part banned, the two main forms of competition that remain in a mature market or industry are: (1) competition for low-cost position, entailing reductions in prime production (labor and raw material) costs, and (2) what is known as "monopolistic competition," that is, oligopolistic rivalry directed at marketing or the sales effort.[4]

In terms of international production it is important to understand that the giant firms constantly strive for the lowest possible costs globally in order to expand their profit margins and reinforce their degree of monopoly within a given industry. This arises from the very nature of oligopolistic rivalry. As Michael E. Porter of the Harvard Business School wrote in his *Competitive Strategy* in 1980:

> Having a low-cost position yields the firm above-average returns in its industry.... Its cost position gives the firm a defense against rivalry from competitors, because its lower costs mean that it can still earn returns after its competitors have competed away their profits through rivalry.... Low cost provides a defense against powerful suppliers by providing more flexibility to cope with input cost increases. The factors that lead to a low-cost position usually also provide substantial entry barriers in terms of scale economies or cost advantages.[5]

The continuous search for low-cost position and higher profit margins led, beginning with the expansion of foreign direct investment in the 1960s, to the "offshoring" of a considerable portion of production. This, however, required the successful tapping of huge potential pools of labor in the third world to create a vast low-wage workforce. Expansion of the global labor force available to capital in recent decades has occurred mainly as a result of two factors: (1) the depeasantization of a large portion of the global periphery by means of agribusiness—removing peasants from the land, with the resulting expansion of the population of urban slums; and (2) the integration of the workforce of the former "actually existing socialist" countries into the world capitalist economy. Between 1980 and 2007 the global labor force, according to the International Labor Organisation (ILO), grew from 1.9 billion to 3.1 billion, a rise of 63 percent—with 73 percent of the labor force located in the developing world, and 40 percent in China and India alone.[6]

The change in the share of "developing countries" (referred to here as the global South, although it includes some Eastern European nations), in world industrial employment, in relation to "developed

Chart 5.1. Distribution of Industrial Employment

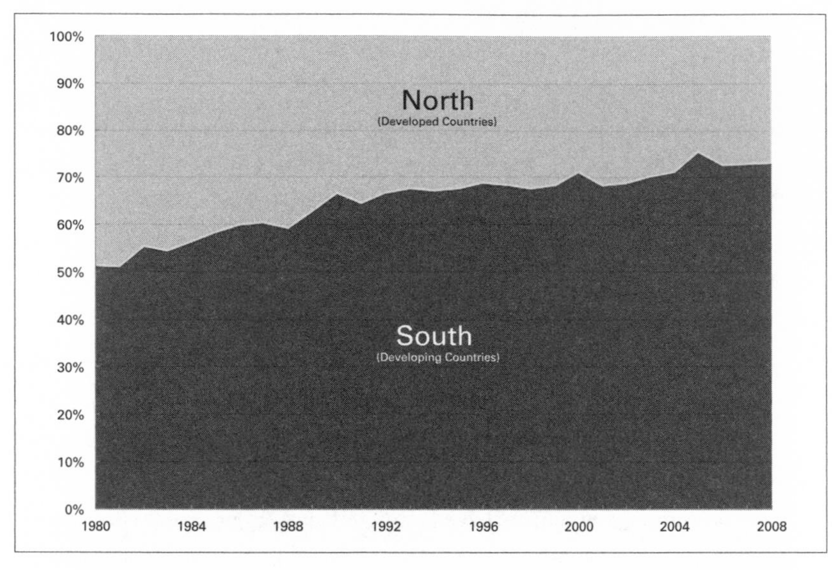

Sources: ILO, "Key Indicators of the Labour Market (KILM), Sixth Edition," Software Package (Geneva: International Labour Organization, 2009); UNCTAD, "Countries, Economic groupings," UNCTAD Statistical Databases Online, http://unctadstat.unctad.org (Geneva: Switzerland, 2011), generated June 28, 2011.

Notes: "Industrial employment" is a broad category that includes mining, manufacturing, utilities (electricity, gas, and water supply), and construction. From 2003 to 2007, manufacturing and mining averaged 58.1 percent of total industrial employment in the United States, while in China the ratio was 75.2 percent (see "Table 4b. Employment by 1-digit sector level [ISIC-Rev.3, 1990]"). Based on the two largest economies, therefore, the broad category of "industrial employment" systematically understates the extent to which the world share of manufacturing has grown in developing countries. Classification of countries as "developing" (South) and "developed" (North) is taken from UNCTAD. The sample averaged 83 countries over the entire period and there were breaks in the country-level series depending on ILO data availability. For example, data were only available for India in 2000 and 2005, and this explains the spikes in these two years.

countries" (the global North) can be seen in Chart 5.1. It shows that the South's share of industrial employment has risen dramatically from 51 percent in 1980 to 73 percent in 2008. Developing country imports as a proportion of the total imports of the United States more than quadrupled in the last half of the twentieth century.[7]

The result of these global megatrends is the peculiar structure of the world economy that we find today, with corporate control and profits concentrated at the top, while the global labor force at the bottom is confronted with abysmally low wages and a chronic insufficiency of productive employment. Stagnation in the mature economies and the resulting financialization of accumulation have only intensified these tendencies by helping to drive what Stephen Roach of Morgan Stanley dubbed "global labor arbitrage," i.e., the system of economic rewards derived from exploiting the international wage hierarchy, resulting in outsized returns for corporations and investors.[8]

Our argument here is that the key to understanding these changes in the imperialist system (beyond the analysis of the multinational corporation itself, discussed in the two previous chapters) is to be found in the growth of the global reserve army—as Hymer was among the first to realize. Not only has the growth of the global capitalist labor force (including the available reserve army) radically altered the position of third world labor, it also has had an effect on labor in the rich economies, where wage levels are stagnant or declining for this and other reasons. Everywhere multinational corporations have been able to apply a divide-and-rule policy, altering the relative positions of capital and labor worldwide.

Mainstream economics is not of much help in analyzing these changes. In line with the Panglossian view of globalization advanced by Thomas Friedman, most establishment analysts see the growth of the global labor force, the North-South shift in jobs, and the expansion of international low-wage competition as simply reflecting an increasingly "flat world" in which economic differences (advantages/disadvantages) between nations are disappearing.[9] As Krugman, representing the stance of orthodox economics, has declared: "If policy makers and intellectuals think it is important to emphasize the adverse effects of low-wage competition [for developed countries and the global economy], then it is at least equally important for economists and business leaders to tell them they are wrong." Krugman's reasoning here is based on the assumption that wages will invariably adjust to productivity growth, and the inevitable result will be a new world-economic equilibrium.[10] All is for the best in the best of all capitalist worlds. Indeed, if there are worries in the orthodox economic camp in this respect, they have to do, as we shall see, with concerns about how long the huge gains derived from global labor arbitrage can be maintained.[11]

In sharp contrast, we shall develop an approach emphasizing that behind the phenomenon of global labor arbitrage lies a new global phase in the development of Marx's "absolute general law of capitalist accumulation," according to which:

> The greater the social wealth, the functioning capital, the extent and energy of its growth, and therefore also the greater the absolute mass of the proletariat and the productivity of its labour, the greater is the industrial reserve army.... But the greater this reserve army in proportion to the active labour-army, the greater is the mass of a

> consolidated surplus population, whose misery is in inverse ratio to the amount of torture it has to undergo in the form of labour. The more extensive, finally, the pauperized sections of the working class and the industrial reserve army, the greater is official pauperism. *This is the absolute general law of capitalist accumulation.*[12]

"Nowadays...the field of action of this 'law,'" as Magdoff and Sweezy stated in 1986,

> is the entire global capitalist system, and its most spectacular manifestations are in the third world where unemployment rates range up to 50 percent and destitution, hunger, and starvation are increasingly endemic. But the advanced capitalist nations are by no means immune to its operation: more than 30 million men and women, in excess of 10 percent of the available labor force, are unemployed in the OECD countries; and in the United States itself, the richest of them all, officially defined poverty rates are rising even in a period of cyclical upswing.[13]

The new imperialism of the late twentieth and twenty-first centuries is thus characterized, at the top of the world system, by the domination of monopoly-finance capital, and, at the bottom, by the emergence of a massive global reserve army of labor. The result of this immense polarization, is an augmentation of the "imperialist rent" extracted from the South through the integration of low-wage, highly exploited workers into capitalist production. This then becomes a lever for an increase in the reserve army and the rate of exploitation in the North as well.[14]

Marx and the General Law of Accumulation

In addressing the general law of accumulation, it is important first to take note of a common misconception directed at Marx's tendential law. It is customary for establishment critics to attribute to Marx—on the basis of one or at most two passages taken out of context—what these critics have dubbed an alleged "immiseration theory" or a "doctrine of ever-increasing misery."[15] Illustrative of this is John Strachey in his 1956 book *Contemporary Capitalism*, the larger part of which was devoted to polemicizing against Marx on this point. Strachey repeatedly contended that Marx had "predicted" that real wages would not rise under capitalism, so that workers' average standard of living must remain constant or decline—presenting this as a profound error on Marx's part. However, Strachey, together with all subsequent critics who have advanced this view, managed only to provide a single partial sentence in *Capital* (plus one early on in *The Communist Manifesto*—not one of Marx's economic works) as purported evidence for this. Thus in the famous summary paragraph on the "expropriation of the expropriators" at the end of volume one, Marx (as quoted by Strachey) wrote: "While there is thus a progressive diminution in the number of the capitalist magnates (who usurp and monopolise all the advantages of this transformative process) there occurs a corresponding increase in the mass of poverty, oppression, enslavement, degeneration and exploitation...."[16]

Hardly resounding proof of a crude immiseration thesis! Marx's point rather was that the system is polarized between the growing monopolization of capital by a relatively smaller number of individual capitals at the top and the relative impoverishment of the great mass of people at the bottom. This passage said nothing about the movement of real wages. Moreover, Strachey deliberately excluded the sentence immediately preceding the one he quoted, in which Marx indicated that he was concerned in this context not simply with the working class of the rich countries but with the entire capitalist world and the global working class—or as he put it, "the entanglement of all peoples in the net of the world market, and, with this, the growth of the international character of the capitalist regime." Indeed, the "kernel of truth" to the "theory of immiseration," Roman Rosdolsky wrote in *The Making of Marx's 'Capital'*, lay in the fact that such tendencies toward an absolute increase in human misery can be found "in two spheres: firstly (temporary) in all times of crisis, and secondly (permanent) in the so-called underdeveloped areas of the world."[17]

Far from being a crude theory of immiseration, Marx's general law was an attempt to explain how the accumulation of capital could occur at all: that is, why the growth in demand for labor did not lead to a continual rise in wages, which would squeeze profits and cut off accumulation. Moreover, it served to explain: (1) the functional role that unemployment played in the capitalist system; (2) the reason why crisis was so devastating to the working class as a whole; and (3) the tendency toward the pauperization of a large part of the population. Today it has its greatest significance in accounting for "global labor arbitrage," i.e., capital's earning of enormous monopolistic returns or imperial rents by shifting certain sectors of production to underdeveloped regions of the world to take advantage of the global immobility of labor, and the existence of subsistence (or below subsistence) wages in much of the global South.

As Fredric Jameson recently noted in *Representing Capital*, despite the "mockery" thrown at Marx's general law of accumulation in the early post-Second World War era, "it is...no longer a joking matter." Rather, the general law highlights "the actuality today of *Capital* on a world scale."[18]

It is therefore essential to engage in close examination of Marx's argument. In his best-known single statement on the general law of accumulation, Marx wrote:

> *In proportion* as capital accumulates, the situation of the worker, *be his payment high or low*, must grow worse.... The law which always holds the relative surplus population *in equilibrium* with the extent and energy of accumulation rivets the worker to capital more firmly than the wedges of Hephaestus held Prometheus to the rock. It makes an accumulation of misery a necessary condition, *corresponding to* the accumulation of wealth. Accumulation at one pole is, therefore, at the same time accumulation of misery, the torment of labour, slavery, ignorance, brutalization and moral degradation at the opposite pole, i.e. on the side of the class that produces its own product as capital [italics added].[19]

By pointing to an "equilibrium" between accumulation of capital and the "relative surplus population" or reserve army of labor, Marx was arguing that, under "normal" conditions, the growth of accumulation is able to proceed unhindered only if it also results in the displacement of large numbers of workers. The resulting "redundancy" of workers checks any tendency toward a too rapid rise in real wages, which would bring accumulation to a halt. Rather than a crude theory of "immiseration," then, the general law of accumulation highlighted that capitalism, via the constant generation of a reserve army of the unemployed, naturally tended to polarize between relative wealth at the top and relative poverty at the bottom—with the threat of falling into the latter constituting an enormous lever for the increase in the rate of exploitation of employed workers.

Marx commenced his treatment of the general law by straightforwardly observing, as we have noted, that the accumulation of capital, all other things being equal, increased the demand for labor. In order to prevent this growing demand for labor from contracting the available supply of workers, and thereby forcing up wages and squeezing profits, it was necessary that a counterforce come into being that would reduce the amount of labor needed at any given level of output. This was accomplished primarily through increases in labor productivity with the introduction of new capital and technology, resulting in the displacement of labor. (Marx specifically rejected the classical "iron law of wages" that saw the labor force as determined primarily by population growth.) In this way, by "constantly revolutionizing the instruments of production," the capitalist system is able, no less constantly, to reproduce a relative surplus population or reserve army of labor, which competes for jobs with those in the active labor army.[20] "The industrial reserve army," Marx wrote, "during periods of stagnation and average prosperity, weighs down the active army of workers; during the period of over-production and feverish activity, it puts a curb on their pretensions. The relative surplus population is therefore the background against which the law of the demand and supply of labour does its work. It confines the field of action of this law to the limits absolutely convenient to capital's drive to exploit and dominate the workers."[21]

It followed that if this essential lever of accumulation were to be maintained, the reserve army would need to be continually restocked so as to remain in a constant (if not increasing) ratio to the active labor army. While generals won battles by "recruiting" armies, capitalists won them by "discharging the army of workers."[22]

It is important to note that Marx developed his well-known analysis of the concentration and centralization of capital as part the argument on the general law of accumulation. Thus the tendency toward the domination of the economy by bigger and fewer capitals was as much a part of his overall argument on the general law as was the growth of the reserve army itself. The two processes were inextricably bound together.[23]

Marx's breakdown of the reserve army of labor into its various components was complex, and was clearly aimed both at comprehensiveness and at deriving what were for his time statistically relevant categories. It included not only those who were "wholly unemployed" but also those who were only "partially employed." Thus the relative surplus population, he wrote, "exists in all kinds of forms." Nevertheless, outside of periods of acute economic crisis, there were three major forms of the relative surplus population: the floating, latent, and stagnant. On top of that there was the whole additional realm of official pauperism, which concealed even more elements of the reserve army.

The floating population consisted of workers who were unemployed due to the normal ups and downs of accumulation or as a result of technological unemployment: people who have recently worked, but who were now out of work and in the process of searching for new jobs. Here Marx discussed the age structure of employment and its effects on unemployment, with capital constantly seeking younger, cheaper workers. So exploitative was the work process that workers were physically used up quickly and discarded at a fairly early age well before their working life was properly over.[24]

The latent reserve army was to be found in agriculture, where the demand for labor, Marx wrote, "falls absolutely" as soon as capitalist production has taken it over. Hence, there was a "constant flow" of labor from subsistence agriculture to industry in the towns: "The constant movement towards the towns presupposes, in the countryside itself, a constant latent surplus population, the extent of which only becomes evident at those exceptional times when its distribution channels are wide open. The wages of the agricultural labourer are therefore reduced to a minimum, and he always stands with one foot already in the swamp of pauperism."[25]

The third major form of the reserve army, the stagnant population, formed, according to Marx, "a part of the active reserve army but with extremely irregular employment." This included all sorts of part-time, casual (and what would today be called informal) labor. The wages of workers in this category could be said to "sink below the average normal level of the working class" (i.e., below the value of labor power). It was here that the bulk of the masses ended up who had been "made 'redundant'" by large-scale industry and agriculture. Indeed, these workers represented "a proportionately greater part" of "the general increase in the [working] class than the other elements" of the reserve army.

The largest part of this stagnant reserve army was to be found in "modern domestic industry," which consisted of "outwork" carried out through the agency of subcontractors on behalf of manufacture, and dominated by so-called "cheap labor," primarily women and children.

Often such "outworkers" outweighed factory labor in an industry. For example, a shirt factory in Londonderry employed 1,000 workers but also had another 9,000 outworkers attached to it stretched out over the countryside. Here the most "murderous side of the economy" was revealed.[26]

For Marx, pauperism constituted "the lowest sediment of the relative surplus population" and it was here that the "precarious... condition of existence" of the entire working population was most evident. "Pauperism," he wrote, "is the hospital of the active labor-army and the dead weight of the industrial reserve army." Beyond the actual "lumpenproletariat" or "vagabonds, criminals, prostitutes," etc., there were three categories of paupers. First, those who were able to work and who reflected the drop in the numbers of the poor in every period of industrial prosperity when the demand for labor was greatest. These destitute elements employed only in times of prosperity were an extension of the active labor army. Second, it included orphans and pauper children, who in the capitalist system were drawn into industry in great numbers during periods of expansion. Third, it encompassed "the demoralized, the ragged, and those unable to work, chiefly people who succumb to their incapacity for adaptation, an incapacity that arises from the division of labour; people who have lived beyond the worker's average life-span; and the victims of industry whose number increases with the growth of dangerous machinery, of mines, chemical workers, etc., the mutilated, the sickly, the widows, etc." Such pauperism was a creation of capitalism itself, "but capital usually knows how to transfer these [social costs] from its own shoulders to those of the working class and the petty bourgeoisie."[27]

The full extent of the global reserve army was evident in periods of economic prosperity, when much larger numbers of workers were temporarily drawn into employment. This included foreign workers. In addition to the sections of the reserve armies mentioned above, Marx noted that Irish workers were drawn into employment in English industry in periods of peak production—such that they constituted part of the relative surplus population for English production.[28] The temporary reduction in the size of the reserve army in comparison to the active labor army at the peak of the business cycle had the effect of pulling up wages above their average value and squeezing profits—though Marx repeatedly indicated that such increases in real wages were not the principal cause of crises in profitability, and never threatened the system itself.[29]

During an economic crisis, many of the workers in the active labor army would themselves be made "redundant," thereby increasing the numbers of unemployed on top of the normal reserve army. In such periods, the enormous weight of the relative surplus population would tend to pull wages down below their average value (i.e., the historically determined value of labor power). As Marx himself put it: "Stagnation in production makes part of the working class idle and hence places the employed workers in conditions where they have to accept a fall in wages, even below the average."[30] Hence, in times of economic crisis, the working class as an organic whole, encompassing the active labor army and the reserve army, was placed in dire conditions, with a multitude of people succumbing to hunger and disease.

Marx was unable to complete his critique of political economy, and consequently never wrote his projected volume on world trade. Nevertheless, it is clear that he saw the general law of accumulation as extending eventually to the world level. Capital located in the rich countries, he believed, would take advantage of cheaper labor abroad—and of the higher levels of exploitation in the underdeveloped parts of the world made possible by the existence of vast surplus labor pools (and noncapitalist modes of production). In his speech to the Lausanne Congress of the First International in 1867 (the year of the publication of the first volume of *Capital*) he declared: "A study of the struggle waged by the English working class reveals that, in order to oppose their workers, the employers either bring in workers from abroad or else transfer manufacture to countries where there is a cheap labor force. Given this state of affairs, if the working class wishes to continue its struggle with some chance of success, the national organisations must become international."[31]

The reality of unequal exchange, whereby, in Marx's words, "the richer country exploits the poorer, even where the latter gains by the exchange," was a basic, scientific postulate of classical economy, to be found in both Ricardo and J. S. Mill. These higher profits were tied to the cheapness of labor in poor countries—attributable in turn to underdevelopment and a seemingly unlimited labor supply (albeit much of it forced labor). "The profit rate," Marx observed, "is generally higher there [in the colonies] on account of the lower degree of development, and so too is the exploitation of labour, through the use of slaves, coolies, etc." In all trade relations, the richer country was in a position to extract what were in effect "monopoly profits" (or imperial rents) since "the privileged country receives more labour in exchange for less" while, inversely, "the poorer country gives more objectified labour in kind than it receives." Hence, as opposed to a single country where gains and losses evened out, it was quite possible and indeed common, Marx argued, for one nation to "cheat" another. The growth of the relative surplus population, particularly at the global level, represented such a powerful influence in raising the rate of exploitation, in Marx's conception, that it could be seen as a major "counterweight" to the tendency of the rate of profit to fall, "and in part even paralyse[s] it."[32]

The one classical Marxist theorist who made useful additions to Marx's reserve army analysis with respect to imperialism was Rosa Luxemburg. In *The Accumulation of Capital* she argued that in order for accumulation to proceed "capital must be able to mobilise world labour power without restriction." According to Luxemburg, Marx had been too "influenced by English conditions involving a high level of capitalist development." Although he had addressed the latent reserve in agriculture, he had not dealt with the drawing of surplus labor from noncapitalist modes of production (e.g., the peasantry) in his description of the reserve army. However, it was mainly here that the surplus labor for global accumulation was to be found. It was true, Luxemburg acknowledged, that Marx discussed the expropriation of the peasantry in his treatment of "so-called primitive accumulation," in the chapter of *Capital* immediately following his discussion of the general law. But that argument was concerned primarily with the "genesis of capital" and not with its contemporary forms. Hence, the reserve army analysis had to be extended in a global context to take into account the enormous "social reservoir" of noncapitalist labor.[33]

Global Labor Arbitrage

The pursuit of "an ever extended market" Marx contended, is an "inner necessity" of the capitalist mode of production.[34] This inner necessity took on a new significance, however, with the rise of monopoly capitalism in the late nineteenth and early twentieth centuries. The emergence of multinational corporations, first in the giant oil companies and a handful of other firms in the early twentieth century, and then becoming a much more general phenomenon in the post–Second World War years, was a product of the concentration and centralization of capital on a world scale, but equally involved the transformation of world labor and production.

It was the increasing multinational corporate dominance over the world economy, in fact, that led to the modern concept of "globalization," which arose in the early 1970s as economists, particularly those on the left, tried to understand the way in which the giant firms were reorganizing world production and labor conditions.[35] This was clearly evident by the early 1970s—not only in Hymer's work, but also in Barnet and Müller's *Global Reach*, which introduced the term "globalization" to account for expanding foreign direct investment. Explaining how oligopolistic rivalry now meant searching for the lowest unit labor costs worldwide, Barnet and Müller argued that this had generated "the 'runaway shop' which becomes the 'export platform' in an underdeveloped country" and a necessity of business for U.S. companies, just like their European and Japanese competitors.[36]

Over the past half century, these global oligopolies have been offshoring whole sectors of production from the rich/high-wage to the poor/low-wage countries, transforming global labor conditions in their search for global low-cost position, and in a divide-and-rule approach to world labor. Some leading U.S. multinationals now employ more workers abroad than they do in the United States—even without considering the vast number of workers they employ through subcontractors. Other major corporations, such as Nike and Reebok, rely on third world subcontractors for 100 percent of their production workforce—with domestic employees confined simply to managerial, product development, marketing, and distribution activities.[37] The result has been the proletarianization, often under precarious conditions, of much of the population of the underdeveloped countries, working in massive export zones under conditions dictated by foreign multinationals, such as General Electric and Ford.

Two realities dominate labor at the world level today. One is global labor arbitrage, or the system of imperial rent. The other is the existence of a massive global reserve army, which makes this world system of extreme exploitation possible. "Labour arbitrage" is defined quite simply by *The Economist* as "taking advantage of lower wages abroad, especially in poor countries." It is thus an unequal exchange process in which one country, as Marx said, is able to "cheat" another due to the much higher exploitation of labor in the poorer country.[38] A study of production in China's industrialized Pearl River Delta region (encompassing Guangzhou, Shenzhen, and Hong Kong) found in 2005 that some workers were compelled to work up to sixteen hours continuously, and that corporal punishment was routinely employed as a means of worker discipline. Some 200 million Chinese are said to work in hazardous conditions, claiming over 100,000 lives a year.[39]

It is such *superexploitation* that lies behind much of the expansion of production in the global South.[40] The fact that this has been the basis of rapid economic growth for some emerging economies does not alter the reality that it has generated enormous imperial rents for multinational corporations and capital at the center of the system. As labor economist Charles Whalen has written, "The prime motivation behind offshoring is the desire to reduce labor costs...a U.S.-based factory worker hired for $21 an hour can be replaced by a Chinese factory worker who is paid 64 cents an hour.... The main reason offshoring is happening now is because it can."[41]

How this system of global labor arbitrage occurs by way of global supply chains, however, is enormously complex. Dell, the PC assembler, purchases some 4,500 parts from 300 different suppliers in multiple countries around the world.[42] As the Asian Development Bank Institute indicated in a 2010 study of iPhone production: "It is almost impossible [today] to define clearly where a manufactured product is made in the global market. This is why on the back of iPhones one can read 'Designed by Apple in California, Assembled in China.'" Although both statements on the back of the iPhones are literally correct, neither answers the question of where the real production takes place. Apple does not itself manufacture the iPhone. Rather the actual manufacture (that is, everything but its software and design) takes place primarily outside the United States. The production of iPhone parts and components is carried out principally by eight corporations (Toshiba, Samsung, Infineon, Broadcom, Numonyx, Murata, Dialog Semiconductor, and Cirrus Logic), which are located in Japan, South Korea, Germany, and the United States. All of the major parts and components of the iPhone are then shipped to the Shenzhen, China, plants of Foxconn, a subsidiary of Hon Hai Precision Industry, Co. headquartered in Taipei, for assembly and export to the United States.

Apple's enormous, complex global supply chain for iPod production is aimed at obtaining the lowest unit labor costs (taking into consideration labor costs, technology, etc.), appropriate for each component, with the final assembly taking place in China, where production occurs on a massive scale, under enormous intensity, and with ultra-low wages. In Foxconn's Longhua, Shenzhen, factory 300,000 to 400,000 workers eat, work, and sleep under horrendous conditions, with workers, who are compelled to do rapid hand movements for long hours for months on end, finding themselves twitching constantly at night. Foxconn workers in 2009 were paid the minimum monthly wage in Shenzhen, or about 83 cents an hour. (Overall in China in 2008 manufacturing workers were paid $1.36 an hour, according to U.S. Bureau of Labor Statistics data.)

Despite the massive labor input of Chinese workers in assembling the final product, their low pay means that their work amounts only to 3.6 percent of the total manufacturing cost (shipping price) of the iPhone. The overall profit margin on iPhones in 2009 was 64 percent. If iPhones were assembled in the United States—assuming labor costs ten times that in China, equal productivity, and constant component costs—Apple would still have an ample profit margin, but it would drop from 64 percent to 50 percent. In effect, Apple makes 22 percent of its profit margin on iPhone production from the much higher rate of exploitation of Chinese labor.[43]

Of course in stipulating a mere tenfold difference in wages between the United States and China, in its calculation of the lower profit margins to be gained with United States as opposed to Chinese assembly, the Asian Development Bank Institute was adopting a very conservative assumption. Overall Chinese manufacturing workers in 2008, according to the U.S. Bureau of Labor Statistics, received only 4 percent of the compensation for comparable work in the United States, and 3 percent of that in the European Union.[44] In comparison, hourly manufacturing wages in Mexico in 2008 were about 16 percent of the U.S. level.[45]

In spite of the low-wage "advantage" of China, some areas of Asia, such as Cambodia, Vietnam, and Bangladesh, have hourly compensation levels still lower, leading to a divide-and-rule tendency for multinational corporations (commonly acting through subcontractors) to locate some sectors of production, such as light industrial textile production, primarily in these still lower wage countries. Thus the *New York Times* indicated in July 2010 that Li & Fung, a Hong Kong-based company "that handles sourcing and apparel manufacturing for companies like Wal-Mart and Liz Claiborne," increased its production in Bangladesh by 20 percent in 2010, while China, its biggest supplier, slid 5 percent. Garment workers in Bangladesh earned around $64 a month, compared "to minimum wages in China's coastal industrial provinces ranging from $117 to $147 a month."[46]

For multinational corporations there is a clear logic to all of this. As General Electric CEO Jeffrey Immelt stated, the "most successful China strategy"—with China here clearly standing for global labor arbitrage in general—"is to capitalize on its market growth while exporting its deflationary power." This "deflationary power" has to do of course with lower labor costs (and lower costs of reproduction of labor in the North through the lowering of the costs of wage-consumption goods). It thus represents a global strategy for raising the rate of surplus value (widening profit margins).[47]

Today Marx's reserve army analysis is the basis, directly and indirectly (even in corporate circles), for ascertaining how long the extreme exploitation of low-wage workers in the underdeveloped world will persist. In 1997 Jannik Lindbaek, executive vice president of the International Finance Corporation, presented an influential paper entitled "Emerging Economies: How Long Will the Low-Wage Advantage Last?" He pointed out that international wage differentials were enormous, with labor costs for spinning and weaving in rich countries exceeding that of the lowest wage countries (Pakistan, Madagascar, Kenya, Indonesia, and China) by a factor of seventy-to-one in straight dollar terms, and ten-to-one in terms of purchasing power parity (taking into account the local cost of living).

The central issue from the standpoint of global capital, Lindbaek indicated, was China, which had emerged as an enormous platform for production, due to its ultra-low wages and seemingly unlimited supply of labor. The key strategic question then was, "How long will China's low wage advantage last?" His answer was that China's "enormous 'reserve army of labor'... will be released gradually as agricultural productivity improves and jobs are created in the cities." Looking at various demographic factors, including the expected downward shift in the number of working-age individuals beginning in the second decade of the twenty-first century, Lindbaek indicated that real wages in China would eventually rise above subsistence. But when?[48]

In mainstream economics, the analysis of the role of surplus labor in holding down wages in the global South draws primarily on W. Arthur Lewis's famous article "Economic Development with Unlimited Supplies of Labour," published in 1954. Basing his argument on the classical economics of Smith and Marx (relying in fact primarily on the latter), Lewis argued that in third world countries with vast, seemingly "unlimited" supplies of labor, capital accumulation could occur at a high rate while wages remained constant and at subsistence level. This was due to the very high reserve army of labor, including "the farmers, the casuals, the petty traders, the retainers (domestic and commercial), women in the household, and population growth." Although Lewis (in his original article on the subject) erroneously confined Marx's own reserve army concept to the narrow question of technological unemployment—claiming on this basis that Marx was wrong on empirical grounds—he in fact adopted the broader framework of Marx's reserve army analysis as his own. Thus he pointed to the enormous latent surplus population in agriculture. He also turned to Marx's notion of primitive accumulation, to indicate how the depeasantization of the noncapitalist sector might take place.

Lewis, however, is best known within mainstream economics for having argued that eventually a *turning point* would occur. At some point capital accumulation would exceed the supply of surplus labor (primarily from a slowdown in internal migration from the countryside) resulting in a rise in the real wages of workers in industry. As he put it, "the process" of accumulation with "unlimited labor," and hence constant real wages, must eventually stop "when capital accumulation has caught up with the labour supply."[49]

Today the Lewisian framework, overlapping with Marx's reserve army theory and in fact derived from it—but propounding the view (which Marx did not) that the reserve army of labor will ultimately be transcended in poor countries as part of a smooth path of capitalist development—is the primary basis on which establishment economics raises the issue of how long global labor arbitrage can last, particularly in relation to China. The concern is whether the huge imperial rents now being received from the superexploitation of labor in the poor countries will rapidly shrink or even disappear. *The Economist*, for example, worries that a Lewisian turning point, combined with growing labor revolts in China, will soon bring to an end the huge surplus profits from the China trade. Chinese workers "in the cities at least," it complains, "are now as expensive as their Thai or Filipino peers." "The end of surplus labor," *The Economist* declares, "is not an event, but a process. And that process may already be under way." A whole host of factors, such as demography, the stability of Chinese rural labor with its family plots, and the growing organization of workers, may cause labor constraints to come into play earlier than had been expected. At the very least, *The Economist* suggests, the enormous gains of capital in the North that occurred "between 1997 and 2005 [when] the price of Chinese exports to America fell by more than 12%" are unlikely to be repeated. And if wages in China rise, cutting into imperial rents, where will multinational corporations turn? "Vietnam is cheap: its income per person is less than a third of China's. But its pool of workers is not that deep."[50]

Writing in *Monthly Review*, economist Minqi Li notes that since the early 1980s 150 million workers in China have migrated from rural to urban areas. China thus experienced a 13 percentage-point drop (from 50 percent to 37 percent) in the share of wages in GDP between 1990 and 2005. Now "after many years of rapid accumulation, the massive reserve army of cheap labor in China's rural areas is starting to become depleted." Li focuses mainly on demographic analysis, indicating that China's total workforce is expected to peak at 970 million by 2012, and then decline by 30 million by 2020, with the decline occurring more rapidly among the prime age working population. This he believes will improve the bargaining power of workers and strengthen industrial strife in China, raising issues of radical transformation. Such industrial strife will inevitably mount if China's non-agricultural population passes "the critical threshold of 70 percent by around 2020."[51]

Others think that global labor arbitrage with respect to China is far from over. Yang Yao, an economist at Peking University, argues that "the countryside still has 45% of China's labour force," a huge reserve army of hundreds of millions, much of which will become available to industry as mechanization proceeds. Stephen Roach has observed that with Chinese wages at 4 percent of U.S. wages, there is "barely...a dent in narrowing the arbitrage with major industrial economies"—while China's "hourly compensation in manufacturing" is "less than 15% of that elsewhere in East Asia" (excluding Japan), and well below that of Mexico.[52]

The Global Reserve Army

In order to develop a firmer grasp of this issue it is crucial to look both empirically and theoretically at the global reserve army as it appears in the current historical context—and then bring to bear the entire Marxian critique of imperialism. Without such a comprehensive critique, analyses of such problems as the global shift in production, the global labor arbitrage, deindustrialization, etc., are mere partial observations suspended in midair.

The data on the global workforce compiled by the ILO conforms closely to Marx's main distinctions with regard to the active labor army and the reserve army of labor. In the ILO picture of the world workforce in 2011, 1.4 billion workers are wage workers—many of whom are precariously employed, and only part-time workers. In contrast, the number of those counted as unemployed worldwide in 2009 consisted of only 218 million workers. (In order to be classified as unemployed, workers need to have actively pursued job searches in the previous few weeks.) The unemployed, in this sense, can be seen as conforming roughly to Marx's "floating" portion of the reserve army.

A further 1.7 billion workers are classified today as "vulnerably employed." This is a residual category of the "economically active population," consisting of all those who work but are not wage workers—or part of the active labor army in Marx's terminology. It includes two categories of workers: "own-account workers" and "contributing family workers."

"Own-account workers," according to the ILO, encompasses workers engaged in a combination of "subsistence and entrepreneurial activities." The urban component of the "own-account workers" in third-world countries is primarily made up of workers in the informal sector, i.e. street workers of various kinds, while the agricultural component consists largely of subsistence agriculture. "The global informal working class," Mike Davis observed in *Planet of the Slums*, "is about one billion strong, making it the fastest-growing, and most unprecedented, social class on earth."[53]

The second category of the vulnerably employed, "contributing family workers," consists of unpaid family workers. For example, in Pakistan "more than two-thirds of the female workers that entered employment during 1999/00 to 2005/06 consisted of contributing family workers."[54]

The "vulnerably employed" thus includes the greater part of the vast pools of underemployed outside official unemployment rolls, in poor countries in particular. It reflects the fact that, as Michael Yates writes, "In most of the world, open unemployment is not an option; there is no safety net of unemployment compensation and other social welfare programs. Unemployment means death, so people must find work, no matter how onerous the conditions."[55] The various components of vulnerably employed workers correspond to what Marx described as the "stagnant" and "latent" portions of the reserve army.

Additionally, many individuals of working age are classified as not belonging to the economically active population, and thus as economically inactive. For the prime working ages of 25–54 years this adds up, globally, to 538 million people in 2011. This is a very heterogeneous grouping including university students, primarily in wealthier countries; the criminal element engendered at the bottom of the capitalist economy (what Marx called the lumpenproletariat); discouraged and disabled workers who have been marginalized by the system; and in general what Marx called the pauperized portion of the working class—that portion of working age individuals, "the demoralized, the ragged," and the disabled, who have been almost completely shut out of the labor force. It is here, he argued, that one finds the most "precarious... condition of existence." Officially designated "discouraged workers" are a significant number of would-be workers. According to the ILO, if discouraged workers are included in Botswana's unemployment rate in 2006 it nearly doubles from 17.5 percent to 31.6 percent.[56]

If we take the categories of the unemployed, the vulnerably employed, and the economically inactive population in prime working ages (25–54) and add them together, we come up with what might be called the *maximum size of the global reserve army* in 2011: some 2.4 billion people, compared to 1.4 billion in the active labor army. It is the existence of a reserve army that in its maximum extent is more than 70 percent larger than the active labor army that serves to restrain wages globally, and particularly in the poorer countries. Indeed, most of this reserve army is located in the underdeveloped countries of the world, though its growth can be seen today in the rich countries as well. The breakdown in percentages of its various components can be seen in Chart 5.2.

The enormous reserve army of labor depicted in Chart 5.2 is meant to capture its maximum extent. Some will no doubt be inclined to argue

Chart 5.2. The Global Workforce and the Global Reserve Army

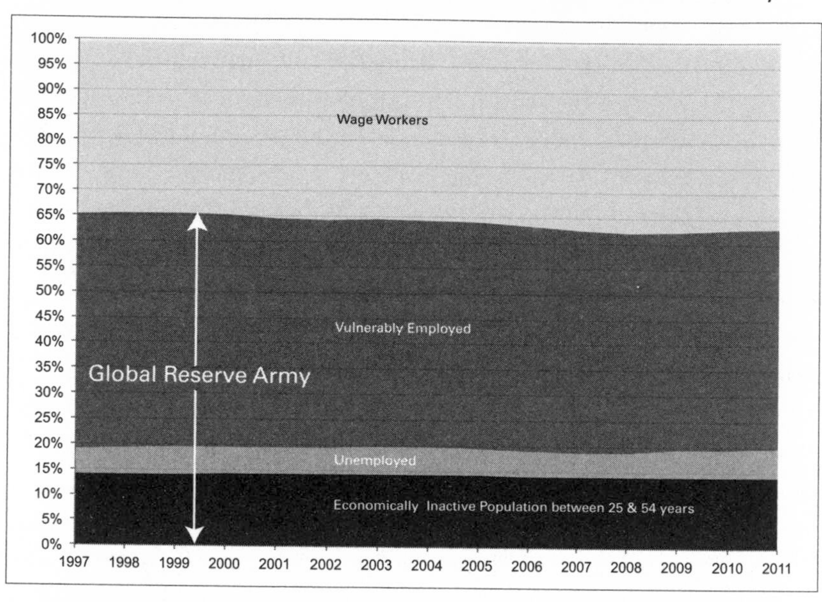

Sources: International Labour Office (ILO), "Economically Active Population Estimates and Projections (5th edition, revision 2009)," LABORSTA internet (Geneva: International Labour Organisation, 2009); ILO "Global Employment Trends," 2009, 2010 and 2011 (Geneva: International Labour Office).

Notes: The proportion of "vulnerably employed" and "unemployed" were estimated based on percentages from the "Global Employment Trends" reports cited below. The chart includes total world population (15 years and over) excluding the economically inactive population less than 25 and greater than 54 years of age.

that many of the workers in the vulnerably employed do not belong to the reserve army, since they are peasant producers, traditionally thought of as belonging to noncapitalist production—including subsistence workers who have no relation to the market. It might be contended that these populations are altogether outside the capitalist market. Yet this is hardly the viewpoint of the system itself. The ILO classifies them generally, along with informal workers, as "vulnerably employed," recognizing they are economically active and employed, but not wage workers. From capital's developmental standpoint, the vulnerably employed are all *potential* wage workers—grist for the mill of capitalist development. Workers engaged in peasant production are viewed as future proletarians, to be drawn more deeply into the capitalist mode.

In fact, the figures we provide for the maximum extent of global reserve army, in an attempt to understand the really existing relative surplus population, might be seen in some ways as underestimates. In Marx's conception, the reserve army also included part-time workers. Yet, due to lack of data, it is impossible to include this element in our global reserve army estimates. Further, figures on the economically inactive population's share of the reserve army include only prime age workers between 24 and 54 years of age without work, and exclude all of those ages 16–23 and 55–65. Yet, from a practical standpoint, in most countries those in these ages too need and have a right to employment.

Despite uncertainties related to the ILO data, there can be no doubt about the enormous size of the global reserve army. We can understand the implications of this more fully by looking at Samir Amin's analysis of "World Poverty, Pauperization, and Capital Accumulation" in *Monthly Review* in 2003. Amin argued that "Modern capitalist agriculture—encompassing both rich, large-scale family farming and agribusiness corporations—is now engaged in a massive attack on third world peasant production." According to the core capitalist view propounded by the WTO, the World Bank, and the IMF, rural (mostly peasant) production is destined to be transformed into advanced capitalist agriculture on the model of the rich countries. The 3 billion-plus rural workers (peasant population) would be replaced in the ideal capitalist scenario, as Amin puts it, by some "twenty million new modern farmers."

In the dominant view, these workers would then be absorbed by industry, primarily in urban centers, on the model of the developed capitalist countries. But Britain and the other European economies, as Amin and Indian economist Prabhat Patnaik point out, were not themselves able to absorb their entire peasant population within industry. Rather, their surplus population emigrated in great numbers to the Americas and to various colonies. In 1820 Britain had a population of 12 million, while between 1820 and 1915 emigration was 16 million. Put differently, more than half the increase in British population emigrated each year during this period. The total emigration from Europe as a whole to the "new world" (of "temperate regions of white settlement") over this period was 50 million.

While such mass emigration was a possibility for the early capitalist powers, which moved out to seize large parts of the planet, it is not possible for countries of the global South today. Consequently, the kind of reduction in peasant population currently pushed by the system points, if it were effected fully, to mass genocide. An unimaginable 7 percent annual rate of growth for fifty years across the entire global South, Amin points out, could not absorb even a third of this vast surplus agricultural population. "No amount of economic growth," Yates adds, will "absorb" the billions of peasants in the world today "into the traditional proletariat, much less better classes of work."

The problem of the absorption of the massive relative surplus population in these countries becomes even more apparent if one looks at the urban population. There are 3 billion-plus people who live in urban areas globally, concentrated in the massive cities of the global South, in which people are crowded together under increasingly horrendous, slum conditions. As the UN Human Settlements Programme declared in *The Challenge of the Slums*: "Instead of being a focus of growth and prosperity, the cities have become a dumping ground for a surplus population working in unskilled, unprotected and low-wage informal service industries and trade."

For Amin, all of this is tied to an overall theory of unequal exchange/imperialist rent. The "conditions governing accumulation on a world scale... reproduce unequal development. They make clear that underdeveloped countries are so because they are superexploited and not because they are backward." The system of imperialist rent associated with such superexploitation reaches its mature form and is universalized with the development of "the later capitalism of the generalized, financialized, and globalized oligopolies."[57]

Prabhat Patnaik has developed a closely related perspective, focusing on the reserve army of labor in *The Value of Money* and other recent works. He begins by questioning the standard economic view that it is low labor productivity rather than the existence of enormous labor reserves that best explains the impoverishment of countries in the global South. Even in economies that have experienced accelerated growth and rising productivity, such as India and China, he argues, "labour reserves continue to remain non-exhausted." This is because with the high rate of productivity growth (and labor displacement) associated with the shift toward production of high-technology goods, "the rate of growth of labour demand... does not adequately exceed the rate of growth of labor supply"—*adequately enough*, that is, to draw down the labor reserves sufficiently, and thus to pull wages up above the subsistence level. An illustration of the productivity dynamic and how it affects labor absorption can be seen in the fact that, despite rock-bottom wages in China, Foxconn is planning to introduce a million robots in its plants within three years as part of its strategy of displacing workers in simple assembly operations.

Foxconn currently employs a million workers in mainland China, many of whom assemble iPhones and iPads.

Patnaik's argument is clarified by his use of a dual reserve army model: the "precapitalist-sector reserve army" (inspired by Luxemburg's analysis) and the "internal reserve army." In essence, capitalism in China and India is basing its exports more and more on high-productivity, high-technology production, which means the displacement of labor, and thus the creation of an expanding internal reserve army. Even at rapid rates of growth therefore it is impossible to absorb the precapitalist-sector reserve army, the outward flow of which is itself accelerated by mechanization.[58]

Aside from the direct benefits of enormously high rates of exploitation, which feed the economic surplus flowing into the advanced capitalist countries, the introduction of low-cost imports from "feeder economies" in Asia and other parts of the global South by multinational corporations has a deflationary effect. This protects the value of money, particularly the dollar as the hegemonic currency, and thus the financial assets of the capitalist class. The existence of an enormous global reserve army of labor thus forces income deflation on the world's workers, beginning in the global South, but also affecting the workers of the global North, who are increasingly subjected to neoliberal "labour market flexibility."

In today's phase of imperialism—which Patnaik identifies with the development of international finance capital—"wages in the advanced countries cannot rise, and if anything tend to fall in order to make their products more competitive" in relation to the wage "levels that prevail in the third world." In the latter, wage levels are no higher "than those needed to satisfy some historically-determined subsistence requirements," due to the existence of large labor reserves. This logic of world exploitation is made more vicious by the fact that "even as wages in the advanced countries fall, at the prevailing levels of labor productivity, labor productivity in third world countries moves up, at the prevailing level of wages, towards the level reached in the advanced countries. This is because the wage differences that still continue to exist induce a diffusion of activities from the former to the latter. *This double movement means that the share of wages in total world output decreases*," while the rate of exploitation worldwide rises.[59]

What Patnaik has called "the paradox of capitalism" is traceable to Marx's general law of accumulation: the tendency of the system to concentrate wealth while expanding relative (and even absolute) poverty.

"In India, precisely during the period of neoliberal reforms when output growth rates have been high," Patnaik notes,

> there has been an increase in the proportion of the rural population accessing less than 2400 calories per person per day (the figure for 2004 is 87 percent). This is also the period when hundreds of thousands of peasants, unable to carry on even simple reproduction, have committed suicide. The unemployment rate has increased, notwithstanding a massive jump in the rate of capital accumulation; and the real wage rate, even of the workers in the organized sector, has at best stagnated, notwithstanding massive increases in labor productivity. In short our own experience belies Keynesian optimism about the future of mankind under capitalism.[60]

In the advanced capitalist countries, the notion of "precariousness," which Marx in his reserve army discussion employed to describe the most pauperized sector of the working class, has been rediscovered, as conditions once thought to be confined to the third world are reappearing in the rich countries. This has led to references to the emergence of a "new class"—though in reality it is the growing pauperized sector of the working class—termed the "precariat."[61]

At the bottom of this precariat developing in the rich countries are so-called "guest workers." As Marx noted, in the nineteenth century, capital in the wealthy centers is able to take advantage of lower-wage labor abroad either through capital migration to low-wage countries or through the migration of low-wage labor into rich countries. Although migrant labor populations from poor countries have served to restrain wages in rich countries, particularly the United States, from a global perspective the most significant fact with respect to workers migrating from South to North is their low numbers in relation to the population of the global South.

Overall the share of migrants in total world population has shown no appreciable change since the 1960s. According to the ILO, there was only "a very small rise" in the migration from developing to developed countries "in the 1990s, and... this is accounted for basically by increased migration from Central American and Caribbean countries to the United States." The percentage of adult migrants from developing to developed countries in 2000 was a mere 1 percent of the adult population of developing countries. Moreover, those migrants were concentrated among the more highly skilled so that "the effect of international migration on the low-skilled labour force" in developing countries themselves "has been negligible for the most part.... Migration from developing to developed countries has largely meant brain drain.... In short," the ILO concludes, "limited as it was, international migration" in the decade of the 1990s "served to restrain the growth of skill intensity of the labour force in quite a large number of developing countries, and particularly in the least developed countries." All of this drives home the key point that capital is internationally mobile, while labor is not.[62]

If the new imperialism has its basis in the superexploitation of workers in the global South, it is a phase of imperialism that in no way can be said to benefit the workers of the global North, whose conditions are also being dragged down—both by the disastrous global wage competition introduced by multinationals and, more fundamentally, by the overaccumulation tendencies in the capitalist core, enhancing stagnation and unemployment.[63]

Indeed, the wealthy countries of the triad (the United States, Europe, Japan) are all bogged down in conditions of deepening stagnation, resulting from their incapacity to absorb all of the surplus capital that they are generating internally and pulling in from abroad—a contradiction that is manifested in weakening investment and employment. Financialization, which helped to boost these economies for decades, is now arrested by its own contradictions, with the result that the root problems of production, which financial bubbles served to cover up for a time, are now surfacing. This is manifesting itself not only in diminishing growth rates, but also rising levels of excess capacity and unemployment. In an era of globalization, financialization, and neoliberal economic policy, the state is unable effectively to move in to correct the problem, and is increasingly geared simply to bailing out capital at the expense of the rest of society.

The imperial rent that these countries appropriate from the rest of the world only makes the problems of surplus absorption or overaccumulation at the center of the world system worse. "Foreign investment, far from being an outlet for domestically generated surplus," Baran and Sweezy famously wrote in *Monopoly Capital*, "is a most efficient process for transferring surplus generated from abroad to the investing country. Under these circumstances, it is of course obvious that foreign investment aggravates rather than helps to solve the surplus absorption problem."[64]

The New Imperialism

As we have seen, there can be no doubt about the sheer scale of the relative shift of world manufacturing to the global South in the period of the internationalization of monopoly capital since the Second World War—and accelerating in recent decades. Although this is often seen as a post–1974 or a post–1989 phenomenon, Hymer, Magdoff, Sweezy, and Amin captured the general parameters of this broad movement in accumulation and imperialism associated with the development of multinational corporations (the internationalization of monopoly capital) as early as the 1970s. Largely as a result of this epochal shift in the center of gravity of world manufacturing production toward the South, about a dozen emerging economies have experienced phenomenal growth rates of 7 percent or more for a quarter century.

Most important among these of course is China, which is not only the most populous country but has experienced the fastest growth rates, reputedly 9 percent or above. At a 7 percent rate of growth an economy doubles in size every ten years; at 9 percent every eight years. Yet the process is not, as mainstream economics often suggests, a smooth one. The Chinese economy has doubled in size three times since 1978, but wages remain at or near subsistence levels, due to an internal reserve army in the hundreds of millions. China may be emerging as a world economic power due to its sheer size and rate of growth, but wages remain among the lowest in the world. India's per capita income, meanwhile, is about one-third of China's. China's rural population is estimated at about 50 percent, while India's is around 70 percent.[65]

Orthodox economic theorists rely on an abstract model of development that assumes all countries pass through the same phases, and eventually move up from labor-intensive manufacturing to capital-intensive, knowledge-intensive production. This raises the issue of the so-called "middle-income transition" that is supposed to occur at a per capita income of somewhere between $5,000 and $10,000 (China's per capita income at current exchange rates is about $3,500). Countries in the middle-income transition have higher wage rates and are faced with uncompetitiveness unless they can move to products that capture more value and are less labor-intensive. Most countries fail to make the transition and the middle-income level ends up being a developmental trap. Based on this framework, New York University economist Michael

Spence argues in *The Next Convergence* that China's "labor-intensive export sectors that have been a major contributor to growth are losing competitiveness and have to be allowed to decline or move inland and then eventually decline. They will be replaced by sectors that are more capital, human-capital, and knowledge intensive."[66]

Spence's orthodox argument, however, denies the reality of contemporary China, where the latent reserve army in agriculture alone amounts to hundreds of millions of people. Moving toward a less labor-intensive system under capitalism means higher rates of productivity and technological displacement of labor, requiring that the economy absorb a mounting reserve army by conquering ever-larger, high-value-capture markets. The only cases where anything resembling this has taken place—aside from Japan, which first emerged as a rapidly expanding, militarized-imperialist economy in the early twentieth century—were the Asian tigers (Korea, Taiwan, Singapore, and Hong Kong), which were able to expand their external export markets for high-value-capture production in the global North during a period of world economic expansion (not the deepening stagnation of today). This is unlikely to prove possible for China and India, which must find employment between them for some 40 percent of the world's labor force—and to a mounting degree in the urban industrial sector. Unlike Europe during its colonial period the emigration of large pools of surplus labor as an escape valve is not possible: they have nowhere to go. China's capacity to promote internal-based accumulation (not relying primarily on export markets), meanwhile, is hindered under today's capitalist conditions by this same reserve army of low-paid labor, and by rapidly rising inequality.

All of this suggests that at some point the contradictions of China's unprecedented accumulation rates combined with massive labor reserves that cannot readily be absorbed by the accumulation process—particularly with the growing shift to high-technology, high-productivity production—are bound to come to a head.

Meanwhile, international monopoly capital uses its combined monopolies over technology, communications, finance, military, and the planet's natural resources to control (or at least constrain) the direction of development in the South.[67]

As the contradictions between North and South of the world system intensify, so do the internal contradictions within them—with class differences widening everywhere. The relative "deindustrialization" in the global North is now too clear a tendency to be altogether denied. Thus the share of manufacturing in U.S. GDP has dropped from around 28 percent in the 1950s to 12 percent in 2010, accompanied by a dramatic decrease in its share (along with that of the OECD as a whole) in world manufacturing.[68] Yet it is important to understand that this is only the tip of the iceberg where the growing worldwide destabilization and overexploitation of labor is concerned.

Indeed, one should never forget the moral barbarism of a system that in 1992 paid Michael Jordan $20 million to market Nikes—an amount equal to the total payroll of the four Indonesian factories involved in the production of the shoes, with women in these factories earning only 15 cents an hour and working eleven-hour days.[69] Behind this lies the international "sourcing" strategies of increasingly monopolistic multinational corporations. The field of operation of Marx's general law of accumulation is now truly global, and labor everywhere is on the defensive.

The answer to the challenges facing world labor that Marx gave at the Lausanne Congress in 1867 remains the only possible one: "If the working class wishes to continue its struggle with some chance of success the national organisations must become international." It is time for a new International.[70]

CHAPTER 6

The Great Stagnation and China

FIVE YEARS AFTER THE Great Financial Crisis of 2007–09 began there is still no sign of a full recovery of the world economy. Consequently, concern, as we noted at the beginning of this book, has increasingly shifted from financial crisis and recession to slow growth or stagnation, causing some to dub the current era the Great Stagnation.[1] Stagnation and financial crisis are now seen as feeding into one another. Thus IMF Managing Director Christine Lagarde declared in a speech in China on November 9, 2011, in which she called for the rebalancing of the Chinese economy:

> The global economy has entered a dangerous and uncertain phase. Adverse feedback loops between the real economy and the financial sector have become prominent. And unemployment in the advanced economies remains unacceptably high. If we do not act, and act together, we could enter a downward spiral of uncertainty, financial instability, and a collapse in global demand. Ultimately, we could face a lost decade of low growth and high unemployment.[2]

To be sure, a few emerging economies have seemingly bucked the general trend, continuing to grow rapidly—most notably China, now the world's second largest economy after the United States. Yet, as Lagarde warned her Chinese listeners, "Asia is not immune" to the general economic slowdown, "emerging Asia is also vulnerable to developments in the financial sector." So sharp were the IMF's warnings, dovetailing with widespread fears of a sharp Chinese economic slowdown, that Lagarde in late November was forced to reassure world business, declaring that stagnation was probably not imminent in China (the Bloomberg.com headline ran: "IMF Sees Chinese Economy Avoiding Stagnation.")[3]

Nevertheless, concerns regarding the future of the Chinese economy are now widespread. Few informed economic observers believe that the current Chinese growth trend is sustainable; indeed, many believe that if China does not sharply alter course, it is headed toward a severe crisis. Stephen Roach, non-executive chairman of Morgan Stanley Asia, argues that China's export-led economy has recently experienced two warning shots: first the decline beginning in the United States following the Great Financial Crisis, and now the continuing problems in Europe. "China's two largest export markets are in serious trouble and can no longer be counted on as reliable, sustainable sources of external demand."[4]

In order to avoid looming disaster, the current economic consensus suggests that the Chinese economy needs to rebalance its shares of net exports, investment, and consumption in GDP—moving away from an economy that is dangerously over-reliant on investment and exports, characterized by an extreme deficiency in consumer demand, and increasingly showing signs of a real estate/financial bubble. But the very idea of such a fundamental rebalancing—on the gigantic scale required—raises the question of contradictions that lie at the center of the whole low-wage accumulation model that has come to characterize contemporary Chinese capitalism, along with its roots in the current urban-rural divide.

Giving life to these abstract realities is the burgeoning public protest in China, now consisting of literally hundreds of thousands of mass incidents a year—threatening to halt or even overturn the entire extreme "market-reform" model.[5] China's reliance on its "floating population" of low-wage internal migrants for most export manufacture is a source of deep fissures in an increasingly polarized society. And connected to these economic and social contradictions—that include huge amounts of land seized from farmers—is a widening ecological rift in China, underscoring the unsustainability of the current path of development.

Nor are China's contradictions simply internal. The complex system of global supply chains that has made China the world's factory has also made China increasingly dependent on foreign capital and foreign markets, while making these markets vulnerable to any disruption in the Chinese economy. If a severe Chinese crisis were to occur it would open up an enormous chasm in the capitalist system as a whole. As the *New York Times* noted in May 2011, "The timing for when China's growth model will run out of steam is probably the most critical question facing the world economy."[6] More important than the actual timing, however, are the nature and repercussions of such a slowdown.

Capitalist Contradictions with Chinese Characteristics

For many the idea that the Chinese economy is rife with contradictions may come of something as a surprise since the hype on Chinese growth has expanded more rapidly than the Chinese economy itself. As the *Wall Street Journal* sardonically queried in July 2011, "When exactly will China take over the world? The moment of truth seems to be coming closer by the minute. China will become the largest economy by 2050, according to HSBC. No, it's 2040, say analysts at Deutsche Bank. Try 2030, the World Bank tells us. Goldman Sachs points to 2020 as the year of reckoning, and the IMF declared several weeks ago that China's economy will push past America's in 2016." Not to be outdone, Harvard historian Niall Ferguson declared in his 2011 book, *Civilization: The West and the Rest*, that "if present rates persist China's economy could surpass America's in 2014 in terms of domestic purchasing power."[7]

This prospect is generally viewed with unease in the old centers of world power. But at the same time the new China trade is an enormous source of profitability for the Triad of the United States, Europe, and Japan. The latest round of rapid growth that has enhanced China's global role was an essential component of the recovery of global financialized capitalism from the severe crisis of 2007–09, and is counted on in the future.

There are clearly some who fantasize, in today's desperate conditions, that China can carry the world economy on its back and keep the developed nations from what appears to be a generation of stagnation and intense political struggles over austerity politics.[8] The hope here undoubtedly is that China could provide capitalism with a few decades of adequate growth and buy time for the system, similar to what the U.S.-led debt and financial expansion did over the past thirty years. But such an "alignment of the stars" for today's world capitalist economy, based on the continuation of China's meteoric growth, is highly unlikely.

"Let's not get carried away," the *Wall Street Journal* cautions us. "There's a good deal of turmoil simmering beneath the surface of China's miracle." The contradictions it points to include mass protests (rising to as many as 280,000 in 2010), overinvestment, idle capacity, weak consumption, financial bubbles, higher prices for raw materials, rising food prices, increasing wages, long-term decline in labor surpluses, and massive environmental destruction. It concludes: "If nothing else, the colossal challenges that lie ahead for China provide an abundance of good reasons to doubt long-term projections of the country's economic supremacy and global dominance." The immediate future of China is therefore uncertain, throwing added uncertainty on the entire global economy. As we shall see, not only might China *not* bail out global capitalism at present; an argument can be made that it constitutes the single weakest link for the global capitalist chain.[9]

At question is the extraordinary rate of Chinese expansion, especially when compared with the economies of the Triad. The great divergence in growth rates between China and the Triad can be seen in Chart 6.1, showing ten-year moving averages of annual real GDP growth for the United States, the European Union, Japan, and China from 1970 to 2010. While the rich economies of the United States, Western Europe, and Japan have been increasingly prone to stagnation—overcoming this in 1980–2006 only by means of a series of financial bubbles—China's economy over the same period (beginning in the Mao era) has continually soared. China managed to come out of the Great Financial Crisis period largely unaffected with a double-digit rate of growth, at the same time that what *The Economist* has dubbed "the moribund rich world" was laboring to achieve any positive growth at all.[10]

To give a sense of the difference that the divergence in growth rates shown in Chart 6.1 makes with respect to exponential growth, an economy growing at a rate of 10 percent will double in size every seven years or so, while an economy growing at 2 percent will take thirty-six years to double in size, and an economy growing at 1 percent will take seventy-two years.[11]

The economic slowdown in the developed, capital-rich economies is long-standing, associated with deepening problems of surplus capital absorption or overaccumulation. As the *New York Times* states, "Mature countries like the United States and Germany are lucky to grow about 3 percent annually"—indeed, today we might say lucky to grow

Chart 6.1. Percent Change from Previous Year in Real GDP

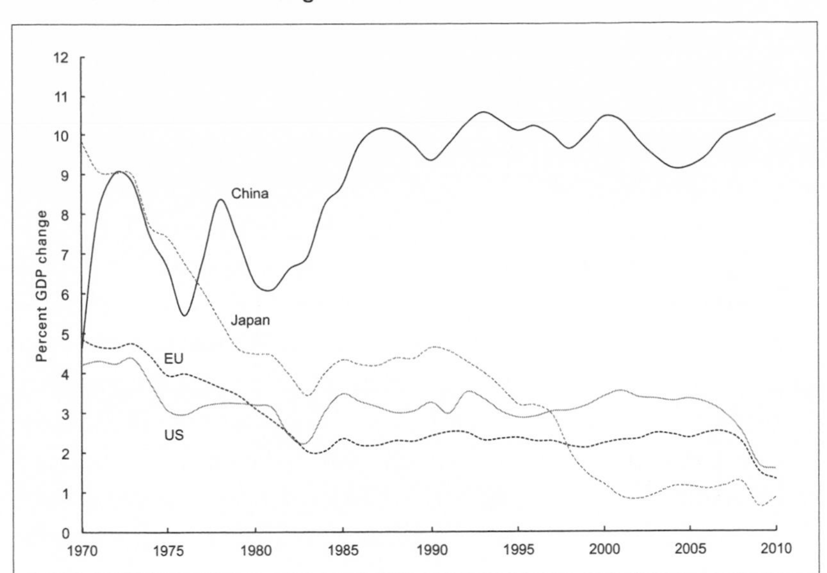

Sources: WDI database for China, Japan, and the European Union (http://databank.worldbank.org) and St. Louis Federal Reserve Database (FRED) for the United States (http://research.stlouisfed.org/fred2/).

at 2 percent. Japan's growth rate has averaged less than 1 percent over the period 1992 to 2010. As Lagarde noted in a speech in September 2011, according to the latest IMF projections, "the advanced economies will only manage an anemic 1½–2 percent" growth rate over the years 2011–12. Recent developments make even this sound optimistic. China, in contrast, has been growing at 10 percent.[12]

The problems of the mature economies are complicated today by two further features: (1) the heavy reliance on financialization to lift the economy out of stagnation, but with the consequence that the financial bubbles eventually burst, and (2) the shift toward the corporate outsourcing of production to the global South. World economic growth in recent decades has gravitated to a handful of emerging economies of the periphery; even as the lion's share of the profits derived from global production are concentrated within the capitalist core, where they worsen problems of maturity and stagnation in the capital-rich economies.[13]

As the structural crisis within the center of the capitalist world economy has deepened, the hope has been raised by some that China will serve to counterbalance the tendency toward stagnation at the global level. However, even as this hope has been raised it has been quickly dashed—as it has become increasingly apparent that cumulative contradictions are closing in on China's current model, producing growing panic within world business.

Ironically, today's fears regarding the Chinese economy stem in part from the way China engineered its way out of the global slump brought on by the Great Financial Crisis—a feat that was regarded initially by some as conclusive proof that China had "decoupled" itself from the West's fate and represented an unstoppable growth machine. Faced with the world crisis and declining foreign trade, the Chinese government introduced a massive $585 billion stimulus plan in November 2008, and urged state banks to be aggressive in making new loans. Local governments in particular ran up huge debts associated with urban expansion and real estate speculation. As a result, the Chinese economy rebounded almost instantly from the crisis (in a V-shaped turnaround). The growth rate was 7.1 percent in the first half of 2009 with state-directed investments estimated as accounting for 6.2 percentage points of that growth.[14] The means of accomplishing this was an extraordinary increase in fixed investment, which served to fill the gap left by falling exports.

This can be seen in Table 6.1, which shows the percent contribution to China's GDP of consumption, investment, government, and trade (net exports). The sharp increase in investment as a share of GDP, which rose 7 percentage points between 2007–10, mirrored the sharp decrease in the share of both trade and consumption over the same period, which dropped 5 and 2 percentage points, respectively. Meanwhile, the share of government spending in GDP remained steady. Investment alone now constitutes 46 percent of GDP, while investment plus trade equals 53 percent.

As Michael Pettis, a professor at Peking University's Guanghua School of Management and a specialist in Chinese financial markets, explained, the sharp drop in the trade surplus in the crisis might "have forced GDP growth rates to nearly zero." However, "the sudden and violent expansion in investment" served as "the counterbalance to keep growth rates high." Of course behind the dramatic ascent of the investment share of GDP, rising 10 percentage points during the years 2002–10, lay the no less dramatic descent of the consumption share, which dropped 10 percentage points over the same period, from 44 percent to 34 percent, the smallest share of any large economy.[15]

Table 6.1. Percent Contribution to China's GDP

	A	B	C	D	B+D
	Consumption	Investment	Government	Trade	Investment + Trade
2002	44.0	36.2	15.6	4.2	40.4
2003	42.2	39.1	14.7	4.0	43.1
2004	40.6	40.5	13.9	5.1	45.6
2005	38.8	39.7	14.1	7.4	47.1
2006	36.9	39.6	13.7	9.7	49.3
2007	36.0	39.1	13.5	11.4	50.5
2008	35.1	40.7	13.3	10.9	51.6
2009	35.0	45.2	12.8	7.0	52.2
2010	33.8	46.2	13.6	6.4	52.6

Sources: Michael Pettis, "Lower Interest Rates, Higher Savings?" http://mpettis.com, October 16, 2011; *China Statistical Yearbook.*

With investment spending running at close to 50 percent in this period the Chinese economy is facing widening overaccumulation problems. For New York University economist Nouriel Roubini:

> The problem, of course, is that no country can be productive enough to reinvest 50% of GDP in new capital stock without eventually facing immense overcapacity and a staggering non-performing loan problem. China is rife with overinvestment in physical capital, infrastructure, and property. To a visitor, this is evident in sleek but empty airports and bullet trains (which will reduce the need for the 45 planned airports), highways to nowhere, thousands of colossal new central and provincial government buildings, ghost towns, and brand-new aluminum smelters kept closed to prevent global prices from plunging.
>
> Commercial and high-end residential investment has been excessive, automobile capacity has outstripped even the recent surge in sales, and overcapacity in steel, cement, and other manufacturing sectors is increasing further.... Overcapacity will lead inevitably to serious deflationary pressures, starting with the manufacturing and real-estate sectors.
>
> Eventually, most likely after 2013, China will suffer a hard landing. All historical episodes of excessive investment—including East Asia in the 1990's—have ended with a financial crisis and/or a long period of slow growth.[16]

Overinvestment has been accompanied by increasing financial frailty raising the question of a "China Bubble." The government's fixed investment stimulus worked in part through encouragement of massive state bank lending and a local borrowing binge, resulting in a further speculative boom centered primarily on urban real estate. China's urban expansion currently consumes half of the world's steel and concrete production as well as much of its heavy construction equipment. Construction accounts for about 13 percent of China's GDP.

Although insisting that the bursting of China's "big red bubble" still is "ahead of us," *Forbes* magazine cautioned its readers in 2011 that "China's real estate bubble is multiplying like a contagious disease," asking: "China's housing market: when will it pop, and how loud of an explosion will it make when it goes boom?" But for all of that, *Forbes* added reassuringly that "China's property bubble is different," since it is all under the watchful eyes of state banks that operate like extensions of government departments.

This notion of a visionary and wise Chinese state that can demolish any obstacles put before the economy on its current path is the corollary of the notion that the Chinese economy as it now exists will grow at double-digit annual rates far into the future. It is an illusion—or delusion. The Chinese model of integration into global capitalism contains contradictions that will obstruct its extension.

This is certainly true in finance. While *Forbes* is hopeful, the *Financial Times* reports something quite different. State banks, supposedly at the center of the financial system, have been hemorrhaging in the last few years due to the loss of bank deposits to an unregulated shadow banking system that now supplies more credit to the economy than the formal banking institutions do. Indicative of a shift toward Ponzi finance, the most profitable activity of state banks is now loaning to the shadow banking system. A serious real estate downturn began in August 2011 when China's top ten property developers reported that they had unsold inventories worth $50 billion, an increase of 46 percent from the previous year. Property developments are highly leveraged and developers have become increasingly dependent on underground (shadow) lenders, who are demanding their money. As a result, prices on new apartments have been slashed by 25 percent or more, reducing the value of existing apartments. China in late 2011 was experiencing a significant property price downturn, with sharp drops in home prices, which had risen by 70 percent since 2000.

Mizuho Securities Asia bank analyst Jim Antos, a close observer of the sector, estimates that bank lending doubled between December 2007 and May 2011, and although the rate of increase declined subsequently, it was to remain far higher than the growth in GDP. As a result, Antos calculates that bank loans stood at $6,500 per capita in 2010 compared to GDP per capita of $4,400, and that the disproportion is continuing to increase, a situation he terms "unsustainable." In addition there are unknown amounts of off-balance-sheet loans, and the current reporting of non-performing loans at 1 percent of total loans only serves to guarantee a sharp increase in this rate in the near future by 100 percent and up. Antos and others note that the banks' capitalization was inadequate even prior to the break in real estate prices. Despite the vast financial resources that the Chinese government has in its role as lender of last resort, a sharp decline in real estate prices and in construction, and therefore in GDP, would produce a full-blown crisis of market confidence in a situation marked by great uncertainty and fear.[17]

Already in 2007 Chinese premier Wen Jiabao declared that China's economic model was "unstable, unbalanced, uncoordinated and ultimately unsustainable." Five years later this is now more obvious than ever. The most intractable problem, the root cause of instability, is the low and declining share of GDP devoted to household consumption, which has dropped around 11 percentage points in a decade, from 45.3 percent of GDP in 2001 to 33.8 percent in 2010. All the calls for rebalancing thus boil down to the need for a massive increase in the share of consumption in the economy.

Such rebalancing has been a major goal of the Chinese government since 2005, and there is no shortage of proposals on how to accomplish it. But they all founder in the face of the underlying reality. As Michael Pettis states: "Low consumption levels are not an accidental coincidence. They are fundamental to the growth model." First among the relevant factors is the (super)exploitation of workers in the new export sectors, where wages grow slowly while productivity with advanced technology grows rapidly. The rise in wages necessary to yield an increase in consumption as a share of GDP would drive the large foreign-owned assembly plants to countries with lower wages. And the surrounding penumbra of small- and middle-scale plants run by Chinese capitalists would also begin to disappear, squeezed by tightening credit and already increasingly prone to embezzlement and flight.[18]

The declining share of consumption in GDP is sometimes attributed to China's high savings rate, largely associated with the attempts by people to put aside funds to safeguard their future due to the lack of national safety net. Between 1993 and 2008 more than 60 million state sector jobs were lost, the majority through layoffs due to the restructuring of state-owned enterprises beginning in the 1990s. This represented a smashing of the "iron rice bowl" or the *danwei* system of work-unit socialism that had provided guarantees to state-enterprise workers.[19] Social provision in such areas as unemployment compensation, social insurance, pensions, health care, and education have been sharply reduced. As Minxin Pei, senior associate in the China Program at the Carnegie Endowment for International Peace, has written:

> Official data indicate that the government's relative share of health-care and education spending began to decline in the 1990s. In 1986, for example, the state paid close to 39 percent of all health-care expenditures.... By 2005, the state's share of health-care spending fell to 18 percent.... Unable to pay for health care, about half of the people who are sick choose not to see a doctor, based on a survey conducted by the Ministry of Health in 2003. The same shift has occurred in education spending. In 1991, the government paid 84.5 percent of total education spending. In 2004, it paid only 61.7 percent.... In 1980, almost 25 percent of the middle-school graduates in the countryside went on to high school. In 2003, only 9 percent did. In the cities, the percentage of middle-school graduates who enrolled in high school fell from 86 to 56 percent in the same period.[20]

The growing insecurity arising from such conditions has compelled higher savings on the part of the relatively small proportion of the population in a position to save.

However, the more fundamental cause of rapidly weakening consumption is growing inequality, marked by a falling wage share and declining incomes in a majority of households. As *The Economist* put it in October 2007, "The decline in the ratio of consumption to GDP does not reflect increased saving; instead, it is largely explained by a sharp drop in the share of national income going to households (in the form of wages, government transfers and investment income).

Most dramatic has been the fall in the share of wages in GDP. The World Bank estimates that this has dropped from 53 percent in 1998 to 41 percent in 2005."[21]

The core contradiction thus lies in the extreme form of exploitation that characterizes China's current model of class-based production, and the enormous growth of inequality in what was during the Mao period one of the most egalitarian societies. Officially the top 10 percent of urban Chinese today receive about twenty-three times as much as the bottom 10 percent. But if undisclosed income is included (which may be as much as $1.4 trillion annually), the top 10 percent of income recipients may be receiving sixty-five times as much as the bottom 10 percent.[22] According to the Asian Development Bank, China is the second most unequal country in East Asia (of twenty-two countries studied), next to Nepal. A Boston Consulting Group study found that China had 250,000 U.S. dollar millionaire households in 2005 (excluding the value of primary residences), who together held 70 percent of the country's entire wealth. China is a society that still remains largely rural, with rural incomes less than one-third those in cities. The majority of workers in export manufacturing are internal migrants still tied to the rural areas, who are paid wages well below those of workers based in the cities.[23]

China's "Opening" and the Global Supply Chain

Today's Chinese economy is a product of both the Chinese Revolution of 1949 and of what William Hinton called "The Great Reversal," or what is more often referred to as the "reform period," which began in 1978 under Deng Xiaoping, two years after Mao Zedong's death. The Chinese Revolution introduced a massive land reform, the greatest in history, expropriating the land from the landlord class and creating a system of collective agriculture. Industry, meanwhile, came to be dominated by state enterprises. The twofold system of worker rights took the form of what Hinton called the "clay rice bowl" in the countryside, which guaranteed peasants a permanent relation to the land as usufruct, or user rights, organized in the form of collective agriculture; while workers in state enterprises benefitted from the "iron rice bowl" or a system of guaranteed lifetime jobs and benefits. (There was also what was called a "golden rice bowl," representing the privileges of state bureaucrats.)[24]

Economic growth in the Mao period was impressive, despite periodic setbacks and internal struggles that developed within the party itself (culminating in the Cultural Revolution). Economic growth during the entire 1966–76 period reached an annual average rate of 6 percent according to World Bank data, while industrial production grew at an annual average rate of around 10 percent. An immense industrial infrastructure, both heavy and light, was created virtually from scratch in these years, complete with a transportation and power network, that by the end of the Mao period employed 100 million people. This then was exploited in the market-reform period that followed. The output of Chinese agriculture was improved during the Cultural Revolution period and productivity reached remarkable levels. As Mark Selden, then coeditor of the *Bulletin of Concerned Asian Scholars*, wrote, "In 1977 China grew 30 to 40 percent more food per capita [than India] on 14 percent less arable land and distributed it far more equitably to a population...50 percent larger."[25]

The market reforms associated with the Great Reversal were aimed at eliminating or expropriating collective agriculture and state enterprises, while proletarianizing the population by weakening both the iron rice bowl and the clay rice bowl, i.e., the economic gains made by peasants and workers in the revolution. In the countryside, collective farms were broken up and replaced with a family contract system. The land was divided into strips (still allocated by the collective) to which peasants had user rights. Each noodle-like strip of land was small and made working the land less efficient, providing a very marginal existence for peasant families. As Hinton wrote: "This was not 'postage stamp' land such as used to exist before land reform, but 'ribbon land,' 'spaghetti land,' 'noodle land'—strips so narrow that often not even the right wheel of a cart could travel down one man's land without the left wheel pressing down on the land of another."[26]

Although some left analysts of China's development, such as world-system theorist Giovanni Arrighi, have called China a case of "accumulation *without* dispossession," the market reform period was in fact characterized from the start by massive accumulation by dispossession (primitive accumulation), and hundreds of millions of people were proletarianized.[27] As geographers Richard Walker and Daniel Buck succinctly explained in *New Left Review* in 2007:

There are three major routes to proletarianization in China: from the farming countryside, out of collapsing state companies in the cities, and through the dissolution of former village enterprises. To take the first of these: rural displacement to the cities is vast, numbering roughly 120 million since 1980—the largest migration in world history. The abolition of the communes and instigation of the household responsibility system allowed some farmers to prosper in the richest zones, but it has left marginal producers increasingly exposed to low price, poor soils, small plots, lack of inputs, and the corruption of predatory local cadres. In the cities, peasant migrants do not have residency rights and become long-term transients. This is due to the household registration or *hukou* system, created in the Maoist era to limit rural-to urban migration....

A second route into the new wage-labour class is out of state-owned enterprises (SOEs). These were the centerpiece of Maoist industrialization, accounting for nearly four-fifths of non-agricultural production. Most are in the cities, where they employed 70 million people in the 1980s. This form of employment has been steadily dismantled, starting with a law that allowed temporary hire without social protection [i.e. minus the iron rice bowl] and a 1988 bankruptcy law terminating workers' guarantee of lifelong employment.... Most decisive was the massive layoffs at the end of the 1990s.... By the early 2000s employment in state-owned enterprises had halved, from 70 to 33 per cent of the urban workforce, with some 30 to 40 million workers displaced.

Finally, a transition to wage-labour followed from the collapse of rural township and village enterprises (TVEs). These flourished in the wake of the dissolution of the communes, with the first phase of liberalization in the early 1980s, especially in Guangdong, Fujian, and around Tianjin and Shanghai. By the early 1990s, they had mushroomed to 25 million firms, employing well over 100 million people—with as much as 40 percent of the total manufacturing output. Owned and operated by local governments, they usually embodied socialist obligations to provide jobs, wages and social benefits to villagers, and to support agriculture and rural infrastructure. Many worked as subcontractors to urban state enterprises. Hence, when many lead-firm SOEs went bankrupt in the 1990s or found more cost-effective suppliers, thousands of TVEs were left in the lurch.... As these small enterprises imploded, millions of workers were stranded. The result has been a two-stage incorporation of peasants into the

> proletariat, first as TVE workers nominally protected by the obligations of local government, then as proletarians subject to the full force of the market—Marx's shift from "formal" to "real" subsumption of labor.[28]

More recently, as we shall see in a later section of the paper, the robbing of many peasants (indeed entire villages) of the small plots that were allocated at the time of the breaking up of the collectives in the early 1980s has now accelerated into a national struggle, leading to massive rural protests.

The privatization of state assets and the robbing of state enterprises have produced enormous wealth at the top in China, with the leading capitalists obtaining their wealth through cronyism. More than 90 percent of the richest 20,000 people in China are said to be "related to senior government or Communist Party officials," creating a whole class of millionaire and billionaire "princelings," the offspring of top officials.[29] In addition, land expropriated from farmers for sale to developers has enriched an untold number of local officials.

The market reforms included what Deng called an "open door" policy, in which China put out the welcome sign for multinational corporations—in sharp contrast to other East Asian nations like South Korea, which at a similar stage in its development placed heavy restrictions on foreign direct investment in industry. Production in China was increasingly geared to exports of manufactured goods associated with the supply chains of Triad-based multinational corporations. China was the second biggest recipient of foreign direct investment in the world in 2009, after the United States. According to a 2006 report by the Development Research Center of the State Council (China's cabinet), foreign capital (concentrated in the export sector) controlled 82 percent of market share in communications, calculator, and related electronics; 72 percent in instrumentation products, cultural, and office machinery; 48 percent in textile apparel, footwear, and hats; 49 percent in leather, fur, feather, and related industries; 51 percent in furniture; 60 percent in educational and sports products; 41 percent in plastics; and 42 percent in transport equipment.[30]

As indicated by Shaun Breslin, professor of politics and international studies at the University of Warwick, after factoring in re-exports through Hong Kong and elsewhere, roughly 30 percent of all exports from China in 1996–2005 ended up in the United States; about 26 percent in Japan; and around 16 percent in the European Union. Others, in determining the effects of re-exports, have estimated the U.S. share of China's exports even higher, at 50 percent.[31]

In the complex global supply lines of multinational corporations, China primarily occupies the role of final assembler of manufactured goods to be sold in the rich economies. Export manufacturing is directed not at the actual production of goods but at commodity assembly using parts and components produced elsewhere and then imported to China. The final commodity is then shipped from China to the developed economies.

China is the world's biggest supplier of final information, communications, and technology goods, and multinational corporations accounted for about 87 percent of China's high-tech exports at the beginning of 2006. But the parts and components for these high-tech goods are almost all imported to China by multinationals for assembly prior to their export via multinationals to the markets within the Triad.[32] Consequently, most of the costs of goods associated with exports from China typically do not represent value captured by the Chinese economy. According to the Federal Reserve Bank of San Francisco, "In 2009, it cost about $179 in China to produce an iPhone, which sold in the United States for about $500. Thus, $179 of the U.S. retail cost consisted of Chinese imported content. However, only $6.50 was actually due to assembly costs in China. The other $172.50 reflected costs of parts produced in other countries."[33]

Within the East Asia region as a whole, China's is the final production platform, with other East Asian nations like Japan, South Korea, and Singapore producing the parts and components. China's imports of parts and components increased almost twenty-four times in 1992–2008, while its final goods trade increased only around twelve times in the same period. In 2009, 17 percent of its parts and components imports came from Japan, 17 percent from South Korea, 15 percent from the ASEAN6 (Brunei, Indonesia, Malaysia, Philippines, Singapore, and Thailand), 10 percent from Europe, and 7 percent from North America. Hence, it is not so much China that is the producer of electronic goods and information, communication, and technology products, but rather East Asia as a whole, within a global supply chain still dominated by multinational corporations within the Triad.[34]

The Chinese economy today is thus structured around the offshoring needs of multinational corporations geared to obtaining low unit labor costs by taking advantage of cheap, disciplined labor in the global South, a process known as "global labor arbitrage." In this global supply-chain system, China is more the world assembly hub than the world factory.

In an article written in 1997, Jin Bei, head of the Research Group for a Comparative Study of the International Competitiveness of China's Manufactured Goods, Chinese Academy of Sciences, contended that most goods being exported from China were not Chinese domestically manufactured goods, but rather should be identified as "para-domestically manufactured goods" reflecting a supply chain under the control of foreign multinationals. "Foreign partners," he wrote,

> obtain the bulk of the direct economic benefits from manufactured goods turned out by wholly foreign-owned businesses and Sino-foreign joint ventures in which they have controlling shares. Such goods do not primarily involve the actualization of China's productive forces, but the actualization of foreign productive forces in China, or the economic actualization achieved by turning Chinese resources into productive forces subject to the control of foreign capital owners. These goods should not, therefore, be identified in principle as manufactured goods made in China.... For example, of the ten top brands of shirts in the world, seven are produced by the Beijing Shirt Factory, yet for producing a shirt bearing the Pierre Cardin label that retails for 300 yuan, the factory only receives three to four yuan in processing fees. How can these shirts be convincingly identified as Chinese-made?[35]

In order to understand the effects of global supply chains, and the way they make it possible for the wealthy countries of the Triad to capture the great bulk of the value created in production, it is useful to look at the famous example of Barbie and the world economy. A Barbie doll ("My First Tea Party Barbie") marketed in California in 1996 sold at a price of $9.99 and was labeled "Made in China." Nearly all of the raw materials and parts that made up the doll, however, were imported, while Chinese workers put together the final Barbie. (At the time there were two Barbie factories in China and one each in Indonesia and Malaysia.) Each factory in China employed around 5,500 workers. Most of the plastic resin in the form of pellets or "chips" was probably imported via the Chinese Petroleum Corporation, Taiwan's state-owned oil importer. The nylon hair came from Japan. The cardboard packaging and many of the paint pigments and oils used for decorating the dolls came from the United States. Only the cotton cloth for Barbie's dress came from China, which otherwise simply supplied labor to assemble the dolls. The workers operated the plastic mold-injection machines, painted the details on the doll (requiring fifteen different paint stations), and sewed the clothing. Workers were paid around $40 a month. The total labor cost for each Barbie was a mere 35 cents, or 3.5 percent of the final retail price.[36]

In 2008 Chinese manufacturing workers, on average, according to the U.S. Bureau of Labor Statistics, received only 4 percent of the wage compensation of manufacturing workers in the United States. Hence, the added margin of profit to be obtained by producing in China (with the same technology) instead of the United States or other developed countries can be enormous. Chinese workers that assemble iPhones for Foxconn, which subcontracts for Apple, are paid wages that represent only 3.6 percent of the final total manufacturing cost (shipping price), contributing to Apple's huge 64 percent gross profit margin over manufacturing cost on iPhones, according to the Asian Development Bank.[37]

Work under these conditions, especially if it involves migrant labor, often takes the form of superexploitation, since the payment to workers is below the value of labor power (the costs of reproduction of the worker). The KYE factory in China produces manufactured goods for Microsoft and other U.S. factories, employing up to 1,000 "work-study" students 16–17 years of age, with a typical shift running from 7:45 A.M. to 10:55 P.M. Along with the "students," the factory hires women 18–25 years of age. Workers reported spending ninety-seven hours a week at the factory before the recession, working eighty-plus hours. In 2009, given the economic slowdown, the workers were at the factory eighty-three hours a week, and on the production line sixty-eight. Workers race to meet the requirement of producing 2,000 Microsoft mice per shift. The factories are extremely crowded; one workshop, 105 feet by 105 feet, has almost 1,000 toiling workers. They are paid 65 cents an hour, with 52 cents an hour take-home pay, after the cost of abysmal factory food is deducted. Fourteen workers share each dorm room, sleeping on narrow bunk beds. They "shower" by fetching hot water in a small plastic bucket for a sponge bath.[38]

Similar conditions exist at the Meitai Plastics and Electronics Factory in Dongguan City, Guangdong. There two thousand workers, mostly women, assemble keyboards and computer equipment for Microsoft, IBM, Hewlett-Packard, and Dell. The young workers, mostly under thirty, toil while sitting on hard stools as computer keyboards move down the assembly line, one every 7.2 seconds, 500 an hour. A worker is given just 1.1 seconds to snap each separate key into place, continuing the operation 3,250 times every hour, 35,750 times a day, 250,250 times a week, and more than a million times a month. Employees work twelve hour shifts seven days a week, with two days off a month on average. They are at the factory eighty-one hours a week, while working for seventy-four. They are paid 64 cents an hour base pay, which is reduced to 41 cents after deductions for food and room. Chatting with other workers during work hours can result in the loss of a day and a half's pay.

Meitai workers are locked in the factory compound four days of each week and are not allowed to take a walk. The food consists of a thin, watery rice gruel in the morning, while on Fridays they are given a chicken leg and foot as a special treat. Dorm rooms are similar to the KYE factory with bunks lined along the walls and small plastic buckets to haul hot water up several flights of stairs for a sponge bath. They do mandatory unpaid overtime cleaning of the factory and the dorm. If a worker steps on the grass on the way to the dorm she is fined. Workers are regularly cheated out of 14 to 19 percent of the wages due to them. The workers are told that "economizing on capital... is the most basic requirement of factory enterprise."[39]

The Yuwei Plastics and Hardware Product Company in Dongguan pays its workers eighty cents an hour base pay for fourteen-hour shifts, seven days a week, making auto parts, 80 percent of which are sold to Ford. In peak season, workers are compelled to work thirty days a month. In March 2009 a worker who was required to stamp out 3,600 "RT Tubes" a day, one every twelve seconds, lost three fingers when management ordered the infrared safety monitors turned off so that the workers could work faster. The worker was paid compensation of $7,430, a little under $2,500 a finger.[40]

What drives the global labor arbitrage and the superexploitation of Chinese labor of course is the search for higher profits, most of which accrue to multinational corporations. This can be seen in a study carried out by the National Labor Committee and China Labor Watch of Pou Yuen Plant F in Dongguan (owned by the Taiwanese Pou Chen Group). The vast majority of the production in Plant F is carried out for the German sports lifestyle corporation PUMA. Plant F in 2004 had around 3,000 workers with the median age twenty to twenty-two years. The base wage for these workers was 31 cents an hour, $12.56 a week. They worked 13.5–16.5 hour daily shifts from 7:30 A.M. to 9:00 P.M., 11:00 P.M, or midnight, with one, three, or four days off a month. Twelve workers shared a crowded dorm room. The report found:

- From beginning to end the total cost of labor to make a pair of PUMA sneakers in China comes to just $1.16. The workers' wages amount to just 1.66 percent of the sneakers' $70 retail price. It takes 2.96 hours to make a pair of sneakers.
- PUMA's gross profit on a pair of $70 sneakers is $34.09.
- PUMA's hourly profit on each pair of sneakers is more than twenty-eight times greater than the wages workers received to make the sneaker.
- PUMA is making a net profit of $12.24 an hour on every production worker in China, which comes to an annual profit of $38,188.80 per worker. For Pou Yuen Plant F alone, PUMA's net profit gained from the workers exceeds $92 million.
- Even after accounting for all corporate expenditures involved in running its business—which the workers in China are ultimately paying for—PUMA's net profit on each $70 pair of sneakers is still $7.42, or 6.4 times more than the workers are paid to make the sneaker.
- In the first five days and two hours of the year—before the first week is even over—the workers in China have made enough PUMA sneakers to pay their entire year's salary.[41]

In 2010 eighteen workers, aged eighteen to twenty-five, at the Foxconn factory complex in Shenzhen, which produces iPhones and iPads for Apple, attempted suicide, fourteen succeeding, the others injured for life. This created a national and international scandal, and brought world attention to these conditions of extreme exploitation.[42]

Although China has minimum-wage legislation and various labor regulations, more and more workers (primarily migrants) toil in an unregulated, informal sector within industry in which minimum wages do not apply and a portion of workers' wages are withheld. According to Anita Chan in *China's Workers Under Assault: The Exploitation of Labor in a Globalizing Economy* (2001), the minimum wage levels are set "at the lowest possible price...while maintaining [the] workers' physical survival," although many workers are denied even that. "Workers' wages are eroded by a multitude of deductions" for such things as forgetting to turn off lights, walking on the grass, untidy dormitories, and talking to others at work. In a survey carried out by the Guangdong trade union, it was revealed that 32 percent of workers were paid below the legal minimum wage.[43]

The global labor arbitrage that lies behind this system of extreme exploitation is in fact a system of imperial rent extraction that feeds the profits of global monopoly-finance capital.[44] China's extraordinary growth is thus a product of a global system of exploitation and accumulation, the chief rewards of which have been reaped by firms located in the center of the world economy.

The Floating Population

In order to understand the extreme exploitation of labor in China, and the unique class contradictions associated with this, it is necessary to examine the role of its "floating population." In the household registration (*hukou*) system set up in 1955–58, each individual was given a particular household registration in the locality of his/her birth. This places limitations on internal migration within the country. The "floating population" thus consists of those who live in an area outside their place of household registration, of which there are currently 221 million people, 160 million of which are said to be rural migrants outside their home county. Rural migrant labor has accounted for as much as 68 percent of the workers in manufacturing and 80 percent in construction. They occupy the lowest rungs in urban employment and are paid wages far less than the national urban average, while often working 50 percent longer hours. In Beijing around 40 percent of the population in 2011 were migrant workers, with temporary residence. In the city of Shenzhen nearly 12 million out of a total population of 14 million people are rural migrants. In addition to receiving much lower pay, rural migrants lack the benefits provided to urban-based workers in the cities, and frequently live and work at the factory in dormitory conditions. The vast majority of rural migrant laborers are under thirty-five years of age—in 2004 the average age was twenty-eight. They work in industrial centers under superexploitative conditions (i.e., receiving wages below the normal reproduction costs of workers) for a few years and then typically return to the land and their peasant origins.

The enormously long hours worked under hazardous conditions in China, particularly by rural migrant workers, takes its toll in terms of industrial accidents. According to official data, 363,383 serious work-related accidents were recorded in China in 2010, which included 79,552 deaths. This represented a marked improvement since 2003, when there were 700,000 work-related accidents and 130,000 fatalities. Most of the victims are migrant workers.[45]

Although Western scholars have often treated migrant workers in China in terms of the standard model of surplus labor attracted to the cities (based on the development model associated with the work of W. Arthur Lewis and ultimately derived from Marx's reserve army analysis), the conditions of the labor surplus in China are in many ways unique. China's floating population can be seen as constituting a reserve army of labor in Marx's terms but with a distinct difference. Its distinctiveness lies in the temporary and partial nature of proletarianization and in the permanent connection of migrants to the land—a product of the Chinese Revolution and the clay rice bowl. Peasants retain land use rights (a form of equity in that land), which are periodically reallocated by village collectives on a relatively egalitarian basis, taking into consideration their occupation of and work on the land. This provides an incentive for rural migrants to maintain a strong connection to their families and the land. The minuscule peasant holdings—on average 1.2 acres but as small as an eighth of an acre—offer a bare bones existence: a homestead with a roof overhead and enough food to eat. Although market reformers have sought to break up these plots, few families are willing to give up their clay rice bowl—their use rights to the land. However, in order to prosper under these conditions, peasant families must periodically seek nonfarm work to supplement their meager earnings. This gives rise to the growing phenomenon of rural migrant labor, which is intensified due to reductions in state support in rural areas during the market reform period.[46]

Rural migrants send remittances back to their families and attempt to save a part of their income to bring back with them. There is strong evidence to suggest that—above and beyond the enormous obstacles to obtaining permanent urban residence status—rural migrants have a strong desire to return to the countryside due to their continuing links to the land, which provides some security. Land is regarded as a permanent asset that can be passed on to future generations. Thus in a state survey in 2006 only 8 percent of rural migrants indicated that they planned to stay long-term in their urban destination. During the migratory stage of their lives rural migrants float back and forth. One survey in 2002 found that only 5 percent of migrants did not return home that year, while 60 percent spent less than nine months away from their home counties. The return migration serves to cushion the economy in a downturn. During the Great Financial Crisis of 2007–09, which resulted in a sharp drop in Chinese exports, there was a significant drop (14–18 million) in the number of migrant workers, as rural migrants who were unable to find employment returned to the land, and new outward migration decreased. The result of this reverse migration was to hold down unemployment—to the point that wages actually increased during the crisis due to labor shortages in industry (induced in part by China's quick economic turnaround) and in response to food price inflation.[47]

Some analysts have commented on how the structural features of rural migration allow high-quality labor power to be reproduced in the rural regions, effectively outside of the capitalist market economy, which then becomes available on a floating basis for its intensive superexploitation in the cities—without urban industry having to foot the real costs of the reproduction of labor power.[48] Costs are kept low and productivity high because production is carried out by young workers who can be worked extremely intensively—only to return to the countryside and be replaced by a new inflow of rural migrants to industry. The eighty-hour-plus work weeks, the extreme pace of production, poor food and living environment, etc., constitute working conditions and a level of compensation that cannot keep labor alive if continued for many years—it is therefore carried out by young workers who fall back on the land where they have use rights, the most important remaining legacy of the Chinese Revolution for the majority of the population. Yet the sharp divergences between urban and rural incomes, the inability of most families to prosper simply by working the land, and the lack of sufficient commercial employment possibilities in the countryside all contribute to the constancy of the floating population, with the continual outflow of new migrants.

Land, Labor, and Environmental Struggles

Although a number of left analysts, as we have seen, continue to point to China as a case of "accumulation *without* dispossession,"[49] primarily due to the rural peasantry's retention of land use rights, in our view the evidence suggests that China is less of a departure from the standard pattern. Such an extreme, rapid development of a capitalist market economy is impossible without primitive accumulation, i.e., dispossessing the population of their assets and direct relation to the means of production. Hinton argued in *The Great Reversal* in 1990 that in order to carry out the primitive accumulation of capital in China it would be necessary for capitalists to weaken and then smash both the iron rice bowl and the clay rice bowl, the chief gains of the mass of the population in the Chinese Revolution.[50] Both rice bowls have been under attack. In response to this—as well as to the driving exploitation of workers and growing inequality—the protests of workers and peasants have been increasing in leaps and bounds.

The number of large-scale "mass incidents" (petitions, demonstrations, strikes, and riots) in China has risen from 87,000 in 2005 to 280,000 in 2010, according to official Chinese sources.[51] The two main sources of conflict are: (1) land disputes, especially in response to illegal land requisitions, regarded as attacks on the clay rice bowl; and (2) labor disputes, particularly the resistance of workers within state enterprises to relentless privatization and the smashing of the iron rice bowl. In addition, there are rapidly growing struggles by workers and peasants over environmental destruction.

In 2002–05 thousands of peasants were involved in protests in Dongzhou village in Guangdong against the building of an electricity plant that had resulted in a land requisition for which they were not fairly compensated. Workers built sheds outside the plant and attempted to block its construction. Conflict with the authorities led to a major part of the plant being blown away by explosives and the police opening fire on protesters in December 2005, leading to a number of deaths.

In December 2011 an uprising began in Wukan, a coastal village of about 20,000 in Guangdong. Villagers set up roadblocks, chased away government representatives, and began arming themselves with homemade weapons in protest over a land requisition, which appropriated their land with little or no compensation. After a ten-day standoff with the local government the villagers agreed to end their protest and reopen the village, when a number of their demands were met.

These cases reflect struggles going on all over China, increasingly threatening, as *Bloomberg Businessweek* states, "the reversal of one of the core principles of the Communist Revolution. Mao Zedong won the hearts of the masses by redistributing land from rich landlords to penniless peasants. Now, powerful local officials are snatching it back, sometimes violently, to make way for luxury apartment blocks, malls, and sports complexes in a debt-fueled building binge." Local provincial, county, and city governments had accumulated debts of 2.79 trillion yuan ($412 billion) by the end of 2009, spurred on by government's fiscal stimulus in response to the Great Financial Crisis. The local governments used land belonging to villagers to secure the debt in their localities, promising land sales. Hence, cities are grabbing land to finance their mushrooming debt.

Falling real estate prices have accelerated the process, forcing local governments with inadequate tax bases to engineer more land sales. Land sales currently account for around 30 percent of total local government revenues, and in some cities make up more than half the revenue. Land is being sold without the support and at the expense of the villagers who have use rights to plots that are collectively owned, while the proceeds of such land sales are lining the pockets of local officials. Not only do the peasants lose their permanent relation to the land (and the clay rice bowl), they are being compensated at rates far below the value for which the land is being sold to developers by the local authorities. Some 50 million peasants lost their homes during the previous three decades, while the expectation is that some 60 million farmers will be uprooted over the next two decades.[52]

Labor disputes are still the most common form of mass incident, accounting for some 45 percent of the total according to one estimate. In the summer of 2010 China's leading industries in auto, electronics, and textiles were hit by dozens of strikes. Although the role of state-owned enterprises (SOEs) in China has declined under the force of privatization, there still remain some 60 million employees of SOEs in urban areas.[53] "In the Maoist socialist era," as Minqi Li has written, "the Chinese [state] workers enjoyed a level of class power and dignity unimaginable by an average worker in a capitalist state (especially in the peripheral and semi-peripheral context)." In the period of market reforms these workers have been increasingly reduced to a state-sector proletariat, but with remnants of the iron rice bowl (or at least its ghostly memory) remaining where workers are strongest. This has led to intense class struggles. In 2009 workers at the Tonghua Iron and Steel Company in Jilin province revolted against privatization and massive layoffs, carrying out a general strike under the leadership of a Maoist-era worker known as "Master Wu." When the general manager of a powerful private company that was taking over the enterprise threatened to fire all of the workers, the workers beat him to death. The government backed off and canceled the privatization plan.[54]

After land and labor disputes, the largest number of mass incidents in China are associated with environmental factors, particularly struggles over pollution. China's environmental problems are massive and growing. It now has sixteen of the world's twenty most polluted cities. Two-thirds of urban residents are breathing air that is severely polluted. Lung cancer in China has increased 60 percent over the last decade even though the smoking rate has remained unchanged. Desertification is leading to the loss of about 6,000 square miles of grasslands every year, around the size of Connecticut. This contributes to sandstorms, resulting in the dust that represents a third of China's air pollution problem. Water shortages, especially in northern China, and water pollution are both growing. China has only 6 percent of the world's freshwater but over three times that share of the world's population. Its per capita water supply is down to a quarter of the global average, while 70 percent of the country's rivers and lakes are severely polluted. Some 300 million people in the rural areas are drinking unsafe water, while one-fifth of the drinking water sources in the major cities are below standard. Massive dam projects designed to deliver electricity are leading to farmland loss, ecological damage, and the forced migration of millions. In 2008 China surpassed the United States as the leading emitter of greenhouse gases (although far below the latter in per capita emissions). Such conditions have led to an upsurge in environmental mass protests. Complaints to authorities increased by about 30 percent a year between 2002–2004, reaching 600,000 annually, while the official tally of disputes in relation to environmental pollution hit 50,000 in 2005.[55]

Most of China's manufacturing force, as we have seen, consists of a floating population that remains tied to the land and user rights (the clay rice bowl), while also experiencing extreme exploitation and degraded environmental conditions in the cities. Given this, the struggles over land, labor, and the environment are wedded in China as nowhere else—to the point that we may be witnessing the emergence of an environmental proletariat, along with a partially proletarianized, relatively independent, and egalitarian peasantry.[56]

As Samir Amin argues, urban China is incapable of absorbing the hundreds of millions of rural workers in China (a dilemma that exists at various levels throughout the global South). Hence, some 50 percent of the Chinese population will have to remain rural. China does not have the external outlet for surplus population that was available to industrializing Europe during the period of colonial expansion.

In China's case, the legacy of its revolution has created an independent peasantry that feeds 22 percent of the world population with 7 percent of the world's arable land, with an equitable land distribution. Rather than seeing this as an archaic weakness of the society, to be subjected to relentless primitive accumulation, it should be seen as a strength of Chinese society, which reflects the genuine need for access to the land on the part of half of humanity.[57]

China and the World Crisis

With the economic Triad of the United States (and Canada), Europe, and Japan caught in continuing economic stagnation—made more evident following the Great Financial Crisis—the focus has been increasingly on China as the means of lifting the world economy. Thus the Winter 2010 issue of the journal *The International Economy* carried the responses of more than fifty orthodox economists from various countries to the question: *Can China Become the World's Engine for Growth*? The answers varied widely, but most of those questioned emphasized the internal contradictions of the Chinese economy, its tendency toward overinvestment and export dependency, its low consumption, and its need to rebalance.[58] Recently, fears that the contradictions of the Chinese economy may further imperil the entire world accumulation process—if China is not able to rebalance toward higher consumption, lower debt, and a higher renminbi—are voiced daily by international capital. Worries that the days of China's economic miracle are numbered and that it is headed toward a sharp slowdown in growth and financial crisis are now prevalent. As Paul Krugman wrote in a *New York Times* column entitled "Will China Break?" on December 18, 2011:

> Consider the following picture: Recent growth has relied on a huge construction boom fueled by surging real estate prices, and exhibiting all the classic signs of a bubble. There was rapid growth in credit—with much of that growth taking place not through traditional banking but rather through unregulated "shadow banking" neither subject to government supervision nor backed by government guarantees. Now the bubble is bursting—and there are real reasons to fear financial and economic crisis.
>
> Am I describing Japan at the end of the 1980s? Or am I describing America in 2007? I could be. But right now I'm talking about China, which is emerging as another danger spot in a world economy that really, really doesn't need this right now... a new [potential] epicenter of crisis.[59]

But few mainstream analysts, Krugman included, recognize the true intensity of the economic, social, and environmental contradictions in China, which make its development pattern unsustainable in every respect. These contradictions are now giving rise to hundreds of thousands of mass protests annually, as peasants struggle to retain their use rights to the land, the floating population (itself still connected to the land) resists superexploitation, state workers defy privatization, and millions more struggle against environmental degradation.

The story usually presented in the U.S. media of a nation-state competition (and occasional collaboration) between the United States and China hides the deep and growing class inequities in a country where the golden rice bowl of the state bureaucrats has been so enlarged that the families of the most powerful party members control billions of dollars in wealth. For example, the family of China's premier, Wen Jiabao, has a wealth estimated at $4.3 billion—in a country where wage income is among the lowest in the world, and where inequality is skyrocketing.[60]

Chinese low-wage exports have been almost entirely consumer durable goods (Department II in the Marxian reproduction schemes as opposed to Department I, investment goods), notably in the areas of information technology and communications, and electronics—but also including clothing, furniture, toys, and various household products. In 2010 "Made in China" goods accounted for 20 percent of furniture and household equipment sold in the United States, 12 percent of other durables, and 36 percent of clothing and shoes.[61] Such Chinese imported commodities are referred to as "deflationary" goods in corporate lingo, since they reduce the cost of many goods usually purchased with wages, and offset higher prices on other items of mass consumption, such as gasoline. Wal-Mart, which alone accounts for 12 percent of the goods shipped to the United States from China, has even been called the greatest friend of the U.S. working class. Indeed, as W. Michael Cox, chief economist for the Federal Reserve Bank of Dallas, put it, given its low prices, "Wal-Mart is the best thing that ever happened to poor people."[62] Yet these same low-priced imported goods, which Wal-Mart exemplifies, make it possible for real wage levels in the United States and other rich countries to stagnate—as the relative shift of manufacturing employment to the global South pulls down wages directly and indirectly (and as what were well-paying jobs disappear).

The growth of cheap manufactured imports has often led to calls for protectionism on the part of U.S. labor groups. However, there is little acknowledgment that these cheap imports are produced by or for multinational corporations headquartered in the Triad. The real struggle, then, is one of creating international solidarity between Chinese workers, who are suffering from extreme forms of exploitation (even superexploitation), and workers in the developed world, who are currently losing ground in a race to the bottom. Today much of the basis for such international worker solidarity can be found in the struggles of workers and peasants in China, which could conceivably be strengthened further by the resurrection of the revolutionary process in China (a turn to the left).

For the *New York Times*, nothing but "Mao's resurrection or nuclear cataclysm" is likely to arrest China's current course. Yet if what is meant by "Mao's resurrection" is the renewal in some way of the Chinese Revolution itself—which would necessarily take new historical forms as a result of changing historical conditions—the potential remains, and is even growing under current conditions.[63]

In 1853, Karl Marx argued that the Chinese Revolution of those days (the famous Taiping Rebellion) might destabilize the financial conditions of the British Empire and hasten the possibilities of revolt in Europe.[64] Although Marx's expectations were disappointed, his notion that the fates of China and the West were tied together was in many ways prophetic. China's deepening contradictions will undoubtedly have an effect on the Triad and on the world as a whole, in what now appears to be the descending phase of capitalism.[65]

* * *

The case of China points to the startling conclusion that in today's globalized world "the endless crisis" of monopoly-finance capital is *endless both in time and space*. Just as there is no way of historically transcending the growing contradictions of capitalist maturity within the context of the system, so there is no spatial fix that will free us from the fault lines that now encircle the entire globe. This leaves us with only one final choice: "the revolutionary reconstitution of society at large, or... the common ruin of the contending classes."[66]

Notes

Introduction: The Endless Crisis

This Introduction, written for the present book, was published in advance in the May 2012 issue of *Monthly Review* (vol. 64, no. 1).

1. Frederick Engels, *The Condition of the Working Class in England* (Chicago: Academy of Chicago Press, 1964), 32.
2. Menzie D. Chinn and Jeffry A. Frieden, *Lost Decades* (New York: Norton, 2011).
3. Ben S. Bernanke, "The Near- and Longer-Term Prospects for the U.S. Economy," Speech to the Federal Reserve Bank of Kansas City Economic Symposium, Jackson Hole, Wyoming, August 26, 2011, http://federalreserve.gov.
4. Robert E. Hall, "The Long Slump," *American Economic Review* 101 (April 2011): 431-32, 467-68.
5. Paul Krugman, "The Third Depression," *New York Times*, June 27, 2010, http://nytimes.com, "Third Depression Watch," May 25, 2011, http://krugman.blogs.nytimes.com, "The Return of Secular Stagnation," November 8, 2011, http://krugman.blogs.nytimes.com.
6. Tyler Cowen, *The Great Stagnation* (New York: Dutton, 2011), 5-8.
7. Thomas I. Palley, *From Financial Crisis to Stagnation* (Cambridge: Cambridge University Press, 2012), 3, 141-53. An earlier presentation of Palley's views on financialization and stagnation can be found in Thomas I. Palley, "The Limits of Minsky's Financial Instability Hypothesis as an Explanation of the Crisis," *Monthly Review* 61, no. 11 (April 2010): 28-43.
8. Christine Lagarde, "Global Economic Challenges and Global Economic Solutions," Address at the Woodrow Wilson Center, Washington, D.C., September 15, 2011, http://imf.org, "An Address to the 2011 International Finance Forum," Beijing, November 9, 2011, http://imf.org.
9. Others have pointed to the longer-term decline in growth rates. See James H. Stock and Mark W. Watson, "Disentangling the Channels of the 2007-2009 Recession," Brookings Panel on Economic Activity (March 22-23, 2012): 5, 44 (Table 10), http://www.brookings.edu.
10. On the empirical recurrence of financial bubbles see Carmen M. Reinhart and Kenneth S. Rogoff, *This Time Is Different* (Princeton: Princeton University Press, 2009).
11. Paul Krugman, "How Did Economists Get It So Wrong?," *New York Times*, September 2, 2009, http://nytimes.com.

12. John Kenneth Galbraith, *The Economics of Innocent Fraud* (Boston: Houghton Mifflin, 2004), 6–7, 12.
13. Ben S. Bernanke, "Implications of the Financial Crisis for Economics," speech at Conference Co-Sponsored by the Bendheim Center for Finance and the Center for Economic Policy Studies, Princeton, New Jersey, September 24, 2010, http://federalreserve.gov. Bernanke's explanation of the failure of the prevailing economic models was similar to that of his predecessor as chairman of the Federal Reserve Board, Alan Greenspan, who told the House Committee of Government Oversight and Reform on October 23, 2008: "The whole intellectual edifice...collapsed in the summer of last year because the data inputted into the risk management models generally covered only the last two decades, a period of euphoria. Had instead the models been fitted more appropriately to historic periods of stress, capital requirements would have been much higher and the financial world would be in far better shape today." "Greenspan Testimony on Sources of Financial Crisis," *Wall Street Journal*, October 23, 2008, http://blogs.wsj.com.
14. Ironically, Bernanke himself earned his academic reputation for work on the Great Depression—but at a time when this was no longer seen as a historical phenomenon requiring an understanding of developing economic contradictions, but simply as a momentary policy error on the part of central bankers. See Ben Bernanke, *Essays on the Great Depression* (Princeton: Princeton University Press, 2000).
15. Joseph Schumpeter, *History of Economic Analysis* (New York: Oxford University Press, 1954), 13, and *Capitalism, Socialism, and Democracy* (New York: Harper and Brothers, 1942), 44.
16. Alfred North Whitehead, *Science and the Modern World* (New York: Free Press, 1925), 51.
17. Georg Wilhelm Friedrich Hegel, *The Phenomenology of Spirit* (New York: Oxford University Press, 1977), 11.
18. Robert E. Lucas, Jr., "Macroeconomic Priorities," *American Economic Review* 93, no. 1 (March 2003): 1; Ben Bernanke, "The Great Moderation," Address to the Eastern Economic Association, February 20, 2004, http://federalreserve.gov.
19. This paragraph and some other parts of this introduction draw on John Bellamy Foster, "The Age of Monopoly-Finance Capital," *Monthly Review* 61, no. 9 (February 2010): 1–13; see also John Bellamy Foster, Harry Magdoff and Robert W. McChesney, "Crises: One After Another for the Life of the System," *Monthly Review* 54, no. 6 (November 1992): 47–49; John Bellamy Foster, Harry Magdoff, and Robert W. McChesney, "What Recovery?" *Monthly Review* 54, no. 11 (April 2003): 5–6; John Bellamy Foster, "The Household Debt Bubble," *Monthly Review* 58, no. 1 (May 2006): 1–11; and John Bellamy Foster and Fred Magdoff, *The Great Financial Crisis* (New York: Monthly Review Press, 2009).
20. John Cassidy, *How Markets Fail* (New York: Farrar, Strauss and Giroux, 2009), 18–20; Dean Baker, "The Run-Up in Home Prices: Is It Real or Is It Another Bubble?" Center for Economic and Policy Research, Briefing Paper (August 2002), http://www.cepr.net; "Consumer Credit: A Crunch May Be Coming," *BusinessWeek*, August 12, 2002, http://businessweek.com; Stephen S. Roach, "The Costs of Bursting Bubbles," *New York Times*, September 22, 2002, http://newyorktimes.com; John Cassidy, "The Next Crash: Is the Housing Market a Bubble That's About to Burst?," *The New Yorker*, November 11, 2002, http://newyorker.com; "The Global

Housing Boom: In Come the Waves," *Economist*, June 16, 2005, http://economist.com; Karl E. Case and Robert J. Shiller, *Is There a Bubble in the Housing Market?* Cowles Foundation Paper No.1089 (New Haven: Yale University Cowles Foundation); Kevin Phillips, *American Theocracy* (New York: Viking, 2006), 375–78.

21. It was once thought that Keynes had forever vanquished Say's Law as logically and empirically fallacious. See John Kenneth Galbraith, *The Economics of Peace and Laughter* (New York: New American Library, 1971), 62–63. Neoclassical model builders, however, soon saw the need to resurrect it both directly and indirectly, in the process of resurrecting pre-Keynesian views generally. As Robert Skidelsky writes in *Keynes: The Return of the Master* (New York: Perseus, 2009), 112: "Mainstream macroeconomics today is based on supply, not demand. It has reasserted a version of Say's Law—that supply creates its own demand—which Keynes repudiated. Thus, both New Classicals and New Keynesians believe that the growth of real GDP in the long run depends on the increase in the supply of factor inputs and technological progress." For a refutation of attempts to resurrect Say's Law see Steve Keen, *Debunking Economics* (London: Zed Books, 2011), 209–18.
22. See Cassidy, *How Markets Fail*; Krugman, "How Did Economists Get It So Wrong?"
23. Paul M. Sweezy, "More (or Less) on Globalization," *Monthly Review* 49, no. 4 (September 1997): 3–4. The best short introduction to Minsky's theory is Hyman Minsky, "Hyman P. Minsky (1919–1996)" (an autobiographical article originally written in 1992), in Philip Arestis and Malcolm C. Sawyer, eds., *A Biographical Dictionary of Dissenting Economists* (Northampton, MA: Edward Elgar, 2000), 411–16.
24. Cassidy, *How Markets Fail*, 215–16. On the relation of Minsky's and Sweezy's analysis see Harry Magdoff and Paul M. Sweezy, *The End of Prosperity* (New York: Monthly Review Press, 1977), 133–36; Foster and Magdoff, *The Great Financial Crisis*, 17–19.
25. Cassidy, *How Markets Fail*, 332; Harry Magdoff and Paul M. Sweezy, *Stagnation and the Financial Explosion* (New York: Monthly Review Press, 1987), 143.
26. Paul A. Samuelson, *Collected Scientific Papers*, vol. 3 (Cambridge, MA: MIT Press, 1972), 710.
27. See John Bellamy Foster, "On the Laws of Capitalism: 1. Insights from the Sweezy-Schumpeter Debate," and Paul M. Sweezy, "On the Laws of Capitalism: 2. The Laws of Capitalism," *Monthly Review* 63, no. 1 (May 2011): 1–16; "Schumpeter Sees Peaceful Socialist Spread as Sweezy Remains Skeptical," *Harvard Crimson*, March 28, 1947, http://thecrimson.com.
28. Paul A. Baran and Paul M. Sweezy, *Monopoly Capital* (New York: Monthly Review Press, 1966), 108.
29. Although Sweezy was later to fault his and Baran's work in *Monopoly Capital* for the failure to emphasize the role of finance in combating stagnation, the recognition of this was not missing from their book, since the final section of the chapter on the sales effort was devoted to the role of FIRE (finance, insurance, and real estate) in countering stagnation. See Paul M. Sweezy, "Monopoly Capital after Twenty-Five Years," *Monthly Review* 43, no. 7 (December 1991): 52–57; Baran and Sweezy, *Monopoly Capital*, 139–41. An even more developed argument on the increasing structural role of debt was presented by Harry Magdoff in 1965. See Paul M. Sweezy and Harry Magdoff, *The Dynamics of U.S. Capitalism* (New York: Monthly Review Press, 1972), 13–16.

30. Sweezy, "Monopoly Capital after Twenty-Five Years," 52–53.
31. Compare Michael J. Piore and Charles F. Sabel, *The Second Industrial Divide* (New York: Basic Books, 1984), 73.
32. Magdoff and Sweezy, *The End of Prosperity* ,111–24.
33. Ibid., 133–36. On the relation of the Minsky moment to the Sweezy normal state in the context of the present crisis see John Bellamy Foster and Robert W. McChesney, "Listen Keynesians, It's the System!," *Monthly Review* 61, no. 11 (April 2010): 44–56.
34. Magdoff and Sweezy, *Stagnation and the Financial Explosion*, 29–32.
35. On the 1930s stagnation debate see William E. Stoneman, *A History of the Economic Analysis of the Great Depression in America* (New York: Garland Publishing, 1979). The relation of this to the development of left economics in the United States is discussed in John Bellamy Foster, "What Is Stagnation?" in Bob Cherry, et al., *The Imperiled Economy: Macroeconomics from a Left Perspective* (New York: Union for Radical Political Economics, 1987), 59–70.
36. Magdoff and Sweezy, *Stagnation and the Financial Explosion*, 32–34.
37. Ibid., 11–12.
38. Ibid., 93–105.
39. Sweezy, "More (or Less) on Globalization."
40. Much of that analysis was worked out in a series of annual assessments of the economy that we ourselves wrote, together with Harry Magdoff, in the April issues of *Monthly Review* during the years 2001–2004.
41. *Economic Report of the President, 2012*, Table B-108; *Economic Report of the President, 1986*, B-108.
42. The data for employment is to be found in Bureau of Economic Analysis, National Income and Product Accounts, Table 6.4, http://www.bea.gov/national/nipaweb/SelectTable.asp. The relation between FIRE and goods production was highlighted in a table twenty-five years ago by Magdoff and Sweezy, *Stagnation and the Financial Explosion*, 23. The stagnation of employment has been a growing concern throughout the financialization era, with its financial crashes, jobless recoveries, and declining employment-to-population ratios. See John Bellamy Foster, Harry Magdoff, and Robert W. McChesney, "The Stagnation of Employment," *Monthly Review* 55, no. 11 (April 2004): 3–17.
43. The wealth effect in this sense was a persistent theme for Alan Greenspan. See, for example, Alan Greenspan, "The Great Malaise," *Challenge* 30, no. 6 (December 1987): 11–14; "Tracking the Wealth Effect," *New York Times*, February 24, 2000, http://newyorktimes.com.
44. Bureau of Economic Analysis, National Income and Product Accounts, Table 5.2.5, Gross and Net Domestic Investment by Major Type (last Revised August 8, 2011; accessed March 15, 2012), http://bea.gov; Table 1.1.5. Gross Domestic Product.
45. For an analysis of these shifts in investment in the early 1980s see Magdoff and Sweezy, *Stagnation and Financial Explosion*, 68–78.
46. David Welch, "Automakers' Overcapacity Problem," *Bloomberg Businessweek*, December 31, 2008, http://businessweek.com.
47. Foster, Magdoff, and McChesney, "The Stagnation of Employment," 3–17; Fred Magdoff, "The Jobs Disaster in the United States," *Monthly Review* 63, no. 2 (June 2011): 24–37; U.S. Bureau of Labor Statistics, Household Data. Table A-15. Alter-

native Measures of Labor Underutilization (accessed March 19, 2012), http://www.bls.gov/news.release/empsit.t15.htm.

48. On the growing interface between financial and political power see John Bellamy Foster and Hannah Holleman, "The Financial Power Elite," *Monthly Review* 62, no. 1 (May 2010): 1–19; Simon Johnson and James Kwak, *13 Bankers* (New York: Pantheon 2010); and Greta Krippner, *Capitalizing on Crisis* (Cambridge, MA: Harvard University Press, 2011). For a pioneering work in linking neoliberalism to financialization see Gérard Duménil and Dominique Lévy, *Capital Resurgent: Roots of the Neoliberal Revolution* (Cambridge, MA: Harvard University Press, 2004).
49. Council of Economic Advisers, *The Economic Report of the President, 2012*, 64–65.
50. See chapter 3 below.
51. Adam Smith, *The Wealth of Nations* (New York: Modern Library, 1937), 61.
52. Karl Marx, *Capital*, vol. 1 (London: Penguin, 1976), 778–81.
53. John R. Munkirs, *The Transformation of American Capitalism* (New York: M.E. Sharpe, 1985), 20.
54. Edward Hastings Chamberlin, *The Theory of Monopolistic Competition* (Cambridge, MA: Harvard University Press, 1962); Joan Robinson, *The Economics of Imperfect Competition* (London: Macmillan, 1965); Paul M. Sweezy, "Demand under Conditions of Oligopoly," *The Journal of Political Economy* 47, no. 4 (August 1939): 568–73. Robinson's work on imperfect competition was not initially concerned with theorizing oligopoly. See Edward Hastings Chamberlin, *Towards a More General Theory of Value* (New York: Oxford University Press, 1957), 27–28.
55. Robinson, *The Economics of Imperfect Competition*, 307.
56. Chamberlin, *The Theory of Monopolistic Competition*, 11.
57. Sweezy, "Demand under Conditions of Oligopoly"; Paul M. Sweezy, *Four Lectures on Marxism* (New York: Monthly Review Press, 1981), 63.
58. Chamberlin, ibid., 109.
59. Chamberlin, *Towards a More General Theory of Value*, 33.
60. See chapter 3 below.
61. Munkirs, *The Transformation of American Capitalism*, 35.
62. Rudolf Hilferding, *Finance Capital* (London: Routledge, 1981).
63. V. I. Lenin, *Imperialism, the Highest Stage of Capitalism* (New York: International Publishers, 1939), 88.
64. Thorstein Veblen, *The Theory of Business Enterprise* (Clifton, NJ: Augustus M. Kelley, 1975), and *Absentee Ownership and Business Enterprise in Recent Times* (New York: Augustus M. Kelley, 1964).
65. See especially Michal Kalecki, *Theory of Economic Dynamics* (New York: Augustus M. Kelley, 1969); Josef Steindl, *Maturity and Stagnation in American Capitalism* (New York: Monthly Review Press, 1976).
66. Baran and Sweezy, *Monopoly Capital*, 7.
67. Harry Magdoff, *The Age of Imperialism* (New York: Monthly Review Press, 1969); James O'Connor, *The Fiscal Crisis of the State* (New York: St. Martin's Press, 1973); Harry Braverman, *Labor and Monopoly Capital* (New York: Monthly Review Press, 1974).
68. The decline of the steel industry was first explained on the left in terms of the monopoly capital/stagnation argument. See Harry Magdoff and Paul M. Sweezy, *The Deepening Crisis of U.S. Capitalism* (New York: Monthly Review Press, 1981), 23–30.
69. Joan Robinson, *Economic Heresies* (New York: Basic Books, 1973), 103.

70. See Stephen Hymer, *The Multinational Corporation* (Cambridge: Cambridge University Press, 1979).
71. Palley, *From Financial Crisis to Stagnation*, 116.
72. Yanis Varoufakis, *The Global Minotaur* (London: Zed, 2011).
73. Council of Economic Advisers, *Economic Report of the President, 2012*, Table B-91, "Corporate Profits by Industry, 1963–2011" (includes corporate profits with inventory valuation adjustment and without capital consumption adjustment).
74. On the imperial rent of oligopoly-finance capital see Samir Amin, *The Worldwide Law of Value* (New York: Monthly Review Press, 2010).
75. Stephen R. Platt, "Is China Ripe for a Revolution?," *New York Times*, February 12, 2012, http://newyorktimes.org.
76. Che Guevara, "Speech at the Afro-Asian Conference in Algeria," February 24, 1965, http://marxists.org.
77. Michael Yates, "The Great Inequality," *Monthly Review* 63, no. 10 (March 2012): 1–18.
78. On the planetary ecological crisis see John Bellamy Foster, Brett Clark, and Richard York, *The Ecological Rift* (New York: Monthly Review Press, 2010).
79. Gar Alperovitz, *America Beyond Capitalism* (Takoma Park, MD: Democracy Collaborative Press, 2011), 3.

Chapter 1: Monopoly-Finance Capital and the Crisis

This chapter is a slightly revised version of "Monopoly-Finance Capital and the Paradox of Accumulation" which appeared in the October 2009 issue of *Monthly Review* (vol. 61, no. 5).

1. Paul Krugman, "Averting the Worst," *New York Times*, August 10, 2009.
2. Thomas I. Palley, *America's Exhausted Paradigm* (Washington, D.C.: New America Foundation, 2009), 32, http://www.newamerica.net.
3. Larry Elliott, "Comic-Book Economics and the Markets," *The Guardian*, July 6, 2009, http://guardian.co.uk. See also John Bellamy Foster and Fred Magdoff, *The Great Financial Crisis* (New York: Monthly Review Press, 2009).
4. Elliott, "Comic-Book Economics."
5. The next few pages draw heavily on Paul M. Sweezy, *Four Lectures on Marxism* (New York: Monthly Review Press, 1981), 36–38.
6. Joseph A. Schumpeter, *Capitalism, Socialism, and Democracy* (New York: Harper and Row, 1942), 90.
7. Thomas L. Friedman, *The World Is Flat* (New York: Farrar, Strauss and Giroux, 2005). For an opposing view, see John Bellamy Foster, "The Imperialist World System," *Monthly Review* 59, no. 1 (May 2009): 1–16.
8. Mark Blaug, *Economic Theory in Retrospect* (Cambridge: Cambridge University Press, 1996), 245; Sweezy, *Four Lectures*, 34–36. See also Karl Marx, *Capital*, vol. 3 (New York: Vintage, 1981), 352–53.
9. J. B. Clark, "Introduction," in Karl Rodbertus, *Overproduction and Crisis* (New York: Scribner, 1898), 15. Clark himself suggested in the same passage that, while this posed no absolute contradiction, it was nevertheless "an unreal case."
10. Sweezy, *Four Lectures*, 39.

11. Paul A. Baran and Paul M. Sweezy, *Monopoly Capital* (New York: Monthly Review Press, 1966), 108.
12. Harry Magdoff and Paul M. Sweezy, *The End of Prosperity* (New York: Monthly Review Press, 1977), 15–20.
13. The classic "kinked-demand curve" treatment of oligopolistic pricing is to be found in Paul M. Sweezy, "Demand under Conditions of Oligopoly," *Journal of Political Economy* 47 (1939): 568–73.
14. Josef Steindl, *Maturity and Stagnation in American Capitalism* (New York: Monthly Review Press, 1976), 9–14.
15. Martin Mayer, *Madison Avenue* (New York: Harper and Brothers, 1959), xiii.
16. On the role of advertising see Robert W. McChesney, John Bellamy Foster, Hannah Holleman, and Inger L. Stole, "The Sales Effort and Monopoly Capital," *Monthly Review*, 60, no. 11 (April 2009): 1-23.
17. Henry Ford II quoted in Barry Commoner, *Making Peace with the Planet* (New York: Free Press, 1992), 80–81.
18. See John Bellamy Foster, Harry Magdoff, and Robert W. McChesney, "The New Economy: Myth and Reality," *Monthly Review* 52, no. 11 (April 2001): 1–15; Hal R. Varian, Joseph Farrell, and Carl Shapiro, *The Economics of Information Technology* (Cambridge: Cambridge University Press, 2004), 14; Tyler Cowen, *The Great Stagnation* (New York: Penguin, 2011), 49-50.
19. Michal Kalecki, *Theory of Economic Dynamics* (London: George Allen and Unwin, Ltd., 1954), 161.
20. Joseph A. Schumpeter, "Depressions," in Douglas V. Brown, et al., *The Economics of the Recovery Program* (New York: McGraw Hill, 1934), 3–21.
21. John Maynard Keynes, *The General Theory of Employment, Interest and Money* (London: Macmillan, 1936), 249.
22. Alvin H. Hansen, *Full Recovery or Stagnation?* (New York: W.W. Norton, 1938).
23. Alvin H. Hansen, "The Stagnation Thesis," in American Economic Association, *Readings in Fiscal Policy* (Homewood, Illinois: Richard D. Irwin, 1955), 549; Joseph A. Schumpeter, *Business Cycles*, vol. 2 (New York: McGraw Hill, 1939), 1032–1050.
24. Robert Heilbroner, *The Future as History* (New York: Harper and Brothers, 1960), 134.
25. Joan Robinson, *Essays in the Theory of Economic Fluctuations* (London: Macmillan, 1962), 54.
26. Susan Strange and Roger Tooze, eds., *The International Politics of Surplus Capacity* (London: George Allen and Unwin, 1981).
27. Bureau of Economic Analysis, National Income and Product Accounts, Table 1.1.1.
28. See Magdoff and Sweezy's *The Dynamics of U.S. Capitalism* (1972), *The End of Prosperity* (1977), *The Deepening Crisis of U.S. Capitalism* (1981), *Stagnation and the Financial Crisis* (1987), and *The Irreversible Crisis* (1988)—all published by Monthly Review Press.
29. Paul M. Sweezy, "The Triumph of Financial Capital," *Monthly Review* 46, no. 2 (June 1994): 8.
30. Hyman Minsky, *Can "It" Happen Again?* (New York: M.E. Sharpe, 1982), 94–95.
31. Foster and Magdoff, *The Great Financial Crisis*, 121; Henry Kaufman, *The Road to Financial Reformation* (Hoboken, New Jersey: John Wiley and Sons, 2009), 161.
32. Kaufman, *The Road to Financial Reformation*, 174; Federal Reserve Board of San Francisco, *FRBSF Economic Letter*, January 19, 2007.

33. Fourteen of the fifteen major financial crises since the 1970s are listed in Kaufman, *The Road to Financial Reformation*, 134. An additional one was the financial crash in Japan in 1990 that led to a decade or more of stagnation.
34. Kaufman, *The Road to Financial Reformation*, 57; Peter Gowan, "U.S. Hegemony Today," in John Bellamy Foster and Robert W. McChesney, eds., *Pox Americana* (New York: Monthly Review Press, 2004), 57–76.
35. Kaufman, *The Road to Financial Reformation*, 67, 97–103, 229.
36. On the role of military spending see John Bellamy Foster, Hannah Holleman, and Robert W. McChesney, "The U.S. Imperial Triangle and Military Spending," *Monthly Review* 60, no. 5 (October 2008): 1–19.
37. On the repressive aspects of the neoliberal state see James K. Galbraith, *The Predator State* (New York: The Free Press, 2008), and Hannah Holleman, Robert W. McChesney, John Bellamy Foster, and R. Jamil Jonna, "The Penal State in an Age of Crisis," *Monthly Review* 61, no. 2 (June 2009): 1–17. On the class struggle, see Michael D. Yates, *Why Unions Matter* (New York: Monthly Review Press, 2009).
38. In his last book, John Kenneth Galbraith declared that the "renaming of the system" as "the market system" in neoliberal ideology was little more than a circumvention of reality, a "not wholly innocent fraud." Related to this, in his view, was the abandonment within the mainstream (and even among much of the left) of the concept of "monopoly capitalism." John Kenneth Galbraith, *The Economics of Innocent Fraud* (Boston: Houghton Mifflin, 2004), 3–9,12.
39. Lawrence Mishel, Jared Bernstein, and Heidi Shierholz, *The State of Working America, 2008/2009* (Ithaca, New York: Cornell University Press, 2009), Table 3.1; Foster and Magdoff, *The Great Financial Crisis*, 129–31.
40. See "The Household Debt Bubble," in Foster and Magdoff, *The Great Financial Crisis*, 27–38.
41. "Financial Rescue Nears GDP as Pledges Top 12.8 Trillion," Bloomberg.com, March 31, 2009; Kaufman, *The Road to Financial Reformation*, 213.
42. "Dollar, Yen Decline as Recovering Economy Eases Refuge Appeal," Bloomberg.com, April 22, 2009.
43. See, for example, "An Astonishing Rebound," *The Economist*, August 13, 2009. On China as the next hegemon see Giovanni Arrighi, *Adam Smith in Beijing* (London: Verso, 2007). For a more sanguine view taking into account China's (and emerging Asia's) relation to "transnational accumulation" see Martin Hart-Landsberg and Paul Burkett, "China and the Dynamics of Transnational Accumulation," *Historical Materialism* 14, no. 3 (2006): 3–43.
44. Kaufman, *The Road to Financial Reformation*, 223.
45. "Old Banks, New Tricks," *BusinessWeek* (August 17, 2009): 20–23.

Chapter 2: The Financialization of Accumulation

This chapter first appeared in the October 2010 issue of *Monthly Review* (vol. 62, no. 5).

1. Karl Marx, *Capital*, vol. 3 (London: Penguin, 1981), 607–8.
2. Paul M. Sweezy, "More (or Less) on Globalization," *Monthly Review* 49, no. 4 (September 1997): 3. The others were stagnation and monopolization. Globalization was, in Sweezy's view, a much longer and wider phenomenon, char-

acteristic of all stages of capitalism's historical development, and hence not an outgrowth of changing modes of accumulation.

3. The term "the enigma of capital" is taken from David Harvey, *The Enigma of Capital* (London: Profile Books, 2010). Although Harvey does not use the term in precisely this way, the approach outlined here is generally in accord with the outlook in his latest book.
4. Joseph A. Schumpeter, *The Theory of Economic Development* (New York: Oxford University Press, 1961), 107, 126, and *Essays* (Cambridge, MA: Addison-Wesley, 1951), 170.
5. The drop in investment in the crisis is reflected in the fact that in 2009 the total capital stock of business equipment in the United States dropped by 0.9 percent from 2008, its first decline since the 1940s; meaning that firms did not even spend enough on new equipment to offset the wear and tear on their existing equipment. "Firms Spend More—Carefully," *Wall Street Journal*, August 11, 2010.
6. Kari Polanyi Levitt, "The Great Financialization," John Kenneth Galbraith Prize Lecture, June 8, 2008, http://karipolanyilevitt.com/documents/The-Great-Financialization.pdf.
7. For evidence of these trends, see John Bellamy Foster and Fred Magdoff, *The Great Financial Crisis* (New York: Monthly Review Press, 2009). It should be noted that this usage of the term "financialization," as related to a secular trend in today's economy, is quite different from its usage in the work of world-system theorists such as Giovanni Arrighi and Beverly Silver, who basically refer to it as a phase in the hegemonic cycles of the capitalist world-system. See Giovanni Arrighi and Beverly J. Silver, *Chaos and Governance in the Modern World System* (Minneapolis: University of Minnesota Press, 1999), 213.
8. Robert E. Yuskavage and Mahnaz Fahim-Nader, "Gross Domestic Product by Industry for 1947–86," Bureau of Economic Analysis, *Survey of Current Business*, December 2005, 71; U.S. Census Bureau, *The 2010 Statistical Abstract*, Table 656, "Gross Domestic Product by Industry and State: 2008"; Kevin Phillips, *Bad Money* (New York: Viking, 2008), 31.
9. John Maynard Keynes, "A Monetary Theory of Production," in Keynes, *Collected Writings*, vol. 13 (London: Macmillan, 1973), 408–11. As Kenneth Arrow put it: "The view that only real magnitudes matter can be defended only if it is assumed that the labor market (and all other markets) always clear, that is, that all unemployment is essentially voluntary." Kenneth J. Arrow, "Real and Nominal Magnitudes in Economics," *Journal of Financial and Quantitative Analysis* 15, no. 4 (November 1980): 773–74.
10. John Maynard Keynes, *Collected Writings*, vol. 29 (London: Macmillan, 1979), 81–82. See also Dudley Dillard, "Keynes and Marx: A Centennial Appraisal," *Journal of Post Keynesian Economics* 6, no. 3 (Spring 1984): 421–24.
11. Keynes, *Collected Writings*, vol. 13, 89.
12. When Sweezy wrote to Keynes's younger colleague, Joan Robinson, in 1982 about the publication of Keynes's 1930s lecture notes in which he discussed Marx, asking if she had any additional knowledge of this, she replied: "I was also surprised at the note about Keynes and Marx. Keynes said to me that he used to try to get Sraffa to explain to him the meaning of labor value, etc., and recommend passages to read, but that he could never make out what it was about." Quoted in Paul M. Sweezy, "The Regime of Capital," *Monthly Review* 37, no. 8 (January 1986): 2.

13. Harlan Linneus McCracken, *Value Theory and Business Cycles* (Binghamton, New York: Falcon Press, 1933), 46–47.
14. Keynes to McCracken, August 31, 1933, in Steven Kates, "A Letter from Keynes to Harlan McCracken dated 31st August 1933: Why the Standard Story on the Origins of the *General Theory* Needs to Be Rewritten," October 25, 2007, Social Science Research Network, *Working Paper Series*, http://ssrn.com/abstract=1024388.
15. Keynes, *Collected Writings*, vol. 29, 81–82. Some will recognize this as the basis for Keynes's later allusion in *The General Theory* to "the underworlds of economics" in which "the great puzzle of effective demand" has its "furtive" existence—and where mention is made of Marx, Hobson, and Douglas. On this, see Keynes, *The General Theory of Employment, Interest and Money* (London: Macmillan, 1936), 32, 355, 364–71. In referring favorably in his lectures to the American underconsumptionists William T. Foster and Waddill Catchings, Keynes was clearly influenced by McCracken's chapter on these thinkers. See McCracken, *Value Theory and Business Cycles*, 157–68.
16. Keynes, *Collected Writings*, vol. 13, 420. See also Donald Moggridge, "From the Treatise to the General Theory: An Exercise in Chronology," *History of Political Economy* 5, no. 1 (Spring 1973): 82.
17. Sweezy, "The Regime of Capital," 2.
18. Karl Marx, *Theories of Surplus Value*, Part 2 (Moscow: Progress Publishers, 1968), 509–15. For a good rendition of the overlap of the analysis of Marx and Keynes in this area, see Peter Kenway, "Marx, Keynes, and the Possibility of Crisis," *Cambridge Journal of Economics* 4 (1980): 23–36.
19. Marx, *Capital*, vol. 3, 515.
20. Marx, *Capital*, vol. 3, 607-610, 707; Karl Marx and Frederick Engels, *Selected Correspondence* (Moscow: Progress Publishers), 396–402; Jan Toporowski, *Theories of Financial Disturbance* (Northampton, MA: Edward Elgar, 2005), 54. For a detailed description of Marx's theory of "fictitious capital" see Michael Perelman, *Marx's Crises Theory* (New York: Praeger, 1987), 170–217.
21. Hyman P. Minsky, *John Maynard Keynes* (New York: Columbia University Press, 1975), 72–73.
22. Harry Magdoff and Paul M. Sweezy, *Stagnation and the Financial Explosion* (New York: Monthly Review Press, 1987), 94–95. The distinction between production and finance, as representing base and superstructure, should not, of course, be confused—Magdoff and Sweezy argued—with the wider, all-encompassing base-superstructure metaphor of historical materialism. Both sets of relations and processes, to which the base-superstructure metaphors refer, must alike be understood as dialectical. The historical emergence of finance from production gives no warrant for reductive explanations of how the structured process functions (or malfunctions) today. This is an error exactly parallel to a frequent, crude misunderstanding of the base-superstructure metaphor of historical materialism by the critics of Marxism. See István Mészáros, *Social Structure and Forms of Consciousness*, vol. 2 (New York: Monthly Review Press, forthcoming), chapter 1.

   Thus, it is a mistake to argue reductionistically, as even some Marxist theorists have, that "the financial cycle is only a reflection of the economic cycle, monetary and financial movements reflect non-monetary and non-financial internal and international disturbances." Suzanne de Brunhoff, *Marx on Money* (New York: Urizen Books, 1973), 100–1.

It should be added that Keynes, too, distinguished between separate realms of industry and finance—as a complex relation where the latter did not simply "reflect" the former—in his chapter on "The Industrial Circulation and the Financial Circulation" in *The Treatise on Money*. John Maynard Keynes, *Collected Writings*, vol. 5 (London: Macmillan, 1971), 217–30.

23. Hyman P. Minsky, "Hyman P. Minsky" (autobiographical entry), in Philip Arestis and Malcolm Sawyer, *A Biographical Dictionary of Dissenting Economists* (Northampton, MA: Edward Elgar, 2000), 414–15; Minsky, "Money and Crisis in Schumpeter and Keynes," 115. Compare Marx, *Capital*, vol. 3, 608–9.
24. See Magdoff and Sweezy, *Stagnation and the Financial Explosion*, 93–94.
25. Jan Toporowski, *The End of Finance* (London: Routledge, 2000), 1.
26. Keynes, *The General Theory*, 159.
27. Paul M. Sweezy, "The Triumph of Financial Capital," *Monthly Review* 46, no. 2 (June 1994): 8–10. For a discussion of the growing political-economic role of finance in U.S. society, see John Bellamy Foster and Hannah Holleman, "The Financial Power Elite," *Monthly Review* 62, no. 1 (May 2010): 1–19.
28. Nassim Nicholas Taleb, *The Black Swan: The Impact of the Highly Improbable* (New York: Random House, 2007).
29. Nouriel Roubini and Stephen Mihm, *Crisis Economics: A Crash Course in the Future of Finance* (New York: Penguin, 2010), 13–37.
30. Carmen M. Reinhart and Kenneth S. Rogoff, *This Time Is Different: Eight Centuries of Financial Folly* (Princeton: Princeton University Press, 2009).
31. Minsky, "Money and Crisis in Schumpeter and Keynes," 121; also see Minsky, *John Maynard Keynes*.
32. Minsky, *John Maynard Keynes*, 79–80.
33. Minsky, *John Maynard Keynes*, 78.
34. Keynes, *The General Theory*, 31, 228, 242, 249–50, 376–78; John Maynard Keynes, "The General Theory of Employment," *Quarterly Journal of Economics* 51 (February 1937): 216; Dudley Dillard, *The Economics of John Maynard Keynes* (New York: Prentice-Hall, 1948), 146–54.
35. The maturity argument was evident in Sweezy as early as the 1940s in *The Theory of Capitalist Development* (New York: Monthly Review Press, 1972), 220–21. But it took on far greater prominence in his later work beginning in the early 1980s. See *Four Lectures on Marxism* (New York: Monthly Review Press, 1981), 26–45.
36. Michal Kalecki, *Essays in the Theory of Economic Fluctuations* (New York: Russell and Russell, 1939), 149; Alvin H. Hansen, *Full Recovery or Stagnation?* (New York: W.W. Norton, 1938).
37. Paul A. Baran and Paul M. Sweezy, *Monopoly Capital* (New York: Monthly Review Press, 1966), 108.
38. Michal Kalecki, *Theory of Economic Dynamics* (New York: Augustus M. Kelley, 1969), 161. See also Josef Steindl, *Maturity and Stagnation in American Capitalism* (New York: Monthly Review Press, 1976), 130–37.
39. Toporowski argues that Kalecki and Steindl, beginning with Kalecki's 1937 article on "The Principle of Increasing Risk," dealt extensively with the contradictions at the level of the firm of reliance on external financing and rentier savings

(as opposed to the internal funds of corporations) in funding investment. This was never developed, however, into a theory of "credit inflation" or integrated with a notion of finance as a means of boosting aggregate demand. See Toporowski, *Theories of Financial Disturbance*, 109–30; Michal Kalecki, "The Principle of Increasing Risk," *Economica* 4, no. 16 (1937): 440–46.

40. Baran and Sweezy, *Monopoly Capital*, 139–41.
41. Total outstanding debt here includes household, business, and government (national, state, and local); Federal Reserve, Flow of Funds Accounts of the United States, Tables L.1 and L.2; *Economic Report of the President, 2006*, Table B-78; also see Foster and Magdoff, *The Great Financial Crisis*, 45–46.
42. Sweezy, "The Triumph of Financial Capital," 8.
43. Harry Magdoff and Paul M. Sweezy, "Financial Instability: Where Will It All End?" *Monthly Review* 34, no. 6 (November 1982): 18–23, and *Stagnation and the Financial Explosion*, 103–5.
44. Jan Toporowski, "The Wisdom of Property and the Politics of the Middle Classes," *Monthly Review* 62, no. 4 (September 2010): 12.
45. Toporowski, "The Wisdom of Property," 11. Keynes himself pointed to a negative wealth effect whereby stagnation tendencies (the decline in the marginal efficiency of capital) negatively affected stock equities thereby, resulting in declines in consumption by rentiers, which then intensified stagnation. See Keynes, *The General Theory*, 319. Asset-price inflation, together with the subsequent collapse of the financialization era, have extended both the "wealth effect" and the "negative wealth effect" far beyond the relatively few rentiers to the broad intermediate strata ("middle classes").
46. Toporowski, *End of Finance*, 8–9.
47. Harvey, *The Enigma of Capital*, 245.
48. Raghuram G. Rajan, *Fault Lines* (Princeton: Princeton University Press, 2010), 8; Edward N. Wolff, "Recent Trends in Household Wealth in the United States: Rising Debt and the Middle-Class Squeeze—An Update to 2007," Levy Economics Institute, Working Paper no. 589 (March 2010): 11, http://levy.org; Arthur B. Kennickell, "Ponds and Streams: Wealth and Income in the U.S., 1989 to 2007," Federal Reserve Board Working Paper, 2009–23 (2009), 55, 63; Toporowski, "The Wisdom of Property." 12, 14.
49. Bloomberg, *2010 M&A Outlook*, bloomberg.com, 8, accessed 8/28/2010; "M&A in 2007," *Wall Street Journal*, January 3, 2008; "A Record Year for M&A," *New York Times*, December 18, 2006; Floyd Norris, "To Rein in Pay, Rein in Wall Street," *New York Times*, October 30, 2009; Henry Kaufman, *The Road to Financial Reformation* (Hoboken, New Jersey: John Wiley and Sons, 2009), 97–106, 234. Traditionally, economic textbooks have treated new stock issues as raising capital for investment. The proliferation of merger activity highlights the fact that this is, in fact, hardly ever the case, and that most stock activity is directed at increasing financial gains.
50. Paul Krugman, "America Goes Dark," *New York Times*, August 8, 2010. The overwhelming of federal spending by the cuts in state and local spending replicates the experience of the 1930s. See John Bellamy Foster and Robert W. McChesney, "A New Deal Under Obama?" *Monthly Review* 60, no. 9 (February 2009): 2–3.
51. Krugman, "This Is Not a Recovery," *New York Times*, August 6, 2010.

52. Prabhat Patnaik, "The Structural Crisis of Capitalism," *MRzine*, August 3, 2010; Rajan, *Fault Lines*, 6.
53. The gap between the richest and poorest country in 1992 was 72:1. Angus Maddison, *The World Economy: A Millennial Perspective* (Paris: Development Centre, *OECD*, 2001), 125; Branko Milanovic, *Worlds Apart: Measuring International and Global Inequality* (Princeton: Princeton University Press, 2005), 40–50, 61–81; Thomas L. Friedman, *The World Is Flat* (New York: Farrar, Strauss and Giroux, 2005).
54. Naomi Klein, *The Shock Doctrine: The Rise of Disaster Capitalism* (New York: Henry Holt, 2007).

Chapter 3: Monopoly & Competition in Twenty-First-Century Capitalism

This chapter is a slightly revised version of an article coauthored with R. Jamil Jonna that first appeared in the April 2011 issue of *Monthly Review* (vol. 62, no. 11).

1. "U.S. Firms Build Up Record Cash Piles," *Wall Street Journal*, June 10, 2010.
2. Sam Bowles and Richard Edwards note: "The term 'monopoly power' refers both to the situation of a single firm (perfect monopoly) and to that of a small group of firms (oligopoly or shared monopoly); in either case, if some firm or firms can exclude others, monopoly power exists." Sam Bowles and Richard Edwards, *Understanding Capitalism* (New York: Harper and Row, 1985), 141.
3. Paul M. Sweezy, *Modern Capitalism and Other Essays* (New York: Monthly Review Press, 1972), 8.
4. John Kenneth Galbraith, *The Economics of Innocent Fraud* (Boston: Houghton Mifflin, 2004), 12.
5. The twenty-two barriers are: (1) capital requirements, (2) economies of scale, (3) absolute cost advantages, (4) product differentiation, (5) sunk costs, (6) research and development intensity, (7) asset specificity, (8) vertical integration, (9) diversification by conglomerates, (10) switching costs in complex systems, (11) special risks and uncertainties, (12) information asymmetries, (13) formal barriers set up by government, (14) preemptive action by incumbents, (15) excess capacity, (16) selling expenses, including advertising, (17) segmenting of the market, (18) patents, (19) exclusive control over strategic resources, (20) taking actions that raise rivals' costs, (21) high product differentiation, and (22) secrecy about competitive conditions. William G. Shepherd, *The Economics of Industrial Organization* (Prospect Heights, Illinois: Waveland Press, 1997), 210.
6. Karl Marx, *Capital*, vol. 1 (London: Penguin, 1976), 777–80.
7. Simon Johnson, "The Bill Daley Problem," *The Huffington Post*, January 11, 2011.
8. Joel Magnuson, *Mindful Economics* (New York: Seven Stories Press, 2008), 283–87; Barry C. Lynn, *Cornered: The New Monopoly Capitalism and the Economics of Destruction* (Hoboken, New Jersey: John Wiley and Sons, 2010), 42–52. On monopolistic pricing under the specific conditions of monopsony, see Josef Steindl, *Economic Papers, 1941–88* (New York: St. Martin's Press, 1990), 309–10.
9. Eric A. Schutz, *Markets and Power* (Armonk, New York: M.E. Sharpe, 2001), 80–81.

10. Lawrence J. White, "Aggregate Concentration in the Global Economy: Issues and Evidence," Stern School of Business, New York University, *Economic Working Papers*, EC-03-13 (2003), 3–4, http://archive.nyu.edu.
11. Today's giant corporations can be seen as pursuing a twofold, interrelated strategy of the pursuit of maximum sales revenue and maximum profitability, which converge over the long run, since larger market share provides the basis for higher monopoly profits, and higher profits are used to expand market share. See Peter Kenyon, "Pricing," in Alfred S. Eichner, ed., *A Guide to Post-Keynesian Economics* (White Plains, New York: M.E. Sharpe, 1979), 37–38.
12. "Fortune 500: Profits Bounce Back," *Fortune*, April 15, 2010, CNNMoney.com.
13. David Harvey, *The New Imperialism* (Oxford: Oxford University Press, 2003), 97–98.
14. Paul M. Sweezy, "The Triumph of Financial Capital," *Monthly Review* 46, no. 2 (June 1994): 1–11.
15. Thomas Friedman, *The Lexus and the Olive Tree* (New York: Random House, 2000), 13.
16. John Kenneth Galbraith, *The New Industrial State* (New York: New American Library, 1967); James K. Galbraith, *The Predator State* (New York: Free Press, 2008), 115–25.
17. Richard B. Du Boff and Edward S. Herman, "Mergers, Concentration, and the Erosion of Democracy," *Monthly Review* 53, no. 1 (May 2001): 14–29.
18. "M&A Deals Hit Record $1.57 Trillion in 2007," *New York Times*, December 21, 2007.
19. "World Motor Vehicle Production," 2009, OICA Correspondents Survey without double counts, http://oica.net/wp-content/uploads/ranking-2009.pdf.
20. "Global 500 2010," money.cnn.com (accessed February 20, 2011). Data is for fiscal year 2009. Japan Post Holdings, Sinopec, State Grid, and China Petroleum were not included in the top twenty-five here, since state-owned, rather than private, companies.
21. Samir Amin, *The Law of Worldwide Value* (New York: Monthly Review Press, 2010), 110–11, 118.
22. Milton Friedman, *Capitalism and Freedom* (Chicago: University of Chicago Press, 2002), 119–20.
23. Friedman, *Capitalism and Freedom*, 120. Definitions of monopoly and competition similar to Friedman's can be found in the National Resources Committee, *The Structure of the American Economy* (1939), directed by Gardiner Means, which observed that the term "monopoly" could be "used on the whole to refer to situations in which sufficient control would be exercised over price by an individual producer or by a colluding group of producers to make possible monopoly profits, i.e., profits above the rate necessary to induce new investment in other industries not subject to monopoly control." Conversely, "a situation was in general classified as competitive if there was insufficient control over price to make monopoly profits possible." For Means, this suggested that monopoly was pervasive in the key sectors of the U.S. economy. Gardiner C. Means, ed., *The Structure of the American Economy*, Part 1 (Washington, D.C.: U.S. Government Printing Office, 1939), 139.
24. Marx, *Capital*, 776–81; Rudolf Hilferding, *Finance Capital* (London: Routledge and Kegan Paul, 1981); Thorstein Veblen, *The Theory of Business Enterprise* (New York: Charles Scribner's Sons, 1932); V. I. Lenin, *Imperialism, the Highest Stage of Capitalism* (New York: International Publishers, 1939), 88.

25. The natural result would be something closer to the price structure of a single monopolist, which, rather than producing up to the point that marginal cost equals price, instead produces to where marginal cost equals marginal revenue, leading to higher prices and lower output.
26. Joseph A Schumpeter, *Essays* (Cambridge: Addison-Wesley, 1951), 47–72; and *Capitalism, Socialism, and Democracy* (New York: Harper and Brothers, 1942), 90-91.
27. Joan Robinson, *The Economics of Imperfect Competition* (London: Macmillan 1933); Edward Chamberlin, *The Theory of Monopolistic Competition* (Cambridge: Harvard University Press, 1933). "Monopolistic competition" is often used in neoclassical economics to refer to a realm of small and medium firms, excluding almost by definition the typical firm structure of oligopoly. Chamberlin, who himself introduced the term "oligopoly" to economics, is clear that such a separation was not his intention. Edward Hastings Chamberlin, *Towards a More General Theory of Value* (New York: Oxford University Press, 1957), 31–42. See also Mark Blaug, *Economic Theory in Retrospect* (Cambridge: Cambridge University Press, 1978), 415.
28. Paul M. Sweezy, "Demand under Conditions of Oligopoly," *The Journal of Political Economy* 47, no. 4 (August 1939): 568–73; Gavin C. Reid, *The Kinked Demand Curve Analysis of Oligopoly* (Edinburgh: Edinburgh University Press, 1981); John M. Blair, *Economic Concentration: Structure, Behavior and Public Policy* (New York: Harcourt Brace Jovanovich, 1972), 468.
29. John E. Elliott, *Comparative Economic Systems* (Englewood Cliffs, New Jersey: Prentice Hall, 1973), 62–63; Eric A. Schutz, *Markets and Power* (Armonk, New York: M.E. Sharpe, 2001), 7.
30. J. R. Hicks, *Value and Capital* (Oxford: Oxford University Press, 1946), 83–84.
31. See John Bellamy Foster, *The Theory of Monopoly Capitalism* (New York: Monthly Review Press, 1986), 53–55.
32. George J. Stigler, *Memoirs of an Unregulated Economist* (New York: Basic Books, 1988), 95. For a scholarly treatment of the TNEC monopoly studies, see Inger Stole, *Advertising at War: Business, Consumers, and Government Policies during the Second World War* (Urbana: University of Illinois Press, forthcoming, 2012).
33. Adolph A. Berle, and Gardiner C. Means, *The Modern Corporation and Private Property* (New York: Macmillan, 1932); Arthur Robert Burns, *The Decline of Competition* (New York: McGraw-Hill, 1936); Roosevelt quoted in Ellis W. Hawley, *The New Deal and the Problem of Monopoly* (Princeton: Princeton University Press, 1966), 412.
34. Schumpeter, *Capitalism, Socialism, and Democracy*, 83, 87–106; Karl Marx and Frederick Engels, *The Communist Manifesto* (New York: Monthly Review Press, 1964), 7. On Schumpeter's larger system of thought see John Bellamy Foster, "The Political Economy of Joseph Schumpeter: A Theory of Capitalist Development and Decline," *Studies in Political Economy* 15 (Fall 1984): 5–42, and "Theories of Capitalist Transformation: Critical Notes on the Comparison of Marx and Schumpeter," *Quarterly Journal of Economics* 98, no. 2 (May 1983): 327–31.
35. Friedrich Hayek, *The Road to Serfdom* (Chicago: University of Chicago Press, 1944), 49; John Kenneth Galbraith, *American Capitalism* (Boston: Houghton Mifflin, 1952), 14–15.

36. Galbraith, *American Capitalism* 32–44, *The Affluent Society* (New York: New American Library, 1984), 32-34, and *The New Industrial State*, 85-108; Sweezy, *Modern Capitalism*, 33-37. In *The New Industrial State*, Galbraith weakened his argument by attempting to substitute a notion of a planned corporate sphere governed by a technostructure for the capitalist economy itself (a view from which he later backed away). The result of this was to rigidify the U.S. economic conditions of the immediate post–Second World War period, exaggerating the independence of management in the big industrial firms from capitalist ownership and external financial influences, thereby undermining the realism that was the hallmark of Galbraithian critique.
37. Sumner H. Slichter, "The Growth of Competition," *The Atlantic Monthly* (November 1953): 66–70.
38. See Blair's classic treatise: *Economic Concentration*.
39. Michal Kalecki, *Theory of Economic Dynamics* (New York: Monthly Review Press, 1965), 17–18: Sweezy, *Modern Capitalism*, 39–41. Kalecki's basic analysis of the degree of monopoly had been set out earlier in his *Essays in the Theory of Economic Fluctuations* (New York: Farrar and Rinehart, 1939). It was developed further in his *Selected Essays on the Dynamics of the Capitalist Economy* (Cambridge: Cambridge University Press, 1971), 156–64. See also Steindl, *Economic Papers, 1941–88*, 303–16; Robert A. Blecker, "International Competition, Economic Growth, and the Political Economy of the U.S. Trade Deficit," in Robert Cherry, et al., eds., *The Imperiled Economy*, vol. 1 (New York: Union for Radical Political Economics, 1987), 227.
40. Josef Steindl, *Maturity and Stagnation in American Capitalism* (New York: Monthly Review Press, 1976).
41. *Radical Perspectives on the Economic Crisis of Monopoly Capitalism* (New York: Union for Radical Political Economics, 1975). On the influence of *Monopoly Capital* on radical political economics in the United States see Paul A. Attewell, *Radical Political Economy since the Sixties* (New Brunswick, New Jersey: Rutgers University Press, 1984).
42. Paul A. Baran and Paul M. Sweezy, *Monopoly Capital* (New York: Monthly Review Press, 1966), 6.
43. For a statistical accounting of the tendency of actual surplus in the U.S. economy to rise in the two decades following the publication of *Monopoly Capital* see Michael Dawson and John Bellamy Foster, "The Tendency of the Surplus to Rise, 1963-1988," in John B. Davis, ed., *The Economic Surplus in Advanced Economies* (Brookfield, Vermont: Edward Elgar, 1992), 42–70. These results, however, are limited by the fact that they measure actual surplus, not potential surplus (with the difference between the two having its statistical trace in unemployment/underemployment/unused capacity).
44. Sweezy, *Modern Capitalism*, 41; Harry Braverman, *Labor and Monopoly Capital* (New York: Monthly Review Press, 1974). For a general discussion of inequality and the position of labor in the contemporary political economy see Michael D. Yates, *Naming the System* (New York: Monthly Review Press, 2003).
45. U.S. Senate, Subcommittee on Antitrust and Monopoly, *Administered Prices: Steel*, Committee on the Judiciary, 85th Congress Second Session, March 1958, 85–89, 97.
46. Baran and Sweezy, *Monopoly Capital*, 57–64.

47. "A Pricing System that Works Only One Way—Up" *BusinessWeek*, June 15, 1957, 188–98.
48. "Buffett Says Pricing Power Beats Good Management," Bloomberg.com, February 17, 2011.
49. Baran and Sweezy, *Monopoly Capital*, 51.
50. Paul M. Sweezy, *Four Lectures on Marxism* (New York: Monthly Review Press, 1981), 63–65.
51. Baran and Sweezy, *Monopoly Capital*, 73–74; Schumpeter, *Capitalism, Socialism, and Democracy*, 84–85.
52. Sweezy, *Four Lectures on Marxism*, 65–66, and *Modern Capitalism*, 45–47. The hierarchy of profits associated with economic concentration and firm size has been empirically demonstrated numerous times both with respect to the United States and other advanced capitalist countries. See, for example: Bagicha Singh Minhas, *An International Comparison of Factor Costs and Factor Use* (Amsterdam: North Holland Publishing Co., 1963), 54–73; Josef Steindl, *Small and Big Business* (Oxford: Basil Blackwell, 1947); Howard Sherman, *Profits in the United States* (Ithaca, New York: Cornell University Press, 1968), and *The Business Cycle* (Princeton: Princeton University Press, 1991), 307–10; Norman R. Collins and Lee S. Preston, "Price-Cost Margins and Industry Structure," *Review of Economics and Statistics* 51, no. 3 (August 1969): 271–86; Richard C. Edwards, *Contested Terrain* (New York: Basic Books, 1979), 82–83, 219–31; Kathleen Pulling, "Cyclical Behavior of Profit Margins," *Journal of Economic Issues* 12 (June 1978): 287–306; Joseph Bowring, *Competition in a Dual Economy* (Princeton: Princeton University Press, 1986), 151–80.
53. Willard F. Mueller, "Conglomerates: A Nonindustry," in Walter Adams, ed., *The Structure of American Industry* (New York: Macmillan, 1982), 427; William M. Dugger, *Corporate Hegemony* (New York: Greenwood Press, 1989), 17–21.
54. Baran and Sweezy, *Monopoly Capital*, 193–201.
55. Stephen Herbert Hymer, *The International Operations of National Firms: A Study of Direct Foreign Investment* (Cambridge, Massachusetts: MIT Press, 1976), 25, 92–93, 117–22 (Hymer's 1960 doctoral dissertation); Robert B. Cohen, et al., "General Introduction," in Stephen Hymer, *The Multinational Corporation* (Cambridge: Cambridge University Press, 1979), 2–3; John H. Dunning and Alan M. Rugman, "The Influence of Hymer's Dissertation on the Theory of Foreign Direct Investment," *American Economic Review* 75, no. 2 (May 1985): 228–32. Hymer was closely associated in his last years with Sweezy and Magdoff at *Monthly Review* and wrote for the magazine. At his death in an automobile accident in 1974 at age 39, he was scheduled to be part of a debate at the United Nations Staff Club in New York, to consist of himself, Magdoff, and Sweezy in opposition to Kindleberger and other defenders of the multinationals. See Charles P. Kindleberger, "Introduction," in Hymer, *International Operations of National Firms*, xxi.
56. Charles P. Kindleberger, *American Business Abroad* (New Haven: Yale University Press, 1969), 27.
57. John H. Dunning, ed., *The United Nations Library on Transnational Corporations*, vol. 1, *The Theory of Transnational Corporations* (New York: Routledge, 1993), 17–43.

58. Paul M. Sweezy and Harry Magdoff, *The Dynamics of U.S. Capitalism* (New York: Monthly Review Press, 1972), 93–100. For a realistic, post-Keynesian theory of the modern oligopoly see Alfred S. Eichner, *The Megacorp and Oligopoly* (Cambridge: Cambridge University Press, 1976).
59. See Thomas R. Navin and Marian V. Sears, "The Rise of a Market for Industrial Securities, 1887-1902," *The Business History Review* 29, no. 2 (June 1955): 105–38. For a historical treatment of the rise of monopoly capital in the United States, including the role of finance in the process, see Richard B. Du Boff, *Accumulation and Power* (Armonk, New York: M.E. Sharpe, 1989).
60. Frederick Engels, *On Capital* (New York: International Publishers, 1974), 118–20.
61. Sweezy, "The Triumph of Financial Capital," 1–11; John Bellamy Foster and Fred Magdoff, *The Great Financial Crisis* (New York: Monthly Review Press, 2009), 63–88.
62. Similar views on the structural relation of neoliberalism to financialization can be found in a number of different left analyses. See Gérard Duménil and Dominique Lévy, *Capital Resurgent* (Cambridge, MA: Harvard University Press, 2004), 110–18; Harvey, *The Enigma of Capital* (Oxford: Oxford University Press, 2010), 11.
63. Joyce Kolko, *Restructuring the World Economy* (New York: Pantheon, 1988), 178–81.
64. See Kolko, *Restructuring the World Economy*, 297-301; David Harvey, *A Brief History of Neoliberalism* (Oxford: Oxford University Press, 2005).
65. R. H. Coase, "The Nature of the Firm: Meaning," in Williamson and Winter, ed., *The Nature of the Firm*, 54. See also in the same volume: Coase, "The Nature of the Firm," 18–33, "The Nature of the Firm: Influence," 61–74, and Oliver E. Williamson, "Introduction," 6.
66. Coase, "The Nature of the Firm: Influence," 61–63. For a critique of the Coasian theory of the firm see Keith Cowling and Roger Sugden, *Beyond Capitalism* (New York: St. Martin's Press, 1994), 38–42.
67. Justifications for both horizontal and vertical integration of firms are often made in terms of the efficiencies associated with various economies of scale. Yet, as Schutz points out, "given the pervasiveness of significant barriers to entry in real-world markets, it would be a mistake to suppose that wherever monopoly power exists in free markets (i.e., aside from cases of state intervention) it must be due to economies of scale." Logically, barriers to entry, which are assiduously cultivated by firms, would be unnecessary if their superior market power were simply the result of greater efficiency. Schutz, *Markets and Power*, 58.
68. Oliver E. Williamson, *Markets and Hierarchies* (New York: The Free Press, 1975), 258–61; Herbert J. Hovenkamp, "Harvard, Chicago and Transaction Cost Economics in Antitrust Analysis," University of Iowa College of Law, Legal Research Paper, no. 10–35 (December 2010): 1–35, http://ssrn.com/abstract=1592476.
69. Dunning and Rugman, "The Influence of Hymer's Dissertation on the Theory of Foreign Direct Investment," 228–32. Hymer, in some of his later work, before moving more decisively into a Marxian perspective, had himself incorporated Coase's work and transactions costs. But he made it secondary within a perspective that emphasized monopoly capital abroad. See Hymer, "The Large Multi-

national Corporation," in Dunning ed., *The Theory of Transnational Corporations*, 34–43; Paul Marginson, "Firms and Corporations," in Philip Arestis and Malcolm Sawyer, *The Elgar Companion to Radical Political Economy* (Brookfield, Vermont: Edward Elgar, 1994), 158–61.

70. Stigler, *Memoirs of an Unregulated Economist*, 92, 162–63.
71. George Joseph Stigler, Kurt R. Leube, and Thomas Gale Moore, eds., *The Essence of Stigler* (Stanford: Hoover Institution Press, 1986), 269, 284.
72. George J. Stigler, "Competition," *The New Palgrave Dictionary of Economics*, vol. 1 (London: Macmillan, 1987): 531–35, Stigler, *The Organization of Industry* (Homewood, Illinois: R.D. Irwin, 1968); Shepherd, *The Economics of Industrial Organization*, 30.
73. Stigler, *Memoirs of an Unregulated Economist*, 102, 161–63. For systematic refutations of Stigler's point on Standard Oil see Michael Perelman, *Railroading Economics* (New York: Monthly Review Press, 2006) and Richard B. Du Boff and Edward S. Herman, "Alfred Chandler's New Business History: A Review," *Politics and Society* 10, no. 1 (January 1980): 100–1.
74. For a useful assertion of reality-based economics in the face of such irrealism, which he labels "utopian economics," see John Cassidy, *How Markets Fail* (New York: Farrar, Strauss and Giroux, 2009).
75. William J. Baumol, John Panzar, and Robert D. Willig, *Contestable Markets and the Theory of Industry Structure* (New York: Harcourt Brace Jovanovich, 1982), xix.
76. Stephen Martin, *Advanced Industrial Economics* (Oxford: Blackwell, 1993), 324; Shepherd, *The Economics of Industrial Organization*, 30–31; Edwin G. West, "Monopoly," *The New Palgrave Dictionary of Economics*, vol. 3 (London: Macmillan, 1987), 540; Schutz, *Markets and Power*, 54–58.
77. Robert H. Bork, *The Antitrust Paradox* (New York: Basic Books, 1978), 164; Hovenkamp, "Harvard, Chicago and Transaction Cost Economics in Antitrust Analysis," 7.
78. Another area of theoretical innovation in economics that has tended to muddy the waters on the issue of monopoly was a proliferation of formal game-theory models (of which Sweezy's kinked-demand curve analysis was recognized as a forerunner) designed to analyze imperfect competition. The majority of these studies concentrated on abstruse models and anecdotes that were far removed from real-world conditions or empirical testing. See Martin, *Advanced Industrial Economics*, 560–64. In a letter to one of the authors on February 14, 2011, noted industrial organization economist Eric A. Schutz confirmed our conclusions that the most important developments in the theoretical shift away from the traditional industrial organization literature and antitrust, with the conservative shift in economics in the 1980s, were transaction cost economics, contestable markets, game theory, and Bork's "antitrust paradox" argument: the four pinpointed in our argument. Schutz would also add a fifth: public choice theory.
79. Stigler, *Memoirs of an Unregulated Economist*, 104.
80. Thomas E. Weisskopf, Samuel Bowles, and David M. Gordon, "Two Views of Capitalist Stagnation," *Science & Society* 69, no. 3 (Fall 1985): 268–70.
81. Robert J. S. Ross and Kent C. Trachte, *Global Capitalism* (Albany: State University of New York Press, 1990), 38, 49, 145.

82. David Gordon, "The Global Economy: New Edifice or Crumbling Foundation," *New Left Review* 168 (March/April 1988): 24–64.
83. John Weeks, *Capitalism and Exploitation* (Princeton: Princeton University Press, 1981), 165. For other examples of such fundamentalist views see Willi Semmler, "Competition, Monopoly, and Differentials of Profit Rates," *Review of Radical Political Economics* 13 (Winter 1981): 39–52; Ben Fine and Andy Murfin, *Macroeconomics and Monopoly Capitalism* (Brighton, Sussex: Harvester, 1984). For responses from the perspective of monopoly capital theory see Howard J. Sherman, "Monopoly Capital vs. the Fundamentalists," in Stephen Resnick and Richard Wolff, *Rethinking Marxism* (Brooklyn: Autonomedia, 1985), 359–77; Michael A. Lebowitz, *Following Marx* (Boston: Brill, 2009), 225–46; Foster, *The Theory of Monopoly Capitalism.*
84. Magdoff and Sweezy, *The Deepening Crisis of U.S. Capitalism*, 28. Arguing from a left standpoint (and falling prey to the ambiguity of competition), James Clifton insisted, in contradistinction to Baran and Sweezy, that: "The fact that it is typically the modern corporation rather than the individual capitalist that pursues this search [for profits] today does not at all imply a lessening of competition in the capitalist economy.... It seems clear that the large firms which dominate the economic process as a whole cannot be so characterized [as monopolies] for that process [the struggle between large firms] is a highly competitive one." James A. Clifton, "Competition in the Evolution of the Capitalist Mode of Production," *Cambridge Journal of Economics* 1, no. 2 (1977): 143, 150.
85. David Harvey, *The Limits to Capital* (Chicago: University of Chicago Press, 1982); Giovanni Arrighi, *The Long Twentieth Century* (New York: Verso, 1994); Robert Brenner, *The Boom and the Bubble* (New York: Verso, 2002); and Duménil and Lévy, *Capital Resurgent*. Harvey did include a limited discussion of the issue of monopoly capitalism in *The Limits of Capital* but underscored his own hesitation on the issue. Thus he responded to Baran and Sweezy's contention that monopoly should be put at "the very center of the analytical effort" by writing: "The abandonment of the 'competitive model' certainly does entail abandoning the law of value—which, to their credit, Baran and Sweezy are fully prepared to do. The trouble is that we cannot withdraw this, the linchpin of Marx's analysis, without seriously questioning or compromising all of the other Marxian categories." Harvey, *Limits to Capital*, 141.
86. Arrighi, *The Long Twentieth Century*, 218–19, 239–43. For a critique of Chandler's work for its rejection of monopoly power as a central factor in the growth of the firm and its close relation to transaction cost analysis see Du Boff and Herman, "Alfred Chandler's New Business History," 87–110.
87. Financialization, Brenner argued, far from encouraging monopoly, was actually a decided agent of dramatically increased market competition. "Banks most obviously, but other financial bodies as well, tend to have immediately at hand, or to be able to bring together, whatever amount of capital is necessary to enter any field that is displaying an unusually high profit rate." Moreover, "firms can resort to bank finance with particular ease." Brenner added: "The upshot is that more than temporary monopolies are difficult to maintain, without direct political action by governmental authorities to sustain them by controlling en-

try (and, of course, the tendency over the last couple of decades has been in the opposite direction, toward deregulation)." Stigler could not have put it better! Robert Brenner, "Competition and Class," *Monthly Review* 51, no. 7 (December 1999): 35.

88. See especially Harry Magdoff and Paul M. Sweezy, *The End of Prosperity* (New York: Monthly Review Press, 1977), *The Deepening Crisis of U.S. Capitalism* (New York: Monthly Review Press, 1981), *Stagnation and the Financial Explosion* (New York: Monthly Review Press, 1987), and *The Irreversible Crisis* (New York: Monthly Review Press, 1988).
89. Harry Magdoff, *Imperialism: From the Colonial Age to the Present* (New York: Monthly Review Press, 1978), 177.
90. Magdoff and Sweezy, *The Deepening Crisis of U.S. Capitalism*, 23–30.
91. Schutz, *Markets and Power*, 66–67.
92. Keith Cowling, *Monopoly Capitalism* (New York: John Wiley and Sons, 1982), 130–34.
93. Keith Cowling, "Monopoly Capitalism and Stagnation," in Tracy Mott, Nina Shapiro, eds., *Rethinking Capitalist Development: Essays on the Economics of Josef Steindl* (New York: Routledge, 2005), 155–66.
94. Doug Dowd, *Inequality and the Global Economic Crisis* (London: Pluto Press, 2009), 31–32, 67–72, and *Capitalism and Its Economics: A Critical History* (London: Pluto Press, 2000), 89–90, 168–99.
95. Samir Amin, "Seize the Crisis!" *Monthly Review* 61, no. 7 (December 2009): 3.
96. We have in mind here such works as Duménil and Lévy, *Capital Resurgent*; Anwar Shaikh, "The First Great Depression of the 21st Century," in Leo Panitch, Greg Albo, and Vivek Chibber, eds., *The Crisis This Time* (London: The Merlin Press, 2010), 44–63; and Robert Brenner, "What Is Good for Goldman Sachs Is Good for America: The Origins of the Current Crisis," Center for Social Theory and Comparative History, Institute for Social Science Research, UC Los Angeles, October 2, 2009. (This is the Prologue to the Spanish translation of the author's *Economics of Global Turbulence* [Verso, 2006], published by AK Press, 2009.)
97. We are now seeing in just the last few years works bringing all of these elements together, making for compelling results. See Harvey, *The Enigma of Capital*; Amin, *The Law of Worldwide Value;* Michael Perelman, *Railroading Economics* (New York: Monthly Review Press, 2006); and John Bellamy Foster and Fred Magdoff, *The Great Financial Crisis.*

Chapter 4: The Internationalization of Monopoly Capital

This chapter is a revised version of an article coauthored with R. Jamil Jonna that first appeared in the June 2011 issue of *Monthly Review* (vol. 63, no. 2).

1. Paul M. Sweezy, "More (or Less) on Globalization," *Monthly Review* 49, no. 4 (September 1997): 3–4.
2. Richard J. Barnet and Ronald E. Müller, *Global Reach: The Power of the Multinational Corporations* (New York: Simon and Schuster, 1974), 213–14.
3. UNCTAD, *World Investment Report, 2010* (New York: United Nations, 2010), 17–18.

4. Mark Casson, "Multinational Monopolies and International Cartels," in Peter J. Buckley and Mark Casson, eds., *The Economic Theory of the Multinational Enterprise* (London: Macmillan, 1985), 65; V. I. Lenin, *Imperialism, the Highest Stage of Capitalism* (New York: International Publishers, 1939).
5. Galambos quoted in G. Pascal Zachary, "Let's Play Oligopoly! Why Giants Like Having Other Giants Around," *Wall Street Journal*, March 8, 1999.
6. "Let's Play Oligopoly!" *Wall Street Journal*.
7. See the data in chapter 3 above.
8. In accord with UNCTAD data, U.S. totals are for non-bank U.S. parents and non-bank majority-owned Foreign Affiliates. See Chart 1 and Kevin B. Barefoot and Raymond J. Mataloni Jr., "U.S. Multinational Companies: Operations in the United States and Abroad in 2008," *Survey of Current Business* 90, no. 8 (2010), Tables 16.2 and 18.2. The percentages for foreign affiliates are 12, 24.6, and 22.8 percent of assets, sales and employment respectively.
9. Barefoot and Mataloni, "U.S. Multinational Companies," 207.
10. Joseph P. Quinlan, *Global Engagement* (Chicago: Contemporary Books, 2001), 37–41; UNCTAD, *The Universe of the Largest Transnational Corporations* (New York: United Nations, 2007), 3.
11. Wladimir Andreff, "Outsourcing in the New Strategy of Multinational Companies: Foreign Investment, International Subcontracting and Production Relocation," *Papeles de Europa* 18 (2009),19.
12. Keith Cowling and Roger Sugden, *Beyond Capitalism* (London: Pinter Publishers, 1994), 35.
13. Walter LaFeber, *Michael Jordan and the New Global Capitalism* (New York: W.W. Norton, 2002), 107, 126, 147–49; Richard J. Barnet and John Cavanagh, *Global Dreams: Imperial Corporations and the New World Order* (New York: Simon and Schuster, 1994), 326–27; Jeff Ballinger, "Nike Does It to Vietnam," *Multinational Monitor* 18 no. 3 (March 1997).
14. Anita Chan, "Nike and its Satanettes" (1999), http://business.nmsu.edu.
15. "Nike's New Game Plan for Sweatshops," *Bloomberg Businessweek*, September 20, 2004, http://businesweek.com. On the general issue of sweatshops in international textile and shoe production see Robert J. S. Ross, *Slaves to Fashion: Poverty and Abuse in the New Sweatshops* (Ann Arbor: University of Michigan Press, 2004).
16. Mujeres Transformando and Institute for Global Labour and Human Rights, "Ocean Sky Sweatshop in El Salvador: Women Paid Just 8 Cents for Each $25 NFL Shirt They Sew" (Pittsburgh, PA: The National Labor Committee, January 24, 2011), http://www.globallabourrights.org. See also Bernard D'Mello, "Reebok and the Global Sweatshop," *Monthly Review* 54, no. 9 (February 2003): 26–40.
17. Beatrice Appay, "Economic Concentration and the Externalization of Labour," *Economic and Industrial Democracy* 19, no. 1 (1998): 161; Yadong Luo, *Multinational Enterprise in Emerging Markets* (Copenhagen: Copenhagen Business Press, 2002), 199–200. See also Keith Cowling and Roger Sugden, *Transnational Monopoly Capitalism* (New York: St. Martin's Press, 1987), 3, 88–90.
18. Louis Galambos, "The Triumph of Oligopoly," in Thomas Weiss and Donald Schaefer, ed., *American Economic Development in Historical Perspective* (Princeton: Princeton University Press, 1994), 252.
19. See James K. Galbraith, *The Predator State* (New York: Free Press, 2008), 19–24.

20. Milton Friedman, *Capitalism and Freedom* (Chicago: University of Chicago Press, 1962), 119–20.
21. Paul A. Baran and Paul M. Sweezy, *Monopoly Capital* (New York: Monthly Review Press, 1966), 57–59.
22. The basic changes associated with the internationalization of monopoly capital were spelled out as early as the 1960s. See "Notes on the Multinational Corporation" in Paul M. Sweezy and Harry Magdoff, *The Dynamics of U.S. Capitalism* (New York: Monthly Review Press, 1972), pp. 88-112.
23. Edward M. Graham and Paul R. Krugman, *Foreign Direct Investment in the United States* (Washington, D.C.: Institute for International Economics, 1995), 193.
24. John Bellamy Foster and Robert W. McChesney, "The Internet's Unholy Marriage to Capitalism," *Monthly Review* 62, no. 10 (March 2011): 1–30.
25. Competition in economics is largely about competition between firms over product markets/sales markets. Competition between workers within labor markets lies largely outside of this conception. On the importance of this distinction see Cowling and Sugden, *Transnational Monopoly Capitalism*, 4.
26. The role of "divide and rule" as a key strategy governing the actions of multinational corporations is discussed more fully under the section "The Law of Increasing Firm Size and the Rise of the Multinational Corporation" below.
27. Pierre Bourdieu, *Acts of Resistance: Against the Tyranny of the Market* (New York: The New Press, 1999), 98; Insull quoted in Arthur M. Schlesinger, Jr., *The Crisis of the Old Order* (New York: Houghton Mifflin, 1957), 120.
28. Marx, *Capital*, vol. 1 (London: Penguin, 1976), 739.
29. Stephen Herbert Hymer, *The Multinational Corporation: A Radical Approach* (New York: Cambridge University Press, 1979), 54.
30. Stephen A. Marglin, "What Do Bosses Do?: The Origins and Functions of Hierarchy in Capitalist Production," *Review of Radical Political Economics* 6, no. 2 (Summer 1974): 80–104; Cowling and Sugden, *Transnational Monopoly Capitalism*.
31. As John Dunning has argued, Marx, and after him Rudolf Hilferding, were the first to develop the notion of internalization in explaining the growth of the firm; however, in their theories such internalization was not of transaction costs—as in the neoclassical Coasian theory of the firm—but of *labor* within a context of control and exploitation. See John H. Dunning, *Explaining International Production* (London: Unwin Hyman, 1988), 130–32.
32. Karl Marx, *Capital*, vol. 1, part 4.
33. Richard C. Edwards, *Contested Terrain* (New York: Basic Books, 1979), 44, 226–27.
34. Illustrations of the role of the state in the growth of large capitals can be found in Kevin Phillips, *Wealth and Democracy: A Political History of the American Rich* (New York: Broadway Books, 2002).
35. Alfred Marshall, *Principles of Economics*, vol. 1 (London: Macmillan, 1961), 317–18.
36. See Edwards, *Contested Terrain*, 3–71.
37. Marx, *Capital*, vol. 1, 1019–38. The role of scientific management and its relation to monopoly capitalism is examined in great detail in Harry Braverman, *Labor and Monopoly Capital* (New York: Monthly Review Press, 1998).
38. Harry Magdoff, *Imperialism: From the Colonial Stage to the Present* (New York: Monthly Review Press, 1978), 166–67.

39. The best mainstream approach to the rise of the multinationals, accordingly, is the "eclectic paradigm" developed by John Dunning, which emphasizes a large number of factors, including both monopolistic advantages (in line with Hymer) and the internalization of market costs. It, however, has the disadvantage of not putting accumulation at the center of the analysis. For a concise summary of the eclectic paradigm see Geoffrey Jones, *Multinationals and Global Capitalism* (New York: Oxford University Press, 2005), 12.
40. Sweezy and Magdoff, *The Dynamics of U.S. Capitalism*, 99.
41. For a classic expression of this see Robert Gilpin, *U.S. Power and the Multinational Corporation: The Political Economy of Foreign Direct Investment* (New York: Basic Books, 1975).
42. The emphasis on strategic control as the defining trait of the modern giant corporation or multinational—a form of control that evolves out of capital's domination of the labor process from the very beginning of the workshop/factory system—is in many ways the centerpiece of the work of Cowling and Sugden in their *Transnational Monopoly Capitalism*, 8–27. See also Graham and Krugman, *Foreign Direct Investment in the United States*, 36.
43. Graham and Krugman, *Foreign Direct Investment in the United States*, 193.
44. Hymer, *The Multinational Corporation*, 86–88; James Peoples and Roger Sugden, "Divide and Rule by Transnational Corporations," in Christos N. Pitelis and Roger Sugden, eds., *The Nature of the Transnational Firm* (London: Routledge, 2000), 174–92.
45. David Harvey, *The New Imperialism* (New York: Oxford University Press, 2003), 137–82; Richard B. Freeman, "The New Global Labor Market," *Focus* (University of Wisconsin-Madison Institute for Research on Poverty) 26, no. 1 (Summer-Fall 2008): 1–6; Joseph P. Quinlan, *The Last Economic Superpower* (New York: McGraw Hill, 2011), 176.
46. "Inside Foxconn's Factory," *The Telegraph* (UK), May 27, 2010, http://telegraph.co.uk.; "Foxconn Cuts Off Suicide Compensation," *The Australian*, June 12, 2010, http://theaustralian.com.au.
47. Peoples and Sugden, "Divide and Rule," 182–89.
48. On the unequal exchange process that this relies on and reinforces, wherein wage differences are greater than the difference in productivity, see Gernot Köhler, "A Critique of the Global Wage System" (2006), http://caei.com.ar.
49. Keith Cowling, *Monopoly Capitalism* (New York: John Wiley and Sons, 1982), 145.
50. Keith Cowling, "Monopoly Capitalism and Stagnation," 150.
51. Graham and Krugman, *Foreign Direct Investment in the United* States, 193. As Sam Gibara, CEO of Goodyear Tire and Rubber Co., declared in 1999, "What you have is a chain reaction. We're going global because our customers are going global. Then, to the extent that we go global, our suppliers are going global." What Gibara refrained from mentioning was that Goodyear's rivals were going global too—a development that Goodyear sought to address by creating strategic alliances, a form of collusion, with other firms (in 1999 it established a strategic alliance with Sumitomo Rubber Industries Ltd. of Japan). In "Let's Play Oligopoly!" *Wall Street Journal.*
52. John H. Dunning and Sarianna M. Lundan, *Multinational Enterprises and the Global Economy* (Northampton, Massachusetts: Edward Elgar, 2008), 487.
53. See Cowling and Sugden, *Beyond Capitalism*, 67–69.

54. Cowling, "Monopoly Capitalism and Stagnation," 150.
55. On the relation of international oligopoly to stagnation see Cowling and Sugden, *Beyond Capitalism*, 91–113. On monopoly capital and global financialization see Foster and Magdoff, *The Great Financial Crisis*.
56. James B. Davies, Susanna Sandström, Anthony Shorroks, and Edward N. Wolff, "The World Distribution of Household Wealth," in James B. Davies, ed., *Personal Wealth from a Global Perspective* (Oxford: Oxford University Press, 2008), 402.
57. UNCTADStat, "Nominal and Real GDP, Total and Per Capita, Annual, 1970–2009 (US Dollars at constant prices [2005] and constant exchange rates [2005] per capita)" and "Total population, Annual, 1950–2050." UNCTAD only provides aggregate GDP per capita data for the G8 but the series is discontinuous because data for Russia are only available from 1992 to present. For the G7 figures, we excluded Russia and manually calculated GDP per capita using total GDP and population. Today the Least Developed Countries, as designated by the UN, include thirty-three in Africa, fourteen in Asia and one in Latin America and the Caribbean.
58. See Fred Magdoff and Brian Tokar, eds., *Agriculture and Food in Crisis* (New York: Monthly Review Press, 2010).
59. In Daniel Yergin and Joseph Stanislaw's neoliberal triumphalist tract (about how Hayek won over Keynes) the great enemy is the state while corporations are downplayed and "corporation" doesn't even deserve an entry in the index. This is all the more startling since Yergin has spent most of his career in support of the giant oil corporations. See Daniel Yergin and Joseph Stanislaw, *The Commanding Heights* (New York: Simon and Schuster, 2002).
60. Bernard E. Harcourt, *The Illusion of Free Markets: Punishment and the Myth of Natural Order* (Cambridge: Harvard University Press, 2011).

Chapter 5: The Global Reserve Army of Labor and the New Imperialism

This chapter is coauthored with R. Jamil Jonna and first appeared in the November 2011 issue of *Monthly Review* (vol. 63, no. 6).

1. Stephen Herbert Hymer, *The Multinational Corporation* (Cambridge: Cambridge University Press, 1979), 41, 75, 183.
2. Hymer, *The Multinational Corporation*, 81, 86, 161, 262–69.
3. Gary Gereffi, *The New Offshoring of Jobs and Global Development*, ILO Social Policy Lectures, Jamaica, December 2005 (Geneva: International Institute for Labour Studies, 2006), http://ilo.org, 1; Peter Dicken, *Global Shift* (New York: Guilford Press, 1998), 26–28.
4. Thorstein Veblen already understood this in the 1920s. See his *Absentee Ownership and Business Enterprise in Recent Times* (New York: Augustus M. Kelley, 1964), 287.
5. See Paul M. Sweezy, *Four Lectures on Marxism* (New York: Monthly Review Press, 1981), 64–65; Michael E. Porter, *Competitive Strategy* (New York: The Free Press, 1980), 35–36.
6. Ajit K. Ghose, Nomaan Majid, and Christoph Ernst, *The Global Employment Challenge* (Geneva: International Labour Organisation, 2008), 9-10. On

depeasantization see Farshad Araghi, "The Great Global Enclosure of Our Times," in Fred Magdoff, John Bellamy Foster, and Frederick H. Buttel, eds., *Hungry for Profit* (New York: Monthly Review Press, 2000), 145-60.

7. John Smith, *Imperialism and the Globalisation of Production* (Ph.D. Thesis, University of Sheffield, July 2010), 224.
8. Stephen Roach, "How Global Labor Arbitrage Will Shape the World Economy," *Global Agenda Magazine*, 2004,http://ecocritique.free.fr; John Bellamy Foster, Harry Magdoff, and Robert W. McChesney, "The Stagnation of Employment," *Monthly Review*, 55, no. 11 (April 2004): 9-11.
9. Thomas L. Friedman, *The World Is Flat* (New York: Farrar, Strauss and Giroux, 2005). Friedman wrongly claims that his "flat world hypothesis" was first advanced by Marx. See 234-37.
10. Paul Krugman, *Pop Internationalism* (Cambridge, Massachusetts: MIT Press, 1996), 66-67. On the absurdity of expecting wage differences between nations simply to reflect productivity trends see Marx, *Capital*, vol. 1 (London: Penguin, 1976), 705.
11. On fears of an end to global labor arbitrage see "Moving Back to America," *The Economist*, May 12, 2011, http://economist.com.
12. Karl Marx, *Capital*, vol. 1, 798. Immediately after the quoted passage Marx added the following qualification: "Like all other laws, it is modified in its workings by circumstances, the analysis of which does not concern us here." It should be added that Marx used "absolute" here in the Hegelian sense, i.e., in terms of *abstract*.
13. Harry Magdoff and Paul M. Sweezy, *Stagnation and the Financial Explosion* (New York: Monthly Review Press, 1987), 204. By 2010, OECD unemployment had grown by 38 percent, reaching 48.5 million persons. ("Unemployment, Employment, Labour Force and Population of Working Age [15-64]," OECD.Stat Extracts, [OECD, Geneva, 2011], retrieved September 24, 2011.)
14. The concept of "imperialist rent" is developed by Samir Amin in *The Law of Worldwide Value* (New York: Monthly Review Press, 2011) and is discussed further below.
15. See, for example, the discussion in Anthony Giddens, *Capitalism and Modern Social Theory* (Cambridge: Cambridge University Press, 1971), 55-58. Giddens offers a half-hearted and confused defense of Marx that is full of misconceptions.
16. John Strachey, *Contemporary Capitalism*, 101; Marx, *Capital*, vol. 1, 929. Strachey also quotes on the same page the passage from *The Communist Manifesto* where Marx and Engels write, "The modern labourer...instead of rising with the progress of industry, sinks deeper and deeper below the conditions of existence of his own class. He becomes a pauper, and pauperism develops more rapidly than population and wealth." Karl Marx and Frederick Engels, *The Communist Manifesto* (New York: Monthly Review Press, 1964), 23. At first sight this seems to support Strachey's point (though taken from an early and non-economic work). However, as Hal Draper points out: "This may sound as if the class of proletarians, as such, is inevitably pauperized. This language reflected the socialistic propaganda of the day; later in *Capital* I (Chap. 25), Marx made clear that the pauper layer is 'the lowest sediment of the relative surplus population.'" Hal Draper, *The Adventures of the Communist Manifesto* (Berkeley: Center for Socialist History, 1998), 233.
17. Roman Rosdolsky, *The Making of Marx's 'Capital'* (London: Pluto Press, 1977), 307.

18. Fredric Jameson, *Representing* Capital (New York: Verso, 2011), 71.
19. Marx, *Capital*, vol. 1, 799.
20. Marx, *Capital*, vol. 1, 764, 772, 781–94; Marx and Engels, *The Communist Manifesto*, 7; Paul M. Sweezy, *The Theory of Capitalist Development* (New York: Monthly Review Press, 1970), 87–92.
21. Marx, *Capital*, vol. 1, 792.
22. Karl Marx, "Wage-Labour and Capital," in *Wage-Labour and Capital/Value, Price and Profit* (New York: International Publishers, 1935), 45; Sweezy, *The Theory of Capitalist Development*, 89.
23. Marx, *Capital*, vol. 1, 763, 776–81, 929.
24. Marx, *Capital*, vol. 1, 794–95; David Harvey, *A Companion to Marx's* Capital (London: Verso, 2010), 278, 318.
25. Marx, *Capital*, vol. 1, 795–96.
26. Marx, *Capital*, vol. 1, 590–99, 793–77.
27. Marx, *Capital*, vol. 1, 797–98.
28. Engels deserves credit for having introduced the reserve army concept into Marxian theory, and makes it clear that what demonstrates the reserve-army or relative surplus-population status of workers is the fact that the economy draws them into employment at business cycle peaks. See Frederick Engels, *The Condition of the Working Class in England* (Chicago: Academy Chicago Publishers, 1984), 117–22, and *Engels on Capital* (New York: International Publishers, 1937), 19.
29. Karl Marx, *Capital*, vol. 3 (London: Penguin, 1981), *Capital*, vol. 2 (London: Penguin, 1978), 486–87, and *Capital*, vol. 1, 769–70; Rosa Luxemburg, *The Accumulation of Capital—An Anti-Critique*, and Nikolai Bukharin, *Imperialism and the Accumulation of Capital* (New York: Monthly Review Press, 1972), 121.
30. Marx, *Capital*, vol. 3, 363.
31. Karl Marx and Frederick Engels, *Collected Works* (New York: International Publishers, 1975), 422.
32. Karl Marx, *Theories of Surplus Value* (Moscow: Progress Publishers, 1971), part 3, 105–6; *Capital*, vol. 3, 344–46; David Ricardo, *On the Principles of Political Economy and Taxation* (Cambridge: Cambridge University Press, 1951), 135–36; John Stuart Mill, *Essays on Some Unsettled Questions in Political Economy* (London: Longmans, Green, and Co., 1877), 1–46: Rosdolsky, *The Making of Marx's 'Capital'*, 307–12. A wide-ranging analysis/debate regarding unequal exchange occurred within Marxism in the 1970s. See Arghiri Emmanuel, *Unequal Exchange* (New York: Monthly Review Press, 1972); Samir Amin, *Imperialism and Unequal Development* (New York: Monthly Review Press, 1977), 181–252. Some Marxist theorists still deny that the rate of surplus value is higher in the periphery than in the center. See Alex Callinicos, *Imperialism and Global Political Economy* (London: Polity, 2009), 179–81; and Joseph Choonara, *Unraveling Capitalism* (London: Bookmarks Publications, 2009), 34–35. For a contrary view, see Sweezy, *Four Lectures on Marxism*, 76–77.
33. Rosa Luxemburg, *The Accumulation of Capital* (New York: Monthly Review Press, 1951), 361–65.
34. Marx, *Capital*, vol. 3, 344.
35. The term "globalization" was first coined in the 1930s. But the first article to use the concept in its modern economic sense, according to the *Oxford English*

Dictionary, was Fouad Ajami, "Corporate Giants: Some Global Social Costs," *International Studies Quarterly* 16 , no. 4 (December 1972): 513. Ajami introduced the term in a paragraph in which he was addressing Marxian notions of "concentration and centralization"—and in particular Baran and Sweezy's *Monopoly Capital*, which had pointed to the multinational corporation as a manifestation of the growth of monopolistic production at the world level. Although critical of Baran and Sweezy's analysis for its Marxian basis, Ajami (a mainstream political scientist now affiliated with the Hoover Institution and the Council on Foreign Relations) nevertheless saw what he called "the domination of multinational giants and the globalization of markets" as emerging out of the same kinds of developments—with respect to the tendency to international oligopoly—that Baran and Sweezy had raised. Ironically, Ajami failed to notice that other theorists he drew upon in his article in contradistinction to Baran and Sweezy—Stephen Hymer, Michael Tanzer, Bob Rowthorn, and Herbert Schiller—were also Marxian and radical political economists, and in the case of the first two, authors of articles in *Monthly Review*.

36. Richard J. Barnet and Ronald E. Müller, *Global Reach* (New York: Simon and Schuster, 1974), 213–14, 306.
37. See chapter 4 above.
38. "Moving Back to America."
39. Dale Wen, *China Copes with Globalization* (International Forum on Globalization, 2005), http://ifg.org; Martin Hart-Landsberg, "The Chinese Reform Experience," *The Review of Radical Political Economics* 43, no. 1 (March 2011): 56–76; Minqi Li, "The Rise of the Working Class and the Future of the Chinese Revolution," *Monthly Review* 63, no. 2 (June 2011): 40.
40. It should be noted that the term "superexploited" appears to have two closely related, overlapping meanings in Marxist theory: (1) workers who receive less than the historically determined value of labor power, as it is defined here; and (2) workers who are subjected to unequal exchange and overexploited, primarily in the global South. In Amin's framework, however, the two meanings are united. This is because the value of labor power is determined globally, while actual wage rates are determined nationally, and are hierarchically ordered due to imperialism. In the global South therefore workers *normally* receive wages that are less than the value of labor power. This is the basis of imperial rent. See Amin, *The Law of Value and Historical Materialism,* 11, 84. John Smith and Andy Higginbottom have developed a similar approach to superexploitation based on Marx. See John Smith, "Imperialism and the Law of Value," *Global Discourse*, 2, no. 1 (2011), http://global-discourse.com.
41. Charles J. Whalen, "Sending Jobs Offshore from the United States," *Intervention: A Journal of Economics* 2, no. 2 (2005): 35. Quoted in Smith, *The Internationalisation of Globalisation*, 94.
42. William Milberg, "Shifting Sources and Uses of Profits," *Economy and Society* 37, no. 3 (August 2008): 439; Judith Banister and George Cook, "China's Employment and Compensation Costs in Manufacturing through 2008," U.S. Bureau of Labor Statistics, *Monthly Labor Review* (March 2011): 44. It is common for commentators to refer to global supply chains as global value chains, based on the concept of value added. (See, for example, Michael Spence and Sandile Hlatshwayo, *The Evolving Structure of the American Economy*

and the Employment Challenge, Council on Foreign Relations Working Paper, March 2011, http://cfr.org.) This leads to the notion that the value added is much higher in high technology production engaged in the North than in the labor-intensive production now increasingly located in the South. However, more value added in this sense simply means higher relative prices and higher income. It does not tell us where the value is produced but simply who gets it (via monopoly power, imperial rent, etc.). We therefore avoid the value chain terminology in this book, and we refer, when necessary, to "high-value-capture" rather than "high-value" links in the global supply chain. The "value capture" term and a general critique of value-chain theory are presented in John Smith, *Imperialism and the Globalisation of Production*, 254–60, and "Imperialism and the Law of Value."

43. Yuqing Xing and Neal Detert, *How the iPhone Widens the United States Trade Deficit with the People's Republic of China*, ADBI Working Paper, Asian Development Bank Institute (December 2010; paper revised May 2011); David Barboza, "After Spate of Suicides, Technology Firm in China Raises Workers' Salaries," *New York Times*, June 2, 2010, http://nytimes.com. It should be noted that the assembly in China of iPhone parts and components that are produced elsewhere (heavily in other East Asian countries) is actually the dominant pattern of East Asian production. According to the Asian Development Bank, China is "the assembly hub for final products in Asian production networks." Asian Development Bank, *Asian Development Outlook, 2008* (Manila, Philippines), http://adb.org, 22; Martin Hart-Landsberg, "The U.S Economy and China," *Monthly Review* 61, no. 9 (February 2010): 18.
44. Banister and Cook, "China's Employment and Compensation," 49.
45. U.S. Bureau of Labor Statistics, "International Comparisons of Hourly Compensation Costs in Manufacturing," Table I, last updated March 8, 2011, http://bls.gov.
46. Vikas Bajaj, "Bangladesh, with Low Pay, Moves In on China," *New York Times*, July 16, 2010, http://nytimes.com.
47. Immelt quoted in Milberg, "Shifting Sources and Uses of Profits," 433. For a powerful theoretical analysis in Marxian terms of global labor arbitrage see Smith, *Imperialism and the Globalisation of Production*.
48. Jannik Lindbaek, "Emerging Economies: How Long Will the Low-Wage Advantage Last?" October 3, 1997, http://actrav.itcilo.org.
49. W. Arthur Lewis, *Selected Economic Writings* (New York: New York University Press, 1983), 316–17, 321, 348, 387–90.
50. "The Next China," *The Economist*, July 29, 2010, http://economist.com.
51. Li, "The Rise of the Working Class and the Future of the Chinese Revolution," 40–41, and *The Rise of China and the Demise of the Capitalist World Economy* (New York: Monthly Review Press, 2008), 87–92.
52. Yang Yao, "No, the Lewisian Turning Point Has Not Yet Arrived," *The Economist*, July 16, 2010, http://economist.com; Stephen Roach, "Chinese Wage Convergence Has a Long Way To Go," *The Economist*, July 18, 2010, http://economist.com.
53. Theo Sparreboom and Michael P. F. de Gier, "Assessing Vulnerable Employment," *Employment Sector Working Paper*, no. 13 (Geneva: ILO, 2008), 7; James Petras

and Henry Veltmeyer, *Multinationals on Trial* (Burlington, Vermont: Ashgate, 2007), 70; Mike Davis, *Planet of Slums* (London: Verso, 2006), 178.

54. International Labor Organisation, *Key Indicators of the Labour Market* (Geneva: ILO, 2009), chapter 3-3; Sparreboom and de Gier, "Assessing Vulnerable Employment," 11.
55. Michael Yates, "Work Is Hell," May 21, 2009, http://cheapmotelsandahotplate.org.
56. ILO, *Key Indicators*, chapter 1-C, and chapter 5.
57. Samir Amin, "World Poverty, Pauperization and Capital Accumulation," *Monthly Review* 55, no. 5 (October 2003): 1–9, and *The Law of Worldwide Value*, 14, 89, 134; Prabhat Patnaik, "The Myths of Capitalism," *MRzine*, July 4, 2011, http://mrzine.monthlyreview.org; United Nations, *World Economic and Social Survey* (New York: UN, 2004), 3; Yates, "Work Is Hell"; Davis, *Planet of Slums*, 179; United Nations Human Settlements Programme, *The Challenge of the Slums* (London: Earthscan, 2003), 40, 46.
58. Prabhat Patnaik, *The Value of Money* (New York: Columbia University Press, 2009), 212–15; "A Perspective on the Growth Process in India and China," *International Development Economics Associates*, The IDEAs as Working Paper Series, Paper no. 05/2009, http://networkideas.org, abstract, 4; Lee Chyen Yee and Clare Jim, "Foxconn to Rely More on Robots; Could Use 1 Million in 3 Years," Reuters, August 1, 2011, http://reuters.com.
59. Prabhat Patnaik, "Notes on Contemporary Imperialism," *MRzine*, December 20, 2010, http://mrzine.monthlyreview.org; "Capitalism and Imperialism," *MRzine*, June 19, 2011, http://mrzine.monthlyreview.org; "Labour Market Flexibility," *MRzine*, May 9, 2011, http://mrzine.monthlyreview.org; and "Contemporary Imperialism and the World's Labour Reserves," *Social Scientist* 35, no. 5/6 (May–June 2007): 13.
60. Prabhat Patnaik, "The Paradox of Capitalism," *MRzine*, October 22, 2010, http://mrzine.monthlyreview.org.
61. For example, Guy Standing, *The Precariat: The New Dangerous Class* (New York: Bloomsbury Academic, 2011). On the current role of the reserve army of labor at the center of the capitalist system see Fred Magdoff and Harry Magdoff, "Disposable Workers: Today's Reserve Army of Labor," *Monthly Review* 55, no. 11 (April 2004): 18–35.
62. Ghose, et al., *The Global Employment Challenge*, 45–49.
63. On the interrelation of these two negative elements affecting employment in the advanced capitalist countries see Foster, "The Stagnation of Employment."
64. Baran and Sweezy, *Monopoly Capital*, 107–8.
65. Michael Spence, *The Next Convergence* (New York: Farrar, Strauss and Giroux, 2011), 19–23, 48, 53–54, 85–86, 107; "China's Urban Population Exceeds Countryside for First Time," Bloomberg.com, January 17, 2012.
66. Spence, *The Next Convergence*, 100–3, 194–98.
67. Samir Amin, *Capitalism in the Age of Globalization* (New York: Zed, 1977), 4–5.
68. Louis Uchitelle, "Is Manufacturing Falling Off the Radar?" *New York Times*, September 11, 2011, http://nytimes.com.
69. Walter LaFeber, *Michael Jordan and the New Global Capitalism* (New York: W.W. Norton, 1999), 106–7, 14–48.
70. Samir Amin, "The Democratic Fraud and the Universalist Alternative," *Monthly Review* 63, no. 5 (October 2011): 44–45, *The World We Wish to See* (New York: Monthly Review Press, 2008).

Chapter 6: The Great Stagnation and China

This chapter, written for the present book, was published in advance as "The Global Stagnation and China" in the February 2012 issue of *Monthly Review* (vol. 63, no. 9).

1. "From the Great Recession to the Great Stagnation," *Forbes*, October 10, 2011, http://forbes.com; Tyler Cowen, *The Great Stagnation* (New York: Penguin, 2010).
2. Christine Lagarde, "An Address to the 2011 International Finance Forum," Beijing, November 9, 2011, http://imf.org. See also C. Ryan Knight, "Dark Clouds, Over the Boat: On China, Production, and Financialization," November 11, 2011, http://lecoupdoeil.wordpress.com.
3. "IMF Sees Chinese Economy Avoiding Stagnation, El Comercio Says," Bloomberg.com, November 30, 2011, http://bloomberg.com.
4. Stephen Roach, "China's Landing—Soft Not Hard," September 30, 2011, http://project-syndicate.org.
5. "Hangzhou Taxi Drivers Go on Strike," *The China Times*, August 2, 2011, http://www.thechinatimes.com.
6. "Calculating the Coming Slowdown in China," *New York Times*, May 23, 2011, http://nytimes.com.
7. "China's Bumpy Road Ahead," *Wall Street Journal*, July 9, 2011, http://online.wsj.com; Niall Ferguson, *Civilization: The West and the Rest* (New York: Palgrave, 2011), 307–8.
8. See the comments by Paul J. Alapat, Fred Bergsten, Haruhiko Kuroda, Jim O'Neill, and Allen Sinai in "Can China Become the World's Engine for Growth?" *The International Economy* (Winter 2010): 12–13, 17, 27, 31, http://international-economy.com.
9. "China's Bumpy Road Ahead," *Wall Street Journal*, July 9, 2011, http://online.wsj.com; "Indifference as a Mode of Operation at China's Schools," *New York Times*, May 18, 2011, http://nytimes.com.
10. "The Next China," *The Economist*, July 29, 2010, http://economist.com.
11. Michael Spence, *The Next Convergence* (New York: Farrar, Strauss and Giroux, 2011), 18–19.
12. "Calculating the Coming Slowdown in China," *New York Times*; Christine Lagarde, "The Path Forward—Act Now and Act Together," Opening Address to the 2011 Annual Meeting of the Boards of Governors of the World Bank Group and the International Monetary Fund, September 23, 2011, http://imf.org.
13. See chapter 5 above.
14. Martin Hart-Landsberg, "China, Capitalist Accumulation, and the World Crisis," *Marxism 21* 7, no. 1 (Spring 2010): 289; Zhang Hong, "Too Early to Hail China's Stimulus Success," *Guardian*, August 28, 2009, http://guardian.co.uk; "China's Local Debts Threaten Crisis," *Asia Times*, July 14, 2010, http://atimes.com.
15. Michael Pettis, "Lower Interest Rates, Higher Savings?" October 16, 2011, http://mpettis.com; "A Workers' Manifesto for China," *The Economist*, October 11, 2007, http://economist.com.
16. Nouriel Roubini, "China's Bad Growth Bet," April 14, 2011, http://project-syndicate.org. See also Roach, "China's Landing."

17. "Why China's Big Red Bubble Is Ahead of Us," *Forbes*, November 30, 2011, http://forbes.com; "China's Housing Bubble Past, and Its Future," *Forbes*, November 8, 2011, http://forbes.com; "Why China's Property Bubble Is Different," *Forbes*, April 22, 2011; "Rise of the Asian Megacity," *BBC News, Asia Pacific*, June 20, 2011; "Cracks in Beijing's Financial Edifice," *Financial Times*, October 9, 2011, http://ft.com; Patrick Chovanec, "China Data, Part 1: Real Estate Downturn," December 12, 2011, http://chovanec.wordpress.com; Kate Mackenzie, "As China's Apartments Go, So Goes China," *Financial Times* blog, December 14, 2011, http://ftalphaville.ft.com; Michael Pettis, "How Do We Know that China Is Overinvesting?" December 3, 2011, http://mpettis.com; Jim Antos, "China's Debt Situation Not Far Off from Greece," July 12, 2011, http://finance.yahoo.com.
18. Ian Bremmer and Nouriel Roubini, "Whose Economy Has it Worst?" *Wall Street Journal*, November 12, 2011; http://online.wsj.com; Michael Pettis, "Some Predictions for the Rest of the Decade," August 28, 2011, http://mpettis.com, and "Lower Interest Rates, Higher Savings."
19. William Hurst, "Urban China: Change and Contention," in William A. Joseph, ed., *Politics in China: An Introduction* (Oxford: Oxford University Press, 2010), 257.
20. Minxin Pei, "The Color of China: Looming Stagnation," *The National Interest* 100 (March/April 2009): 17.
21. "A Workers' Manifesto for China," *The Economist*, http://economist.com.
22. "China's Growing Income Gap," *Bloomberg Businessweek*, January 27, 2011, http://businessweek.com; "Country's Wealth Divide Past Warning Level," *China Daily*, May 12, 2010, http://chinadaily.com.cn.
23. Wu Zhong, "China's 'Most Wanted' Millionaires," *Asia Times Online*, September 19, 2007, http://atimes.com; Hart-Landsberg, "China, Capitalist Accumulation, and the World Crisis," 280.
24. William Hinton, *The Great Reversal* (New York: Monthly Review Press, 1990), 168–71.
25. World Bank, WDI Database, databank.worldbank.org; Martin Hart-Landsberg and Paul Burkett, *China and Socialism: Market Reforms and Class Struggle* (New York: Monthly Review Press, 2005), 37; William Hinton, *Through a Glass Darkly* (New York: Monthly Review Press, 2006), 130; Selden quoted in Hart-Landsberg and Burkett, *China and Socialism*, 38.
26. Hinton, *The Great Reversal*, 16.
27. Giovanni Arrighi, *Adam Smith in Beijing* (London: Verso, 2007), 389; Ho-fung Hung, "A Caveat: Is the Rise of China Sustainable?" in Ho-fung Hung, ed., *China and the Transformation of Global Capitalism* (Baltimore: Johns Hopkins University Press, 2009), 189.
28. Richard Walker and Daniel Buck, "The Chinese Road: Cities in the Transition to Capitalism," *New Left Review* 46 (July–August 2007): 42–44.
29. Peter Kwong, "The Chinese Face of Neoliberalism," *CounterPunch*, October 7, 2006, http://counterpunch.org; Martin Hart-Landsberg, "The U.S. Economy and China," *Monthly Review* 61, no. 9 (February 2010): 26–27.
30. *Green Left*, May 18, 2007, http://www.greenleft.org; Lan Xinzhen, "A Foreign China," *Beijing Review*, January 11, 2007, http://bjreview.com.cn; Wenzhao Wang, "China New M&A Regulation and Its Impact on Foreign Business in China," *China Trade Law Report* (American Lawyer Media), October 2006, http://avvo.com; "Foreign Direct Investment in China in 2010 Rises to Record

$105.7 Billion," *Bloomberg News*, January 17, 2011, http://bloomberg.com; "The Next China," *The Economist*.

31. Shaun Breslin, *China and the Global Political Economy* (New York: Palgrave Macmillan, 2007), 110; Jephraim P. Gundzik, "What a US Recession Means for China," *Asia Times Online*, September 27, 2006, http://atimes.com.
32. Martin Hart-Landsberg and Paul Burkett, "China, Capitalist Accumulation, and Labor," *Monthly Review* 59, no. 1 (May 2007): 20–22.
33. Galvin Hale and Bart Hobijn, "The U.S. Content of 'Made in China,'" Federal Reserve Board of San Francisco, *FRBSF Economic Letter*, August 8, 2011, http://frbsf.org.
34. Hyun-Hoon Lee, Donghyun Park, and Jing Wang, *The Role of the People's Republic of China in International Fragmentation and Production Networks*, Asian Development Bank, ADB Working Paper Series on Regional Economic Integration, 87 (September 2011): 5, 15–16.
35. Jin Bei, "The International Competition Facing Domestically Produced Goods and the Nation's Industry," *Social Sciences in China* 12, no. 1 (Spring 1997): 65–71.
36. "Barbie and the World Economy," *Los Angeles Times*, September 22, 1996, http://articles.latimes.com.
37. See chapter 5 above.
38. Institute for Global Labour and Human Rights, *China's Youth Meet Microsoft: KYE Factory in China Produces for Microsoft and Other Companies*, April 13, 2010, http://globallabourrights.org; "Microsoft Supplier in China Forces Teenagers to Work 15-hour Shifts under Sweatshop Conditions," *China Labour Net*, April 17, 2010, http://globallabourrights.org.
39. Institute for Global Labour and Human Rights, *High-Tech Misery in China: The Dehumanization of Young Workers Producing Our Computer Keyboards*, February 2, 2009, http://globallabourrights.org.
40. Institute for Global Labour and Human Rights, *Dirty Parts: Where Lost Fingers Come Cheap; Ford in China*, March 22, 2011, http://globallabourrights.org.
41. National Labor Committee and China Labor Watch, *PUMA Workers in China*, November 4, 2004, http://globallabourrights.org.
42. "Foxconn Worker Plunges to Death in China," *Reuters*, Nov. 5, 2010, http://reuters.com; "Struggle for Foxconn Girl Who Wanted to Die," *South China Morning Post*, December 22, 2011, http://topics.scmp.com; "Inside Foxconn's factory," *The Huffington Post*, July 6, 2011, http://huffingtonpost.com.
43. Anita Chan, *China's Workers' under Assault: The Exploitation of Labor in Globalizing Economy* (New York: M.E. Sharpe, 2001), 11–13; Hart-Landsberg and Burkett, "China, Capitalist Accumulation, and Labor," 27–29. But see "Beijing to Raise Minimum Wage," December 29, 2011, http://www.chinadaily.com.cn, for evidence of high-level concern with these questions.
44. Samir Amin, *The Law of Worldwide Value* (New York: Monthly Review Press, 2010).
45. "Migrant Workers in China," *China Labour Bulletin*, June 6, 2008, http://clb.org.hk; "China's 'Floating Population' Exceeds 221 Million," *Peoples' Daily Online*, February 28, 2011, http://english.peopledaily.com.cn; Rachel Murphy, *How Migrant Labor Is Changing Rural China* (Cambridge: Cambridge University Press, 2002), 44, 204, 216; Ke-Qing Han, Chien-Chung Huang, and Wen-Jui Han, "Social Mobility of Migrant Peasant Workers in China," *Sociology Mind* 1, no. 4 (2011): 206.

46. Hinton, *The Great Reversal*, 172, *Through a Glass Darkly*, 128; Murphy, *How Migrant Labor Is Changing Rural China*, 218; Ted C. Fishman, "The Chinese Century," *New York Times*, July 4, 2004, http://nytimes.com.
47. Maëlys de la Rupelle, Deng Quheng, Li Shi, and Thomas Vendryes, *Land Rights Insecurity and Temporary Migration in Rural China*, IZA Discussion Paper Series, Institute for the Study of Labor (Bonn), December 2009, 2–7, ftp.iza.org; Ke-Qing Han, et al., "Social Mobility of Migrant Peasant Workers," 209; Xin Meg, Tao Kong, and Dandan Zhang, "Searching for Adverse Labour Market Effects of the GFC in China," Research School of Economics, Australian National University, www.oecd.org.
48. See He Xuefeng, "New Rural Construction and the Chinese Path," *Chinese Sociology and Anthropology* 39, no. 4 (Summer 2007): 29–30; Murphy, *How Migrant Labor Is Changing Rural China*, 200, 214–18.
49. Arrighi, *Adam Smith in Beijing*, 389; Ho-fung Hung, "A Caveat," 189.
50. William Hinton, *The Great Reversal*, 168–71.
51. See "Hangzhou Taxi Drivers Go on Strike"; "Indifference as a Mode of Operation at China Schools," *New York Times*, May 18, 2011.
52. "Chinese See Communist Land Sales Hurting Mao's Poor to Pay Rich," *Bloomberg Businessweek*, November 2, 2011, http://bloomberg.com; "China's Local Debts Threaten Crisis," *Asia Times Online*, July 14, 2010, http://atimes.com; "China's Stability Landed in Trouble," *Wall Street Journal*, December 16, 2011, http://online.wsj.com; "Village Revolts against Inequities of Chinese Life," *New York Times*, December 14, 2011, http://nytimes.com; "Beijing Set to 'Strike Hard' at Revolt," *Wall Street Journal*, December 16, 2011, http://online.wsj.com; "Demonstrators Who Took Over Chinese Village Halt Protest," *New York Times*, December 21, 2011, http://nytimes.com; Yanqi Tong and Shaohua Lei, "Large Scale Mass Incidents and Government Responses in China," *International Journal of China Studies* 1, no. 2 (October 2010): 492–93; Tong Yanqui and Lei Shaohua, "Large-Scale Mass Incidents in China," *East Asian Policy* 2, no. 2 (April/June 2010): 27; Congressional Research Service, *Social Unrest in China*, CRS Report for Congress, May 8, 2006, www.fas.org.
53. Capital Trade, Inc., *An Analysis of State-Owned Enterprises and State Capitalism in China* (Washington, D.C.: U.S.-China Economic and Security Review Commission, 2011), 27 (Table IV-1), http://www.uscc.gov/researchpapers/research_archive.php.
54. Minqi Li, "The Rise of the Working Class," *Monthly Review* 63, no. 2 (June 2011): 41–44; Tong and Lei, "Large Scale Mass Incidents," 490–91.
55. Carin Zissis and Jayshree Bajoria, "China's Environmental Crisis," Council on Foreign Relations, August 4, 2008, http://cfr.org; Ma Jun, "How Participation Can Help China's Ailing Environment," *China Dialogue*, January 31, 2007, http://chinadialogue.net; "Outrage Grows Over Air Pollution and China's Response," *New York Times*, December 6, 2011, http://nytimes.com; Tong Yanqi and Lei Shaohua, "Large-Scale Mass Incidents in China," 25; "Environmental Issues Addressed More Urgently in China," *China Daily*, May 4, 2006, http://chinadaily.com.cn.
56. On the concept of the environmental proletariat see John Bellamy Foster, Brett Clark, and Richard York, *The Ecological Rift* (New York: Monthly Review Press, 2010), 439–41.

57. Samir Amin, "China, Market Socialism, and U.S. Hegemony," *Review* 3 (2005): 259–79; "Arable Land Decreases to 102.4mln Hectares," Chinese Government's Official Web Portal, http://www.gov.cn/english; Wen Tiejun, "Deconstructing Modernization," *Chinese Sociology and Anthropology* 39, no. 4 (Summer 2007): 10–25.
58. "Can China Become the World's Engine for Growth?: A Symposium of Views," *The International Economy* (Winter 2010), www.international-economy.com.
59. Paul Krugman, "Will China Break?" *New York Times*, December 18, 2011, http://nytimes.com.
60. Li, "The Rise of the Working Class and the Future of the Chinese Revolution," 45.
61. Galvin Hale and Bart Hobijn, "The U.S. Content of 'Made in China,'" Table 1.
62. Ted C. Fishman, *China, Inc.* (New York: Scribner, 2005), 257.
63. Fishman, "The Chinese Century"; Li, "The Rise of the Working Class," 50.
64. Karl Marx, *Dispatches for the New York Tribune* (London: Penguin, 2007), 3; John Newsinger, "The Taiping Peasant Revolt," *Monthly Review* 52, no. 5 (October 2000): 29–37.
65. Since these words were originally written in our article in the February 2012 issue of *Monthly Review*, where this chapter was published in advance (appearing online on the 1st of that month), the same general question about China's fate has been raised elsewhere. Thus the *New York Times*, as noted in the Introduction to this book, asked "Is China Ripe for Revolution?" in an article by Stephen R. Platt in its February 12, 2012, edition. Like our concluding paragraph above that article took as its historical reference point the Taiping Rebellion, and quoted the same passage from Marx as we did. In the case of the *New York Times*, however, this did not lead to our specific conclusion: that the fates of East and West (North and South) are today more and more tied together, in revolution as well as reaction.
66. Karl Marx and Frederick Engels, *The Communist Manifesto* (New York: Monthly Review Press, 1964), 2.

Index